No Ifs, Ands, or Butts

A Smoker's Guide to Kicking the Habit

By Julie Waltz Kembel

NIA INC. TUCSON

Library of Congress Catalog Card Number: 89-91978

ISBN: 0-931836-02-6

Edited by Sabina Dunton
Cover design and illustrations by David Fischer
Design, layout and typography by Robert Kembel

Published by:

Northwest Learning Associates Inc.
3061 N. Willow Creek Drive
Tucson, Arizona 85712-1381
Phone: (520) 881-0877, FAX: (520) 881-0632

Printed in the United States of America

5 6 7 8 9 99 98 97

To all smokers who choose to quit—
to their courage,
their determination,
and their ultimate success.

And, most especially,

to Catherine Stockwell
whose personal courage and love of life have been
a continual inspiration.

Table of Contents

Foreword

I am writing this for all smokers who continue to say, "I don't want to quit smoking," or "I can't quit smoking," or "We all have to die of something." I know, for I was one of them.

When I smoked, I had plenty of excuses for not quitting. I needed cigarettes to relax. Cigarettes were comforting. I liked to smoke. But I knew smoking wasn't good for me, so I'd quit. Then I'd start smoking again. I quit several times using one method or another—sometimes as a New Year's resolution, sometimes because someone challenged me to do it. I'd feel victorious for a while but I always went back to smoking again... until my doctor told me I had lung cancer. Then, I *did* quit for good. No games. No excuses. No cigarettes. It was easy to quit smoking when I was fighting for my life!

Why is it we don't take our health seriously until we are threatened with losing it? I had been a nursing home administrator. I knew the importance of health to quality of life. I ate sensibly. I exercised regularly. I drank alcohol only occasionally. Though I smoked, I thought I was taking good care of myself. I felt good. I didn't let myself think what cigarettes might be doing to my health. I tell myself *now* that if I had it to do all over again, I would do it differently.

If you are reading *No Ifs, Ands, or Butts* with the idea that it will help you quit smoking, take it seriously.

There is so much important information in it about decision and commitment. There are so many practical and helpful tools for quitting smoking, and for living well without cigarettes. This is much more than a "how to do it" book. It is a guide to help you to understand and work with yourself successfully. It teaches you about stability and flexibility, about being realistic and practical. It teaches you about self-management and self-support. And, it teaches you about faith and belief in yourself.

I have known and loved the author, Julie Waltz, for many years. We have laughed and cried together. We have talked about our hopes and feelings until the wee hours of the morning. She is so sensitive and so creative. You will experience that through the stories about Jeremy, and about Bob, Betheny, Martha, Tim, Randy and Louise. She uses them to help you understand more about yourself. They are stories about living, not just about smoking.

I hope that no one who reads this book will be so foolish as to give up his or her most precious possessions—health and life—for a cigarette. Make up your mind to quit smoking now. Be determined. Be optimistic. With a positive attitude and positive thinking, you can accomplish anything. Call upon the strength of your friends and family to give you support. Believe in yourself, for you do have the power to work miracles in your own life. You *can* quit smoking if you really want to do it.

Catherine Stockwell*
April, 1989

---

* Catherine Stockwell died in May 1989, leaving behind a legacy of love, faith and joy in living. She encouraged all of us to try our hardest to achieve our goals. She believed in everyone with absolute sincerity. When she wrote this brief foreword she knew she was dying, yet she faced each day with faith and dignity. Catherine couldn't change what was happening to her, but she hoped her experience, and her words, will help others find the strength they need to quit smoking.

Catherine was my friend and I miss her. My hope is that her words will reach you and help you find your own commitment to health and to life.

Julie Waltz Kembel

Preface

How This Book Came To Be

All my life I have had the philosophy that what happens to each of us in our own lives is the result of a combination of factors: our own experiences and personalities, the teachings of others, our skills and points of view, and perhaps most importantly, circumstance. I've always viewed circumstance as a very peculiar marriage, or blend, of timing with opportunity, which probably accounts for why we pass the same opportunities by at certain times in our lives and act on them at other times.

How this book came to be is just such a marriage of timing and opportunity. I had remarried and relocated from Seattle, Washington, to Tucson, Arizona. In January of 1987 I went to work at Canyon Ranch, a world-famous health and fitness resort located right in my own neighborhood.

I came to Canyon Ranch to teach food habit management, a combination of dietary and habit change training to help people manage themselves successfully with food and with eating. This was an area I knew well, having personally battled and overcome my own weight problems and detrimental eating habits. I had previously published a book of the same name, *Food Habit Management*, currently used for instructional purposes in a wide variety of health care settings.

One of my first assignments at Canyon Ranch was to further develop and expand the smoking cessation program. My own personal battle with cigarettes had been brief and certainly far less catastrophic than my long-standing struggle with food. But I understood the similarities between the two—and the differences.

As a broad-based counselor trained and experienced in how people learn, change, and maintain habits, I approach smokers in the same way I approach over-eaters.

"Tell me about yourself."

"Why are you here?"

"What do you want to accomplish?"

"What prevents you from accomplishing it?"

"Why is this important to you?"

"Why do you want to tackle it at this particular time?"

"Knowing yourself, where or how do you expect to have trouble reaching your goal?"

"What personal strengths can you rely on to help you reach your goal?"

"What personal weaknesses do you see in yourself that would get in the way of your ability to reach your goal?"

"How do you feel I can best help you at this time?"

Hundreds of bright, intelligent, questioning people have come to Canyon Ranch to tackle and overcome their smoking habits. These people and the program that's been developed for them have been the inspiration for this book, *No Ifs, Ands, or Butts: A Smoker's Guide to Kicking the Habit.*

The Program Behind the Book

When the orientation meeting of the Stop Smoking Program at Canyon Ranch takes place, the people in the room display a variety of emotions. Some are angry, testy or judgmental; others are silent, indifferent, weepy, sad, noncommittal, or fearful. They are on the "hot seat" of decision: to quit or not to quit. At Canyon Ranch, the method for quitting is immediate and complete withdrawal. In other words, quitting "cold turkey" during the five-day program.

During the first two days in the Canyon Ranch program, the withdrawal symptoms from nicotine and from smoking are most strongly felt. Concentration is difficult. Some people are edgy and impatient; others are listless and unresponsive. Most are feeling anxious and not at all certain they will ultimately succeed. During the third day, the situation begins to get better. Complexions become pinker, eyes become clearer, concentration improves.

During the fourth session the group's over-all optimism for personal success rises significantly. Joking and teasing increase. Sincere discussions about lifestyle issues, mood management without cigarettes, and ways to cope with specific difficult situations take place in earnest. The participants have absorbed the medical and physiological information, and have begun using the basic methods they have learned to help them through their cigarette cravings and their own restlessness. They have decided upon specific ways to set the stage for not smoking at home, at work, and in the car. Now they want to deal with more difficult issues: their moods; particular people, places, or events they have always associated with smoking; what will happen if they ever make a mistake and pick up a cigarette again.

Some people are genuinely diabolical: they like to test themselves against the highest odds. They are the ones most likely to see if they can have "just one" cigarette and get away with it. Others are sometimes overconfident and blindly walk into situations destined for potential trouble. Such people might arrange a ski or fishing trip with all of their old smoking buddies, thinking that after three weeks or three months of being smoke-free themselves, they can now handle all challenges. Still others feel unsure of themselves and need to know specifically what to do to get back on track if ever they get de-railed.

The final sessions of the Canyon Ranch program teach the participants how to manage themselves under stress without cigarettes, how to apply what they have learned, how to deal with difficult situations and how to recover from temporary slip-ups. They are taught what is probably the most critical part of the "quitting" process: relapse prevention and recovery.

At Canyon Ranch, we maintain contact with the Stop Smoking participants for at least a year. They let us know what works and what doesn't. Some people have little to absolutely no difficulties; others struggle much harder. A few people have even been coached through a recovery plan by telephone!

All in all, the approach used in the program works. A significant percentage of the people who complete the program quit smoking successfully—sometimes with one trip through the program, sometimes with two. National averages indicate that people make three attempts to quit smoking before permanently giving it up. As the American writer, Mark Twain, once observed, "To cease smoking is the easiest thing I ever did; I ought to know because I've done it a thousand times."

Organization Of This Book

This book is the culmination of several years of intensive research, development, testing, practice and redesign. It is written primarily for cigarette smokers. Pipe and cigar smokers will undoubtedly find some help in the pages of this book as well, but the orientation and presentation of the information is geared toward cigarette users. Whether your ultimate intent is to quit "cold turkey," use a short-term aid like nicotine gum or cut down gradually, the issues of self-management training, skill building, coping strategies, and attitude shaping are much the same.

This book is organized into three primary sections. The chapters within each section reflect the section's main objective. They are designed to inform and involve *you*, the reader, actively.

Section I, "The Decision to Quit," focuses intensively on feelings, attitudes and ways to prepare yourself to begin the process of leaving cigarettes and smoking. Important physiological and psychological information is presented because it is necessary for you to thoroughly understand what happens to your body and your mind when you smoke—and when you quit.

The chapters in **Section II, "Taking Action to Quit,"** are filled with specific information about ways to cope and ultimately succeed at quitting smoking. Self-help exercises will guide you through the processes of self-observation, planning, experimenting and evaluating the various withdrawal and self-management tools in order to help you quit smoking completely and permanently.

Section III, "Maintaining Progress," is designed to help you maintain your skills and your equilibrium over the long haul. These final chapters will help you recover from pitfalls, mistakes and relapses, and teach you some easy-to-live-with ways to maintain your on-going progress. Further, you will learn how to manage your weight, if weight gain is a worry for you when you quit smoking, and how exercise can help you live more comfortably without cigarettes.

Section IV, "Self-Study Exercises," contains the self-help tasks recommended in specific chapters. These pencil and paper exercises will help you apply what you are learning to yourself so you can take effective action.

Woven into the this book's tapestry of factual information, self-discovery exercises, and successful "quitting" techniques is an on-going narrative among a small cast of characters introduced in the first chapter. Their comments, feelings and reactions may sound much like yours, for they represent people like yourself. These characters will progress through the struggle for decision, and will keep you company throughout your process of quitting smoking. Their experiences are actual, blended from true stories of the people I have worked with during the past few years.

The introductory pages of Sections I through IV contain a brief story of their own. This story's purpose is to prepare you for the underlying lessons that are learned through the very personal struggle to break a controlling and harmful, yet pleasurable habit.

If you are feeling anxious or reluctant to quit smoking, read the narrative sections in each chapter first. They are set off in italics and are easy to find. Use them to introduce the concepts and to get your thinking started. If you like to read stories, this is a more gentle way to "get your feet wet."

Using This Book

This book is designed to be used. It contains wide margins for writing notes and comments to yourself. It is small enough to be carried with you, but large enough to read and to write in. Mark it up! Use it! Keep it in the bathroom as the only book there for reading; or leave it on the kitchen table to read while you eat; or leave it by your reading chair for browsing.

Keep a pencil handy as you read for recording important information: your thoughts, feelings, reactions, insights. It is important to let your mind go a bit as you read the book. Recording your seemingly idle thoughts will provide a window for recognizing what is going on inside at the deeper levels of your consciousness. This is valuable information for understanding and managing yourself comfortably and effectively. A separate journal for writing as you read may feel more comfortable and private than writing in the book.

If you are reading this book on your own and using it to help you restructure or eliminate your smoking habits, take each chapter as it comes in its normal sequence. Read it s-l-o-w-l-y. Make notes in the margins. Take time to think about the concepts. Look up additional information to help you gain a broader or deeper understanding of the information. References have been included for this purpose. Do the self-help exercises where suggested. They will involve you in the change process more directly. Take the time you need to do the job well. Arranging a week or so away from your normal activities so that you can concentrate and even practice some techniques more comfortably is an ideal way to begin.

If you are using this book as part of an individual counseling or group program to help you quit smoking, follow your leader's instructions. Any chapters unassigned for reading or study can be pursued later on as background or reinforcement for you.

Reread the book. You will discover ideas and concepts you had not noticed the first or even the second time you read it. If you read this book only once and then put it away on a shelf, it will be much easier for you to revert to old ways of thinking and acting. New concepts and new methods take a while to settle in. Use this book to keep your mind actively engaged in your new ways of thinking and acting. Use it for problem solving and reinforcing your nonsmoking habits. Though the stated topic of the book is quitting smoking, you will gain knowledge and experience in self-management, equally applicable in theory and practice to many other areas in your life.

I wish you success in your quest for freedom from smoking and from cigarettes. I wish you inward peace with the decisions you make for yourself. I wish you the confidence that comes from insight, understanding, and experience. I wish you the courage to keep going. And most of all, I wish you the joy of accomplishment, earned from your own conviction, dedication, patience and effort.

Julie Waltz Kembel
July, 1989

Acknowledgments

No Ifs, Ands, or Butts: A Smoker's Guide to Kicking the Habit is the culmination of two years of research, development and trial. I am deeply grateful to many people for their contributions.

My husband, Bob Kembel, brought my words to the printed page through countless hours at his own computer. His skill, sensitivity and patience are obvious in the design, layout and typography of this book.

Sabina Dunton is more than an editor. Her professional knowledge of smoking cessation techniques, small group instruction, self-help instructional tools and her own experience as author of similar books have been invaluable to me in the design and redesign of the book.

A small group of very dedicated technical advisors coached, advised and supported me throughout the development of this book: Daniel Baker, Ph.D., Psychology; Philip Eichling, M.D., Medicine; Linda Connell Hadfield, R.D., Nutrition; Eric Chesky, Gary Holzsager and Karma Kientzler, Exercise and Fitness. Between them, Dan Baker and Phil Eichling analyzed and reviewed the entire book, guiding me in the appropriateness and accuracy of the information presented.

David Fischer, Carolyn Niethammer and Dr. Lee Vliet all added a very personal as well as professional component to the depth and completeness of this book. Beverely Elliott, Jodina Scazzola Pozo and Chris Chapman taught side by side with me in the Canyon Ranch Stop Smoking Program. Their insight, humor and dedication to helping people quit smoking are reflected throughout the book.

Inspiration is a most important ingredient to any author. Catherine Stockwell, who wrote the foreword, and Mel Zuckerman, owner and founder of Canyon Ranch Health and Fitness Resort, have been important sources of inspiration to me. The Canyon Ranch guests who seek my help to quit smoking or make other healthy lifestyle changes inspire me to find tools and methods of presentation that will make their progress easier and more secure.

The researchers and authors of publications concerning smoking and smoking cessation, drugs, and tools and techniques for healthy living have laid a strong foundation of knowledge and techniques for people who choose to quit smoking. I am indebted to many of these men and women whose expertise shaped my professional growth and development, and who provided facts and inspiration for the writing of this book. Tom Ferguson, M.D., author of *The Smoker's Book of Health*, deserves special mention. His thoroughness and readability provide a standard of excellence for writers of self-help books.

A special acknowledgment belongs to my husband Bob, and my daughters, Lori and Robin, for their love, support and encouragement during the writing of this book.

To all of these people, and to the others I have not specifically named, **THANKS!**

Deciding To Quit

Twelve-year old **Jeremy** sat at his grandmother's kitchen table, drinking a cup of hot chocolate with three marshmallows bobbing on top. He was telling his grandmother about a HAM radio kit he had seen advertised in one of his father's electronics catalogs. His science teacher at school had built one and had demonstrated it to Jeremy's class more than three months ago. Jeremy had not been able to get the radio kit out of his mind. He had approached his mother, then his father, in hopes of receiving one for his upcoming birthday. They told him that he would have to earn the money to buy the kit himself. Now Jeremy was approaching his grandmother.

Jeremy took a folded piece of paper out of his pocket and smoothed it out for his grandmother to see. "Here, Gram," he said, "this is what it looks like."

"Very nice, Jeremy," his grandmother said. "Tell me how you plan to get one for yourself."

"I wish I could have it as a birthday present, or even a birthday and a Christmas present combined," he replied. "But Mom and Dad said I have to earn the money myself. I wish I had enough money already saved up. I wish I had a paper route or something so I would have some money. I wish I could just wish hard enough and make it appear right on top of this table!" he said.

*Gram laughed. She had listened to Jeremy's long wish lists for many years. "Jeremy," she said gently, "if you really and truly want something in this life, **you have to have a backbone instead of a wishbone.**"*

The chapters in this section are designed to help you turn your wishbone into a backbone: to help you develop and strengthen your own commitment to stop smoking for life.

Before You Begin

1

Change takes but an instant. It's the resistance to change that takes the time to overcome.

... Hebrew Proverb

When you lit up your first cigarette you probably didn't think much beyond how you felt, how "cool" or grown-up you looked, or maybe even how much a part of the action you were. If you were like most new smokers you probably didn't think much beyond the present. You very likely had little inkling of how important cigarettes would become in your life. Most new smokers don't realize just how much cigarettes will mean to them: the companionship, the relaxation, the stepping back from life's worries; the tool with which they think deeply or socialize extensively; the companion who greets them first in the morning and bids them the final good-night in the evening. Most smokers have a deep and intimate relationship with their cigarettes. Many smokers consider cigarettes to be their most trusted friend: one that doesn't insult or condemn them, that accepts them as they are and is always available. Perhaps this is why so many smokers feel such deep resistance to permanently leaving cigarettes.

Haven't you noticed how important cigarettes have become in your life? Haven't you worried about how you will get along without them? Haven't you wondered how you will find the strength to give them up? Quitting smoking can be difficult, but thousands of people are able to do it successfully. What helps them achieve that success is an understanding of themselves and of the meaning smoking has for them, a level of motivation to get themselves started, and a commitment to themselves to see the process of quitting all the way through to the end. A good set of practical tools and specific guidelines to follow are important when quitting smoking. But, they cannot replace or be effective without that basic understanding, motivation and commitment—the elements needed to overcome personal resistance to quitting smoking.

This first chapter is designed to cause you to reflect about how you started smoking in order to help you understand more about your reasons for quitting, to help you examine your own motivation to stop smoking, and to show you the steps necessary to ensure your success in leaving cigarettes completely. You will be introduced to six characters who began smoking in high school and who, throughout the chapters of this book, will also be working through the specific tasks and processes to quit smoking entirely. Perhaps you will see yourself in one or more of these individuals. Their presence in the book may offer a little companionship for you in what otherwise may be a lonely journey. Whatever is the case for you, remember that these characters and their role in the book are intended to help you understand, personalize, and relate more fully to the information provided.

Introductions

Let's meet the six people now and look at how each of them became a smoker. They are gathered together at their second high school class reunion, twenty years following graduation.

Bob was among the most popular kids in his graduating class. Very social and easy-going, Bob was easy to talk to and he always took time for his friends. He was introduced to cigarettes at a party one night. Being a joiner, Bob was eager to do what the others were doing. Both of his parents smoked, so he took his first cigarette easily. Sometime during the following week, a friend offered him a cigarette as they were walking to the school parking lot. Bob accepted. Soon Bob was buying his own cigarettes and sharing them with others.

Beth was an achiever. An intense and very focused person, Beth took her studies and the editorship of the school newspaper very seriously. Following a particularly exhausting wrap-up meeting for the February edition of the paper, the whole team of writers and editors headed out for hamburgers and cokes. Five members of the team were smokers. At the restaurant the smokers lit up, leaving their packs and matches on the table. Beth watched them closely, noticing how they seemed to relax with their cigarettes. She thought about the smokers long after the meeting ended.

Beth put smoking out of her mind until the March paste-up session for the paper. Two of the group were smoking while they worked (despite school no smoking rules). Beth studied them and their actions. She asked one of the girls if she could have a cigarette. "Sure," the girl said. "Help yourself." Beth took one, wrapped it carefully in a tissue, and placed it in her eyeglasses case. Later that evening Beth went outside with her cigarette and a pack of matches. She pictured her friends as they smoked and tried to imitate what she saw them do. After the first few puffs and the coughing and choking, she calmed herself down, leaned back against the side of the garage, took a small puff and held the smoke in her mouth. Slowly she inhaled. She coughed, but not as much as before. She tried again. And again. By the time she finished the cigarette, Beth felt light-headed and a little dizzy, but more relaxed than she had been. She borrowed a few more cigarettes that week. By the end of the week Beth was asking her friends where she could get them for herself.

Louise was a rebellious brat, by her own admission. Her parents had strict codes of behavior for all of their seven children. One of those codes was "no smoking;" another was "no drinking." Louise was a sophomore in high school when she tasted her first cigarette. She thought it was awful tasting but exceptionally cool looking.

As time went on Louise had many opportunities to smoke with friends who had cigarettes of their own. She was careful, at first, never to smoke at home. One evening she was confronted by her father soon after arriving home from a party. Her father, smelling the smoke in her hair and on her clothing, accused her of smoking. Louise denied that she had smoked at first. But later, when her father continued his harangue on the virtues of not smoking, Louise became defiant. She boldly told him that she had been smoking for many months and that she planned to continue to smoke. She was punished. She was confined to the house except during the hours of school and church.

Louise became even more intent upon continuing to smoke, which she did at every opportunity, and did nothing to conceal the fact from her parents. This created a tense, hostile environment at home. The more her parents restricted, the more Louise rebelled. Following graduation, Louise left home. She got a job as a waitress and moved in with some friends. She explored alcohol with the same intensity as cigarettes and it wasn't long before she had a major drinking problem. Many hours of therapy and even more hours with Alcoholics Anonymous would be needed to help Louise understand and deal more effectively with herself and her parents.

Randy was an athlete, and he was extremely popular. Everyone thought he was "cool." He did well in football and drove a car that was the envy of everyone. Whatever Randy did, others copied. When Randy smoked, others did too. Randy's high-school picture, brought for the reunion, showed a dark-haired young man, one foot on the bumper of his car, one arm wrapped around an attractive girl, and in his other hand, a lighted cigarette.

Martha waited until she had her first baby before she began to smoke. Married right out of high school, Martha was intent on beginning her family right away. She became pregnant in her third month of marriage. She brought the new baby home and all went well until the baby developed colic. The constant crying grated on Martha's nerves. Her husband gave her some relief from baby tending, but Martha was unable to relax even when she left the baby in someone else's care. A friend of Martha's suggested she try smoking cigarettes to ease her nerves. She told Martha that she had smoked for a long time and that she could not relax without the cigarettes. Martha tried smoking and found that she, too, could relax a little better afterward. She smoked whenever the baby cried and

No Ifs, Ands, or Butts

whenever she needed to unwind. In a very short time she was smoking three packs a day.

Tim first began smoking during boot camp in the Army. "All the tough guys smoked," he explained. "Only the 'wimps' wouldn't at least try." Tim tried. Tim was successful. Tim was tough. Tim was smoking two packs a day.

Do you wonder what's happened to these people?

Bob is married and has a young son named **Jeremy.** He is a social worker with a master's degree. He successfully quit smoking almost three years ago when the public building in which he works was declared a nonsmoking environment. Bob is proud of his achievement and frequently conducts smoking cessation groups as part of his job.

Beth changed her name to **Betheny** and now writes news and features for a major television network. She is very successful. Slim and chic, Betheny is the visual picture of the "perfect woman." She is still intense. She still smokes. She says smoking helps her think more clearly and without cigarettes she cannot focus her attention on her work. Her producer is urging her to quit smoking.

Louise quit drinking and made two unsuccessful attempts to stop smoking. She admits to having some very deep-seated anger and still uses the cigarettes as punishment to her parents and to herself. Her therapist is helping her to express her anger more appropriately. She is also helping Louise to nurture and comfort herself. Louise's AA friends provide a network of support and encouragement.

Randy, the school athlete, coaches high-school football and sells cars on the week-ends. He is still popular and keeps up with the latest trends. He still drives an enviable car. He is a role model for the students he coaches. Randy recently launched a "smoke out" campaign for students and their parents at school and was the first person to toss his cigarettes in the trash can.

Martha has three children now and she still smokes. She is angry about anti-smoking legislation which restricts where she can smoke. Martha has emphysema. Her doctor is insisting that she give up smoking. Martha is ignoring him.

Tim is the corporate head of a large athletic shoe manufacturing company with seven sites in six countries. He is still tough, ruling his empire with a fair but very firm hand. His smoking habit is not in keeping with the health and fitness aspect of the corporate image that the Board of Directors is advocating. Further, Tim is newly married, for the second time, to a woman who does not smoke, and does not like to be in the presence of smokers. Tim is in the process of quitting.

How Smoking Affects Your Mind And Body

Do you see yourself in one or a combination of these people? Do their stories seem common to you? Each person's story represents a true human situation. They are common stories, yet the emotions involved are intensely individual. The underlying issue is that each of us struggles to cope successfully within the arenas of our life: family, education, career, financial security, friends, personal and spiritual growth and development, daily habits and patterns.

These struggles alternately produce elation, frustration, joy, anger, determination, tension, fatigue, relaxation, impatience, irritation and a vast array of unmentioned feelings. Each of these feelings can be a springboard for something. Perhaps you want something you can use to ease the pain or discomfort of bad feelings, or something to use for distracting yourself in order to ease frustration or impatience. Maybe you need something to ease loneliness or boredom or emptiness, or something you can use to soothe irritation. Perhaps you want something you can use to relax or energize yourself. If these somethings are associated with smoking, then you will recognize the desire for one or more of them most clearly when you hear yourself saying, "I want a cigarette!"

Consider, for a moment, the notion that a cigarette is simply a tool, much like a shovel. If you were a new gardener and wanted to plant some rose bushes, you would purchase the bushes, the necessary fertilizer, the pest sprays and a shovel. Now the shovel is probably not something that you want directly, as you do the rose bushes. What you really want is a hole for each rose bush, and the shovel is the tool necessary for producing what you want: the hole.

Following this analogy, what most people want when emotions run high is one or more of the somethings referred to in the previous paragraph. These somethings require a tool of some sort for implementation. The all-purpose tool of choice for smokers is a cigarette. While it is true that meditation, for example, can be a very effective tool for relaxation, or that a telephone call to a good friend can ease loneliness, most smokers think first of a cigarette. It's habit. It requires little or no effort. It's nearly always available. It requires no explanation. Thus, it is easier to smoke than to use almost any other tool to cope with the current emotion. This is a primary reason why smokers are so strongly attached to cigarettes, and to smoking. As long as smokers perceive that they are soothed, comforted, quieted, distracted, stimulated, kept company, occupied and pleasured by cigarettes, the deep-seated need to have these urges satisfied will be stronger than any intellectual decision to quit smoking.

While smokers have given ample evidence of the physically pleasurable effect of inhaling, of having something to do with the hands, of the oral enjoyment of "dragging" on a cigarette, researchers have concluded that there is a physiological basis for the profound impact of cigarettes. They report that nicotine stimulates the activity of several neurochemicals responsible for regulating heart rate, blood pressure, muscle tension, pain sensitivity and blood sugar.

These neurochemicals have powerful psychological effects as well. Several studies support the idea that cigarettes help smokers concentrate and stay alert. Other research demonstrates that nicotine can act directly on the brain to reduce anxiety and increase tolerance to pain. Even more interesting is the idea that smokers can regulate these effects as needed. For example, short, quick puffs supply smaller amounts of nicotine and act as a stimulant to the brain, resulting in greater alertness. Slow, deep drags cause initial stimulation, followed by relaxation or sedation. This adaptability of nicotine's effects is one important reason why the impact of tobacco is so insidious.

Whether for psychological or physiological reasons, or both, quitting smoking is a serious matter, not to be taken lightly. Loss of cigarettes most probably means more than loss of nicotine. Smokers who have quit, stayed abstinent for some lengthy period of time and later returned to smoking most often state psychological or emotional reasons for returning to smoking. Perhaps it is the effect of the cigarette as a tool used to meet emotional or psychological needs, or perhaps it is the effect of the nicotine itself. One thing is certain: **you cannot take something out of your life without replacing it with viable substitutes.** Taking something so compelling and pervasive as cigarettes away without active and useful alternatives to meet the same emotional and psychological needs as were met with the cigarettes will only lead you back to smoking.

The process of changing deep-seated habits is a lengthy one. When the habits are combined with perceived pleasure and with addictive physiological and psychological components, the whole process is more complicated and even harder to change. This is not to say that changing these habits is impossible. It does mean that the person making the changes needs to understand the difficulty involved and to allow sufficient time, consistent effort, daily concentration and a great deal of patience in order to establish the desired changes. This is not meant to sound pessimistic, only serious. The effort and concentration required must be applied continuously if you are to succeed. You need to allow for the added effort and emotional drain that typically accompany changes in daily habits. You also need to allow for the occasional "slip-ups" and "set-backs" that are not failures, but reminders that new learning usually involves some error. It is not the error itself that worries people as much as the recovery from it. For this reason, Chapter 9 is devoted to error prevention and recovery.

You are about to initiate some lifestyle changes with very positive benefits to your health and physiological well-being. The psychological and emotional aspects of your current behavior may get in the way of consistent change. The addictive nature of cigarettes themselves may cause you to cling to old habits. The more you understand about how smoking affects your body, mind and emotions, and the more you understand about behavior and how to change it, the more successful you are likely to be in making the desired changes.

How Motivated Are You?

Many people purchase books like this one or enroll in stop smoking programs seeking motivation for quitting smoking. They hope the book or the program will have something magical to motivate them, or to strengthen their resolve. No one has the ability to motivate you—except you. Others can inspire, push, advise and cheer for you, but they cannot create the drive necessary for you to achieve your goals. The effort expended in achieving a goal is voluntary. If you see no personal gain for reaching a particular goal, your efforts to make the necessary changes will be sporadic and of short duration. Therefore, your first task in the change process is to **make certain that the changes you seek in your smoking behavior are ones that YOU personally want to make, for your very own personal reasons.**

Your Reasons For Quitting

Take some time alone with yourself. Ask yourself a few pointed questions. Take time to answer them thoughtfully and honestly. Writing your responses down helps to focus and clarify your thoughts. This will be invaluable to you later as you try to understand you own motivation for quitting, and to anticipate what the potential obstacles and supports to your quitting smoking will be. Use the space provided in the book for writing down your answers to the questions asked.

1. What is your real reason for wanting to quit smoking? _____

   _____

   _____

   _____

2. Are you doing this for yourself? _____ If not, who are you
   doing it for and why? _____

   _____

   _____

3. Are you doing this to please someone else in order to gain
   their respect or approval? _____

   _____

   _____

4. Are you doing it because you think it's the correct thing to do
   for your health or appearance? _____

   _____

   _____

   _____

5. Is social pressure your main reason for quitting smoking? ____

6. What do you hope to gain for yourself as a result of quitting
   smoking? _____

   _____

   _____

   _____

7. Who will be affected by your quitting and in what ways?

   _____

   _____

   _____

   _____

8. Are you tough enough to quit when others around you are still smoking? _____

9. Are you willing to go out of your way to be with nonsmoking people and be in a nonsmoking environment when necessary to keep yourself from smoking? _____

10. Are you willing to invest a significant amount of time and energy in order to quit smoking successfully? _____

Perhaps it will be more helpful to list your thoughts in a way that makes it easier for you to analyze your own state of readiness. Look at the categories listed below and write your answers on the blank lines provided. Where a 1-5 rating level is indicated, 1 is low and 5 is high.

1. Benefits of smoking? _____
   _____
   _____
   _____

2. Benefits of quitting? _____
   _____
   _____
   _____

3. Consequences of smoking? _____
   _____
   _____
   _____

4. Consequences of quitting? _____
   _____
   _____
   _____

5. Supporters for smoking? _____

_____

_____

_____

6. Supporters for quitting? _____

_____

_____

_____

7. Length of time smoking? _____

8. Length of time not smoking? _____

9. Desire to smoke? (1 - 5)* _____

10. Desire to quit? (1 - 5)* _____

11. Commitment to smoke? (1 - 5)* _____

12. Commitment to quit? (1 - 5)* _____

(* Remember, 1 is low and 5 is high)

Are You Ready To Quit?

Take some time to think about your answers. Look at your desire and commitment to smoking and not smoking. Look at your reasons for quitting, and the effort and energy you claim you are willing to give to quitting smoking. Do your answers point to emotional or psychological preparedness for quitting? Or do they show you that because of commitment, timing, the influence of particular people or even the nature of your reasons, quitting smoking right now is not a priority for you? Whether you decide to quit smoking at this time or wait until later, you need to analyze your answers to the questions in this chapter to make sure that you are ready, willing and able to do whatever is necessary for you to quit smoking successfully.

If you have determined that you are not ready to commit yourself to quitting smoking right now, forcing yourself to enroll in a stop smoking program may only result in failure, defiance or stubborn resistance to using any of the suggested tools or techniques. Trying to trap yourself into compliance is not the most effective way to tackle an important goal.

Just as young children do not learn to read until they are developmentally ready, adults should not begin a serious, detailed program of long-term behavior change until they are psychologically ready. Many people are not committed and ready to accomplish change when they first seek help or enroll in a program. Spending money on programs or books does not always establish commitment, nor does it typically strengthen wavering commitment. It may, however, help the person accumulate enough information and new ways of looking at the same old issues to eventually lead to a firm decision to quit.

Some people with uncertain resolve prefer to become involved in a more detached way. They attend classes, join in group discussion and even go through the motions of setting goals for change. Yet they do not actively work on specific assignments. They go through the motions to "try them on for size," to see if they think they really can or want to stop smoking. For some people this is a good way to begin. It lets them explore the concepts and think about the issues involved. It provides a type of "readiness" training which will be very helpful when they make a sincere decision later on to quit smoking.

If this applies to you, enroll in a private session with a smoking cessation counselor. Give yourself permission to listen and to play with the concepts. Read the information given to you, talk about it, and then, when you feel ready to take on the challenge of totally quitting, enroll in a structured stop smoking program within your community, or take advantage of one of the residential stop smoking programs offered in a variety of specialized settings.

Even totally committed people may struggle with the effort of lifestyle change if they are involved with some other major life event at the same time they are quitting smoking. A job or career change, new marriage, divorce, relocation, severe illness or death of someone important to you are all examples of situations which may absorb great amounts of your available energy. This is energy you need to be able to concentrate on and work hard with the stop smoking techniques you will learn here.

If you are undergoing some major life change or other energy-consuming tasks in your life right now, take the time necessary to settle those issues first and then begin your stop smoking plan of action. It is true that busy people always have energy-draining tasks to deal with. Only you can determine whether these tasks are within your normal routine, or whether they represent more effort than you can reasonably give and still handle the extras necessary to stop smoking successfully.

Steps To Increase Your Success

There are some very necessary steps which you must take in order to increase your success in quitting smoking. They are:

1. **Set specific time aside each week for reading and planning.** Make certain that the time you allocate for study is not cluttered with other tasks requiring attention, and that it is not a normally sleepy time of day or night for you. Impaired concentration will sabotage all your intended efforts to learn effectively.

2. **Experiment with the ideas and techniques suggested.** Keep in mind that you do not need to make habits out of every idea or technique you try. You need to have opportunities to find out what works, what fits your personality and lifestyle, and what feels good to do. Later you can select the "keepers" from everything you've experimented with and follow the steps to making

them habitual. For right now, though, the idea is to explore all the tools and techniques. Try everything, then decide.

3. **Share each week's learning and progress with someone to gain reinforcement and support.** Be cautious in your selection of support people. Someone who needs to quit smoking is not likely to be openly accepting of your continuing success, for your progress only brings home the idea that he or she ought to be able to do as you've done and quit. An "I told you so" support person may anger more than reinforce you. It is critical that the person who agrees to support you be someone you feel good about, and that he or she genuinely feels good about your quitting smoking.

4. **Attend all individual counseling or class sessions if you are enrolled in a formal stop-smoking program, no matter what else you might prefer to do instead.** The time spent in study and practice now will allow for lots of mental and emotional "free time" for yourself later. Get this objective out of your way first. The more time and serious attention you give it now, the sooner you will be able to move comfortably on to other things.

5. **If you are studying this book on your own, select one chapter at a time for reading and study.** Work with it daily until you reach a state of understanding and a moderate working knowledge of the tools presented. Set aside a period for study each day, experiment with the ideas, and share your learning and progress with someone regularly. It may be easier for you to be irregular in your effort to read and practice the tools in this book if you are doing it all on your own.

If you see yourself sabotaging the consistency of your study efforts, enroll yourself in a stop smoking group or enlist the help of a professional to guide you through the process. Some people need to be accountable to someone other than themselves in order to keep their energies and motivation strong. If this applies to you, make certain you have involved yourself with someone you regard highly right from the very beginning. This helps to keep you striving for success. None of us likes to fail in the eyes of someone we look up to.

Determine Your Resistance To Change

If you are unable or unwilling to commit yourself to these steps at this time, don't start yet. Instead, talk with a smoking cessation counselor to develop a good alternative plan to prepare for readiness. This may seem harsh to you but there is a related psychological element that may be at work. This element is called resistance to change. The resistance phenomenon emerges when people attempt to corner, or trap themselves into doing something they are unwilling to do. The impact of this resistance is noticed as noncompliance, sabotage or returning to smoking.

If you recognize these tendencies in yourself, examine your thoughts carefully. If they point to unwillingness to make change, wait until you feel differently before committing yourself to quit "cold turkey." You may realize, though, that your tendencies to sabotage yourself are more a reflection of your frustration with yourself, impatience with your progress, or a particular quirk in your psychological make-up. In these instances, it is helpful to look at sabotage as an indicator for the need to handle yourself differently. Perhaps being more gentle with yourself, setting more reasonable goals, establishing simpler tasks would be useful in reducing frustration. These issues will be discussed later in this book.

Time Out To Think

*When the reunion was over, **Betheny** asked **Bob** to stay for a few more minutes so that they could talk privately. Bob brought two steaming cups of coffee to the table where Betheny sat and they chatted casually about the changes in their high-school friends. The chatter died down. Betheny sat quietly, tracing the rim of her cup with her finger. Bob waited patiently, sensing that Betheny was struggling with something important. She took* *a deep breath, then started to talk. Betheny told Bob that the people she worked for were urging her to quit smoking and that, for some reason, she felt angry about it. She had done a week-long news feature on the health hazards of smoking and she knew all about the medical risks.*

"I've thought about quitting smoking many times," she told Bob, "but I just can't seem to take it all very seriously. You said you sometimes help others quit smoking and I wondered if you could give me some advice to help me change my attitude."

"What's the most positive reason for smoking?" Bob asked Betheny.

She thought for a moment before answering. "Composure," she said.

As they talked further, Bob understood that Betheny's appearance was of utmost importance to her. A normally high-energy, intense person, Betheny was unable to sit still with composure. Thus, she needed cigarettes to occupy her hands when she felt restless and edgy. When faced with the need to make a decision in a hurry, Betheny tended to search for a cigarette while she collected her thoughts and arrived at her decision. While on the telephone, Betheny would light cigarette after cigarette. She told Bob that she didn't see how she could ever handle telephone calls without her cigarettes.

"And I absolutely cannot afford to gain weight!" she exclaimed. "I'm the only person on the set who still smokes. No one will even let me in the editing room if I have a cigarette with me. I've got to get this situation under control, fast."

"Betheny," Bob said gently, "if you could find some other ways to maintain your composure, and if you could learn to control your weight without cigarettes, would you still want to quit smoking?"

"I think so," she replied. "I would miss them very much. They keep me company. I smoke wherever I am. I smoke in the cab, in the tub, while putting on my make-up. I smoke while I read, write and think. I even smoke when I don't want to think. Am I hopeless?"

"No," Bob smiled. "You're not hopeless, but you do have a big job on your hands if you really do want to quit smoking. I think the first step is to decide if you really do want to quit. Everything you mentioned can be handled successfully without cigarettes. You will need some very

structured guidance to help you learn ways of managing yourself without smoking. You will have to decide that quitting smoking is important enough to you to put in the time and effort necessary to get the job done."

Betheny was silent with her thoughts. Again Bob waited patiently. At last she said, "What should I do first?"

His answer was simple. "Think. Think about the pros and the cons, about the benefits and the disadvantages. Think about how much cigarettes control you." Betheny stared at him. "They do control you, you know. If you cannot go anywhere without taking cigarettes along, if you have to calculate how long you can go without a cigarette, if you plan your social activities around your smoking buddies, don't you think cigarettes are controlling you?"

"I hadn't looked at it that way," Betheny replied. "I'll have to think about that."

Closing Thoughts

Like Betheny, you also need to think. This could be one of the most important decisions you will ever make. Reaching the decision to quit or not to quit is, for many people, the hardest task of all. Whatever your decision, remember that it needs to fit you at this time in your life.

If you choose to continue smoking for the time being, there will be other opportunities for you to quit. Read the remaining chapters in this section of the book for they may stimulate your motivation.

If you are prepared to quit smoking now, read each chapter carefully. Do the recommended self-study exercises and experiment with the ideas that appeal to you. Take the time necessary to do the job well.

Whether you are planning to read for motivation or for action, move on to Chapter 2 and let's get started.

Preparing For Change

2

In all things, success depends upon previous preparation.

... Confucius

The beginning steps of change are awareness and knowledge. These are the first steps this book focuses upon. You will be learning many new things: concepts and facts, tasks, processes and points of view. Most people have more than adequately demonstrated their ability to learn effectively and to apply that learning in their educational and professional lives. Yet these same people feel frustrated with their performance when it involves certain types of personal change, like quitting smoking.

The learning process used to change behavior is not so different than the process of learning to play a musical instrument, speak a foreign language or deliver a formal speech. However, there is a special kind of learning handicap that comes from previous failures, reputations earned for only short-term change and feelings of fear and insecurity about one's ability to make the intended changes. If you are a smoker who has quit, then started smoking again, you can certainly relate to this. The more you understand about the learning process, particularly *your* learning process, and how it applies to the accomplishment of change in your life, the easier it will be for you to reach your intended goal.

Right now, at the very beginning of your program to quit smoking, you already possess a set of smoking habits which are well practiced. In fact, they may be so well established that they just happen without conscious thought. Further, these smoking habits may be important to you for a variety of reasons: tension release, relaxation, something to do when you feel fidgety, something to keep you company while you think or read, appetite reduction or any number of other physical, emotional, psychological or social reasons.

Your smoking habits are comfortable and familiar to you. What you are asking of yourself in giving up cigarettes is to exchange old, comfortable, familiar, secure habits and patterns for a new set of habits and patterns which, initially, will feel awkward and strange, inconsistent and not very comfortable or secure. Smoking satisfied some very specific needs in your life. You will be identifying those needs, and you will be learning and practicing new ways to satisfy them.

Keep in mind that all new learning feels awkward and unsure in the beginning. Do you remember learning to drive a car with a manual transmission, or learning to use a computer? It is the daily practice, the repetition of basic techniques that eventually results in feelings of familiarity and security with the new learning. The blending and the molding of new ideas and techniques to fit your personality and lifestyle takes time and repeated practice. Eventually they become habit. The challenge is to "hang in there" long enough for the changes to get established!

This chapter will help you to begin the processes of emotional, psychological and intellectual preparation for stopping smoking. You will learn about the factors that affect significant change in long established habits like smoking. You will be challenged to think about yourself and your daily patterns in ways you may not have considered before. Hopefully you will feel encouraged by the end of this chapter, and excited about your potential for success.

Relax now and let your mind wander over the next several pages. Allow time for daydreaming or unstructured thinking. Write your thoughts down for review at a later date. Give yourself time to think about the concepts. Mold those concepts into your own thinking patterns. There is no rush. The objective is evolution, not revolution.

Confronting Fear

Betheny returned to her hotel room, tired but deeply thoughtful. Bob's words echoed through her mind. "Do cigarettes really control me?" she wondered. "Why else would I fight so hard not to give them up?" Betheny lit a cigarette and paced about the tiny room. "Why?" she demanded of herself. Her mind answered back: "Fear."

Betheny stopped pacing to stare at herself in the mirror. "Fear?" she said aloud to her image. "Fear of what?" The face that looked back from the mirror was drawn, the tension lines deeply etched in the skin around her eyes and mouth. "Fear of failure. Fear of success. Fear of looking stupid. Fear of not knowing how to handle yourself. Fear of losing control."

Betheny stared at herself in amazement. "I guess I hadn't realized just how deeply involved with cigarettes I really am," she thought. "Can I really give them up? Do I really want to?"

Does fear get in your way when you think about giving up cigarettes? What do you fear? Think about it for a few moments. Most of us fear separating ourselves from the people, places and things that we feel emotionally attached to. Whenever we don't have a clear picture in our minds of what we will do, how we will act, even how we will feel without them, the tendency is to hold on tight to them so that we won't feel insecure. There is security in holding on to what is familiar to us, even if what we are holding on to isn't good for us anymore. Isn't that a factor in why we stay with jobs we don't like, relationships that don't feel good, houses that are too big or too small?

Perhaps one way to confront some of the fears you may be having is to first write them down. Then think about what each of them means to you. For example, consider that one of your fears may be loneliness. How could the loss of cigarettes cause loneliness for you?

Perhaps you like the companionship of always having something with you that you take everywhere. Many people like having something familiar to look at, to hold, to take along in a purse or pocket, to touch or caress when they are feeling upset. Some people feel a sense of companionship from the lighted cigarette, almost as though the cigarette smoke represents a living being. Some people have undergone so much change in their lives that cigarettes represent the only consistent part of their lives.

Is loss of control one of your fears? Do you worry that you will become a nasty tempered person, yelling and shouting at others, slamming doors or being sarcastic in your comments? Do you fear that others will think badly of you or want to stay far away from you for ever and ever? Do you fear that without cigarettes to give you a sense of confidence, you will now appear to be unsure of yourself, nervous, confused, flustered or otherwise unsettled?

Whatever your fears are about giving up cigarettes, write them on the lines below and alongside each, include some comments about what that fear actually means to you.

My fear...	What it means to me...

My fear...	What it means to me...

Acknowledging that you have some fears is a very important first step in doing something about them. Writing them down and thinking about the impact each of them has on you will help to make them seem less scary. In a way, seeing them in written form is like turning on a flashlight in a dark room. The light helps you to identify the objects in front of you so that you can walk around without bumping into them. When you can look at your fears and understand what meaning they have for you, it will be more obvious what actions you will need to take in order to deal with them effectively. You will also be able to ask questions of others who have quit smoking to learn how they managed to handle the same things that worry you. Don't be shy about talking to people who have quit smoking successfully to learn about the methods, the coping tools and techniques, they used. People love to talk about their experiences and enjoy giving suggestions when asked.

Emotional Separation

Betheny met *Louise* for lunch the next day. Though not very close friends in high school, Betheny felt drawn to Louise the night of the reunion. Betheny had done a feature on alcoholism in America and was interested in hearing about Louise's experiences with quitting drinking.

The two women talked easily during lunch. Over coffee, the conversation became more serious. Louise was talking about the feelings of grief that engulfed her when she gave up alcohol. She told Betheny that her therapist had helped her to realize that part of her anger really came from a deep sense of loss.

Louise went on to explain that her anger toward her parents came more from a feeling of being pushed away by them, a belief that she was unacceptable to them no matter what she did. She tried to win their approval at first, she said, but when that failed she just wanted to hurt them in some way. Smoking and then drinking had just the effect on them she wanted. The emotional distance between them became greater. Inwardly that hurt; outwardly she became more openly rebellious.

As Betheny questioned Louise further, she became very conscious of how difficult it was for Louise to separate herself emotionally from her parents and also from drinking. Betheny could see that Louise had strong emotional attachment to cigarettes also and she wondered how Louise was going to deal with giving them up, if she ever decided to quit smoking.

Betheny thought about Louise for a long time after they said their good-byes. Louise had left a bleak picture of emptiness and loneliness in Betheny's mind. She telephoned **Bob** that night to ask his views about what Louise had told her.

Bob was very direct with Betheny. He told her that separation from people, things, even behavior patterns that have been very closely associated with a person will usually cause a deep sense of loss and some confusion about how to continue on alone. He told her that grief is a normal part of the separation process. "In fact," he said, "when you decide to give up smoking, you will probably feel a deep sense of loss at first. You may find yourself crying a lot, possibly even feeling empty inside."

"Why?" asked Betheny. "I'm not a very sentimental person and I can't imagine getting all that upset over cigarettes."

Bob explained. "Look at it this way. Imagine that you and your very best friend are soon to be parted. The two of you have gone all through school together. You were even roommates in college. You married at the same time, each of you serving as the attendant of honor at each other's wedding. Your first children even arrived within three months of each other. You've known each other's most intimate thoughts for years, and you've known all the principal friends and family members in each other's lives.

"Now your friend is about to move 1500 miles away. What pain! 'How will I survive?' you think to yourself. 'How can I possibly go on alone?' It hurts, but you have no choice other than to accept the impending loss. The pain of separation is knife-sharp at first, as anyone who has experienced such a loss well knows. It subsides some with time until you recognize it as a dull ache. That is, until you turn on the late show one night on your TV, and there is a wonderful old movie playing—one you saw with your friend. The stab of pain returns as the memories come flooding back. Maybe you shed a tear; maybe you reach for the phone. Whatever you do, the pain of missing your friend will be felt.

"Most of us understand this process," Bob continued, "and accept it where people or pets are concerned. Certainly social customs have taught us the mechanics of how to accept such losses. Social customs have not taught us how to handle the loss of intimate relationships with things. Sure, we feel badly when we break a favorite item, or lose the rosary beads we've carried since childhood. We are told to buck up, buy another item to replace the first one, and 'get on with it.' Nothing has been said about resolving the feelings of loss. You're told that you'll get over it. And you will, eventually."

"Don't you think you're making too much out of this?" Betheny asked.

"Perhaps," Bob answered. "But don't ignore your feelings. If you do, you'll have a much harder time handling yourself."

You may be feeling a bit skeptical of the notion of emotional loss as it applies to cigarettes. Remember, though, that you are about to begin an ending process when you quit smoking, and your ability to handle it successfully can be helped by paying close attention to how you bring other painful situations to a close.

Stop for a moment to think about your relationships with other people. Think about how you have ended specific relationships in the past, what you said, how you felt and even how you acted. Did you try to rekindle any of those relationships? Did you cry much?

Did you hide for awhile, refusing opportunities to get together with other people? What words did you use to comfort yourself?

Your answers to these questions may offer some perspective about what to expect in terms of your own behavior, or what your needs might be for dealing with this degree of personal loss in your life.

New beginnings have their roots in endings. In other words, without an ending there is no new beginning. Endings represent a death of sorts. Our culture supplies a variety of rituals around death to help people cope with their loss. Burial and mourning rites allow a picture of finality and a genteel period of transition to begin the processes of acceptance and adjustment. As you begin your withdrawal from cigarettes, allow for the feelings of grief if they are evident to you. If the grief is very strong, you may need or want a ritual act of closure to give finality to smoking in your life. Bob shared with Betheny his own personal plan for putting cigarettes to rest.

Bob had been a three-pack-a-day smoker. He smoked everywhere, for all reasons. Especially dear to him were his coffee and cigarette breaks. He discovered that coffee was a strong trigger for him to want a cigarette. He tried using herbal teas in the morning, but discovered, to his amazement, that his favorite old coffee cup was the big culprit in causing him to think of and then want a cigarette. He told **Betheny** how hard it was to admit that he had to get rid of his favorite cup, and his small, but precious, collection of unusual lighters. "I couldn't just throw them away," he explained. "I needed to do something more special."

After thinking about other deep personal losses, particularly the death of his father, Bob came upon the idea of a burial rite for his smoking gear. He told Betheny how he placed the cup and the lighters inside a pretty metal box. Then he went outside to his favorite flower bed. Bob was an avid gardener. He had some available garden space in the corner of that flower bed. He buried the box deep in the ground in the center of the corner section. Then, in commemoration of the entire event, he planted a large number of Nicotiana seedlings. "Nicotiana," Bob explained, "is the very beautiful and very fragrant flower of the tobacco plant."

No Ifs, Ands, or Butts

Perhaps burial rites don't strike you as the way to begin quitting smoking, but if you do find yourself immersed in a deep sense of loss, some ritual act of closure to your former smoking life may be in order. Many people are embarrassed by the depth of emotion they feel when making their decision to quit smoking. Some deny their feelings; others become depressed. Some are openly angry and seem short-fused with respect to many things in addition to smoking.

These are typical grief reactions, and they need to be worked through before adjustment can take place. Talk with your instructor or counselor, and with those closest to you. Let them know you are struggling and ask for whatever extra help and "TLC" you might need. Spend time with others who are quitting smoking also. Companionship is helpful, especially when you are experiencing similar feelings. Helping one another work through these feelings can be especially healing. Acquire some new trinkets or talismans with which you can build a sense of strength and freedom from cigarettes. Acknowledge your courage in beginning an important and difficult task. Explore new rituals to help you adjust (e.g., a "bath and book" time before bed). Above all, give yourself room to explore, to feel, to challenge and to learn.

Facing The Challenge

The psychological attachment to cigarettes for most people is imbedded in their needs for managing themselves easily and effectively. **The task of quitting smoking is not a matter of simply replacing cigarettes for a while.** It goes much deeper than that to the very basic needs we have for calming and soothing ourselves, for relaxing, for reducing tension, for taking a much needed break from routine, for pampering and rewarding, for controlling restlessness, for getting away from people for a few moments, for alleviating boredom, for doing something while waiting for the next task to begin, for tuning the mind out, for gathering thoughts, for enduring long conversations, for sitting still while on the telephone, for companionship and for things still unmentioned that affect only you. These are normal human needs, experienced in some way on a frequent basis.

Nonsmokers have learned to meet these needs in a variety of ways; smokers have their all-purpose tool of choice, the cigarette. You will have to learn to handle these needs in alternative ways in order for you to permanently give up cigarettes. To pull a familiar coping tool out of your life and not replace it with something else will leave you feeling confused, less in control, maybe even angry. It will leave you vulnerable to the cigarette—not because of the nicotine, but because of the need to manage yourself effectively, to cope with the emotion or situation.

Perhaps you have quit smoking before and returned to it during a period of challenge, stress or crisis. It would be easy to assume, under these circumstances, that you weren't really ready to quit smoking forever. Perhaps that is true. Consider, though, that under stress or emotional turmoil, your primary objective would have logically been to get some relief, FAST. For many years, relief had been spelled, c-i-g-a-r-e-t-t-e-s. Old, very automatic learning would have taken over at such a moment of need. If circumstance then presented you with the easy opportunity to take or purchase a cigarette, you might have smoked one before you were even aware of your actions.

Situations like these, unfortunately, seem to imply personal failure more than simple error in judgement or technique, or lapse of concentration. If you, in a situation like that, found yourself overwhelmed by negative feelings, wouldn't it impair your ability to think rationally? Not surprisingly, mistakes of this type can lead you back to the old habits you had previously left behind. In such a situation it is not you, the person, who failed but rather, it is a failure of planning or technique or tool. Later in this book you will learn how to recover from errors and return quickly to the desired habits. For now, though, let's continue to look at the concepts underlying change of long-established habits.

Have you ever wondered how it is that you can be so incredibly successful in so many areas of your life and so frustratingly unsuccessful in sustaining long-term personal change like quitting smoking? Have you questioned why you are willing to work so incredibly hard for some things, yet want the easiest way out with others? Have you ever thought about why it is that so many of your actions are superficial and circumstantial while others are so carefully planned and executed? The answers to these questions lie within you. They can be discovered by watching how you cope with daily problems and challenges. Noting your reactions and responses to a variety of people and situations should give you a fairly accurate picture of yourself.

As you read this book you are being asked repeatedly to take time out to think, to reflect upon your thoughts, feelings and actions. Self-observation is an important tool for enabling you to predict how you might act and react in future situations. One of the unsettling aspects of change is its seeming lack of predictability. People appear to be most comfortable when they are able to anticipate what will happen to them and how they will respond when it does happen. Perhaps the issue of control is at the root of this need for predictability.

You will not be able to accurately anticipate everything that will happen to you when you quit smoking. But understanding how you have handled other challenges and changes in the past will help you plan ahead for meeting many of those same needs when you quit smoking.

The Power Of The Mind

In preparing yourself to begin quitting smoking, some preliminary mental "headwork" will be required. The basis of this headwork is embodied in the term "open-mindedness." This refers to a mind open to new ideas and to the exit of old, no longer useful ideas. Opening your thinking may require some focused effort at times, for each of us has attitudes, points of view, opinions and experiences which may hinder the ease and agility with which new ways of thinking are adopted.

Openness in thinking about yourself and your relationship to smoking, your feelings, your needs, even your thinking processes will be crucial to your ultimate success in eliminating cigarettes. Equally important is the attitude of willingness to hear, consider and adopt new ways of looking at things, of doing things differently. Easier to say than to do at times, **keeping yourself mentally open will be one of the most important tasks in accomplishing change.**

Another component of your "headwork" is to stay focused on your close-range goals. Most of us tend to look at "forever" when we set our goals. "I can never have ice cream again," or, "Now that I understand how this works I'll always have to do it this way." Forever is a long time. It feels overwhelming. The Chinese philosopher, Lao-tse, once said, *"A journey of a thousand miles must begin with a single step."*

Remember this as you move along through withdrawal and the development of new habits. Keep your eyes focused on the here and now, on today, on this craving. As you will soon learn, cigarette cravings are short, though frequent in the beginning. You can probably get yourself through ninety seconds of anything. Correct? Cigarette cravings are only thirty to ninety seconds in length. By keeping your vision limited to one craving at a time, rather than to a whole lifetime without cigarettes, the task of quitting smoking suddenly gets easier—and more do-able. The journey of a former smoker begins with overcoming one craving. And another. And another.

To put this same concept another way, most new nonsmokers look at quitting smoking as one, gigantic, monumental task. People experienced at accomplishing broad-range personal change will tell you that such change was made possible by dividing the overall goal into a series of smaller, more manageable steps. You will learn how to set a realistic, manageable step-by-step plan to help you accomplish the necessary changes to start and keep you a nonsmoker, one step at a time.

What Is Your Learning Style?

Betheny's continual questioning stirred up **Bob's** own thoughts about the steps involved in quitting smoking. He searched through his written materials for some practical suggestions and ideas to pass along to her. His search took him to a variety of educational and instructional books used in his daily counseling practice. That got him into thinking about the learning process itself. His enthusiasm grew. He telephoned Betheny at her hotel, hoping to reach her before she left for home.

"Betheny," he said, "I have some information I want to share with you. Do you have time to meet me for coffee?"

"Sure," she replied. They arranged the time and place.

Bob and Betheny settled into a corner of the coffee shop and chatted a bit. Then Bob began. "You were a very good student in high school as I remember," he said to Betheny. She nodded. "That should be helpful to you now," he continued. "Let's look at learning theory and process, and how they relate to changing habits.

"If you decide to quit smoking it will help you to realize that you will be involved in a structured learning process. The process of learning new habits is much the same as the process for learning anything." Betheny looked puzzled. Bob continued. "People accomplish their learning in many ways. Some people **learn by hindsight**. Actually most of life's learning is by hindsight. You see it in performance evaluations and critiques of written material. You probably see it in your work every day." Betheny nodded. "In this learning style," Bob said, "error is essential, for without it much of the concrete illustration and technique will not be brought into discussion."

"That's true," Betheny agreed. "In the editing room we are always critiquing everything. Later this information is passed on to the actors, the lighting and camera crews, everyone who needs to know."

"Good," Bob said. "You already have a positive attitude about learning from mistakes. In changing habits there are many mistakes to deal with and you will have to handle them the same way you handle the ones in the editing room. Mistakes aren't failures. They are errors in technique, judgement, timing. Remember that for later.

"Another learning style is **by rote.** This is typical for most new learning, and requires the conscious application of rules and procedures. Playing a musical instrument is a good example of this. First you learn to read the notes by rote; then tap out the rhythm with a pencil or finger by rote. You start putting them together. It is the continual, disciplined practice that eventually results in flexibility."

"That's great for piano," Betheny commented, "but I don't see how it applies to quitting smoking."

"You will be learning very specific tools and techniques as part of your quit smoking program or plan," Bob explained. "At first you will be doing them just because you are supposed to, not because it naturally occurs to you to do them. They will feel strange and unnatural. The cigarette has felt very natural for a long time. You will have to keep practicing with the nonsmoking tools and techniques by rote, by very conscious application until, at last, they happen more naturally. With piano, it is in the hours and hours spent at the keyboard that you really learn to play. With quitting smoking, it is the hours and hours of doing different things, instead of smoking, that will make you a nonsmoker."

"People are always telling me what to do," Betheny complained. "I can just imagine how much advice I'll get when I let people know I'm giving up cigarettes!"

Bob laughed. "Perhaps you should look at advice in another way. Call it **learning by example.** This is like the advice given to us by others: parents, teachers, people who have previously acquired the learning we are about to experience. Actually, most of us have a harder time learning from others' experiences. That's why we prefer to **learn from personal experience.** As independent as you are," Bob smiled, "I'll bet this will be your preferred learning style."

Betheny shrugged. "This all seems very complicated to me. I always thought the plan was to decide to quit smoking and then just tough it out."

"That's what most people think," Bob told her. "Commitment is the single most important aspect to doing anything substantial, and especially for quitting smoking. For some people, commitment alone provides the needed incentive. But for the many people who struggle with new things, or who have quit and then gone back to smoking, there's much more to be learned.

"Think of it this way, Betheny. You have evolved a very definite set of coping mechanisms with your daily use of cigarettes. You won't suddenly 'unlearn' what you already know. In fact in the early studies of how behavior is learned (classical conditioning), a Russian scientist named Pavlov discovered that if he rang a bell at the same time he fed his laboratory dogs, he could 'teach' them to expect food at the sound of the bell, whether or not food was actually present. He noted that only a few trials were required to teach the dogs this new response. When attempting to retrain the dogs not to expect food at the sound of the bell, Pavlov discovered that the process of retraining (or unlearning) took longer to accomplish than did the initial training."

"That's interesting," Betheny commented.

Bob went on. "Based on information gained from Pavlov and others, behavioral specialists have suggested that **rather than teach people to not do something they have been used to doing, instead teach them to do something different, something new.** Learning is achieved more rapidly this way. What it means in terms of smoking is this: you have smoked for an extensive period of time and to teach you not to smoke in the same situations and states of need where you once smoked would take a very long period of time. Why not teach you something new instead, or in place of smoking? Therefore, when the telephone rings and you make a mad dash for something to fiddle with while you talk, why not place a variety of 'playthings' to amuse yourself with in the places by your telephone where you once kept cigarettes?

"Whether the object is a hand grip to squeeze, pens and a telephone book to doodle with, paper clips to string together or an interesting collection of trinkets to play with, the result is the same: calming superficial tension. When your hand reaches out for a cigarette pack to keep you company while you're trapped on the listening end of a telephone cord, it needs to find something. If your hand finds nothing, the urge for a cigarette may be very strong.

"Remember," Bob added, "once you've completed physical withdrawal from nicotine, **it is less the cigarette itself you crave than it is the need to soothe or relax yourself.** The more proficient you become in training yourself to do other things to meet the same needs as were met by cigarettes, the sooner you will feel secure in your ability to live happily without smoking."

"I can just see me now," Betheny commented wryly. "All these high-powered ad men coming into my office to watch me string paper clips together. That should give them all a good laugh!"

"Perhaps that will be something you will do only in private. Isn't your producer the one who's been pushing you to quit smoking? Do you think he'd prefer to watch you string paper clips than light up a cigarette?"

"Okay," Betheny laughed. "You scored one point for quitting. You'll need a few more points to get me really motivated."

"Well, motivation can be a tricky thing," Bob commented. "The initial spark of motivation to quit has to come from you. But we know something about what kills motivation. One killer is to take on too many things to do at one time. Another is to start off with the toughest tasks first.

"Think about typical instructional books," he suggested. "Remember how the learning objectives were divided into a series of small tasks, beginning with the easiest ones and progressing sequentially into increasingly more difficult ones?"

"Yes, I can see where this applies to typing, math and playing the piano," Betheny replied, "but what does it have to do with not smoking?"

Bob answered. "Keep in mind that all learning progresses in the same way, no matter what the task or topic. **Early learning is based upon very concrete, easy steps.** This allows for ease in grasping basic concepts and procedures. It allows, too, for early success, and nothing motivates someone more than the excitement of succeeding. Don't you agree?" Betheny looked noncommittal.

"As training progresses, the difficulty of the tasks and the conceptual framework increases slowly. Big jumps in difficulty most often result in frustration. As the frustration continues, the motivation diminishes. Most educators and trainers work hard to reduce the size of the steps, or to add extra encouragement until the new understandings or actions have been grasped and tested. **Your stop smoking training begins with concrete learning first, progressing to the more abstract. It begins with simpler tasks, moving to the more complex; from a more regimented style to a more spontaneous, improvisational style.** This is in keeping with basic learning principles."

"That seems too complicated for me to do on my own," Betheny said.

"That's why there are so many informative books, stop smoking programs, specialized counselors and teachers, and even support groups for smokers who have quit and just want additional ideas and reinforcement. They will help you discover how to arrange the sequence and complexity of your learning tasks, as they relate to not smoking."

"You're looking a bit restless, Betheny," Bob remarked. "This is a lot of information to cover at one time."

"Agreed!" Betheny said as she stood up. "I have an early morning flight so I'm going to go to the hotel and pack." Betheny knew she had heard enough for one session. She wanted time to get off by herself to think. She hadn't come to the reunion to force herself to quit smoking. Yet Bob's words made sense to her intellectually. "I don't have to do anything about it right now," she told herself as she left the coffee shop.

Closing Thoughts

You have probably had enough heavy concentration for one session also. Take some time now to put the book aside. Go about your normal routines. Let the information you've read percolate in your mind. Think about how you learn best and what motivates you. If you are feeling a bit overwhelmed, don't worry about that for now. Remember, "the journey of a thousand miles begins with the first step." **Your first step is to think.**

Keep in mind that the value of your stop smoking training is in more than the end result alone. It is in the learning, the personal growth and the confidence you acquire in the process of realizing the goals you set for yourself. Some people, when they hike, look only toward the destination, oblivious to the many enchantments along the way. Others are excited about the wildflowers, the animal tracks, the satisfaction of strenuous exercise. While some people look only toward the destination and measure how far there is yet to go, others prefer to look backward to where they started and measure how far they have come. So what can be learned from this?

One lesson is that the journey itself is perhaps more valuable than the destination, for without the learning and the strengthening of the journey, the destination cannot be reached. The second lesson is to take time to recognize how far you've come in reaching your goals, not just how far you still have to go. The success you will feel in quitting smoking will belong to you, earned with hard work, dedication, and conviction. The victory will be yours. Go for it!

What Happens When You Smoke

3

Roughly 1,000 people a day die from smoking tobacco. That's 350,000 people who die prematurely every year—from cancer..., from heart disease, from... vascular disease... and from... lung disease. It's as though a little better than two 747s filled with people crash every day all year.

... C. Everett Koop, M.D.
Surgeon General of the United States

If we were looking at airplane crashes instead of smoking-related deaths, this information might appear to be more shocking, more newsworthy. It would certainly generate different emotional responses. There appears to be a greater concern about airplane crashes than statistics on smoking and disease. Yet these are factual statistics, gleaned from hundreds of documented studies. The statistics present a picture that you cannot afford to ignore if you are a smoker.

The intent of this chapter is not to present lengthy statistics to demonstrate the negative impact of smoking on health. You are most likely aware of that already. Nor is it to convince you of the addictive aspect of nicotine. Most smokers have known that for years. The purpose of this chapter is to show you how the chemical properties of cigarettes interact with your mind and body in very specific ways. The intent is to help you recognize *why* nicotine is addictive, and *how* smoking adversely affects your body. The more you know about the underlying whys and hows of cigarettes' interaction with your mind and body, the easier it will be for you to understand what happens to you when you smoke, and what to expect when you quit and enter into withdrawal.

Understanding Your Feelings About Smoking

*While Bob continued to help Betheny prepare herself emotionally and psychologically to quit smoking, **Martha** was having a more urgent problem. She had been admitted to the hospital for severe bronchitis. Lung evaluation studies were done as part of her treatment. The bad news was that Martha's emphysema was advancing. Her doctor was being, in Martha's words, "a real pain!"*

***Dr. Anderson** sat at the foot of Martha's hospital bed. "You cannot fool around with this any longer," he told Martha. "Your health, and your life expectancy demand that you give up smoking now!"*

Martha bristled. "You have told me that over and over again. What makes you think I'll change my mind this time?"

"What are you so angry about, Martha?" Dr. Anderson asked gently.

Tears came to her eyes. "It just seems unfair, that's all," she sobbed. "I try so hard to do everything everyone expects of me. The only real pleasure I have is my cigarettes. They calm me down. They make me feel good. They give me the only breaks I get in a day."

Silence filled the room. "I just hate the way nonsmokers act so superior around smokers," she fumed. "And I resent the way laws are being made to keep people from smoking in restaurants and public buildings. I feel like a social leper every time I light up a cigarette. Even my kids are giving me a bad time about my smoking. They tell me it stinks when I smoke. They won't let me kiss them good-night if I've just had a cigarette."

"Martha," Dr. Anderson said carefully, "it sounds to me like your anger is coming from the restrictions placed upon your freedom to smoke."

"Yes," Martha agreed, "that's right. And now my body is joining forces with all those other restrictions. It's not fair!"

Dr. Anderson thought for awhile, then spoke quietly. **"Did you ever look at how many restrictions cigarettes put on your freedom?"**

"What do you mean?" Martha demanded.

"I mean that because of the power you've let cigarettes have over you, you are unable to ignore them, you are uncomfortable in situations where smoking is forbidden, you are rejected by your children when you've been smoking. Now even your body is screaming for your help to stop smoking, and you cannot give the cigarettes up. Your body has no way to heal itself without your quitting smoking. It's trying to tell you something important but you can't hear it because you have let cigarettes become more important to you than your own life and health. Is that really what you want, to be that controlled by the outside influence of cigarettes?"

Martha was silent. There seemed to be nothing to say. Dr. Anderson patted her on the arm and promised to visit her again later on that day.

Do you relate to Martha's feelings? Can you understand the meaning behind Dr. Anderson's words? If you have deep feelings of anger or frustration when it comes to the topic of quitting smoking, perhaps it will be helpful to examine them further before removing cigarettes from your life. Emotions have a way of clouding over rational information. If you are feeling very protective about your smoking habits, take time to figure out why this is so. You will need to clear your emotions out of the way in order for you to actually accept the information in this chapter.

As you read further, you will be taken on a "mental excursion" through the body to learn how tobacco smoking affects your mind and body. Take time to read this information carefully. Stop for breaks when necessary. Think about what you have read. Look for the meaning this information has for you. There is no hurry in terms of the speed with which you read this chapter. Make margin notes in the book. Ask questions of your instructor, physician or other people who have the knowledge to answer them accurately. Use your imagination to actually visualize what happens to you when you smoke.

The Power Of The Cigarette

Dr. Anderson returned to *Martha's* room late in the afternoon. She seemed more subdued than she had been earlier. He smiled at her, then asked, "Are you willing to do a little talking about just why cigarettes have so much control over you?"

Martha shrugged. After a few minutes she said, "I guess the information can't hurt me."

Dr. Anderson began slowly. "Nicotine is a psychoactive drug, which means that it works through the central nervous system. It is as addictive as heroin and just as serious. Nicotine is contained in tobacco leaves and smoke. You retain ninety percent of the nicotine contained in the smoke you inhale. The job of the lungs is to get oxygen from the air you breathe and transfer it to your blood which transports it immediately to your brain. The nicotine you inhale travels in the blood along with the oxygen, reaching your brain in just seven seconds. The nicotine causes an immediate and noticeable chain of chemical and physical reactions. Your response to these reactions is where you feel the power of the cigarette.

"Nicotine," Dr. Anderson continued, *"is unusual because it both stimulates and sedates the central nervous system.* When you take short, rapid puffs from your cigarette, you get smaller amounts of nicotine than when you take long, deep drags. The smaller amounts of nicotine activate the central nervous system, causing you to feel stimulated. The higher doses of nicotine that come from the deep drags on the cigarette cause depression, or slowing, of the passage of nerve impulses. This produces a mild sedative effect which you probably interpret as soothing and relaxing."

Dr. Anderson had Martha's attention now, so he continued. "You can adjust your style of smoking to match your needs for stimulation or

No Ifs, Ands, or Butts

sedation. You may not be very conscious of your ability to regulate nicotine dosage in this way, but I'll bet you can see it in other smokers."

"I hadn't thought about that before," Martha said, "but now that you mention it, I think I see what you mean. When I try to relax and unwind, I usually stretch out on the couch or bed, or sit back in my chair. I really take my time with the cigarette. I hold the smoke in longer."

"And when you are smoking in a hurry," Dr. Anderson questioned, "do you sit forward more, puff more quickly, hold the smoke in for less time?"

"Oh, sure," Martha answered.

"How do you feel when you smoke that way?" the doctor asked.

"Mostly charged up," Martha replied.

"Can you see how your style of smoking can affect how much energy you feel?" Dr. Anderson asked. "This affects your emotions, too."

Dr. Anderson was trying to help Martha begin to understand the power behind the cigarette. Let's look more closely at how this works. Once in the brain, nicotine appears to cause an increase in the production of several of the brain's most powerful chemical messengers. Four of them are epinephrine (adrenaline), norepinephrine, dopamine, and beta-endorphine. These chemical messengers are clearly connected to mood or emotional states, with sensations of excitement or stimulation on the "up" side, and sensations of tranquilization and loss of anxiety on the "down" side.

The neurochemicals affecting the "up" side are epinephrine (adrenaline) and norepinephrine. Nicotine causes an increase in epinephrine which creates an effect similar to the "fight or flight" reflex which we experience during times of high anxiety. Heart and breathing rates increase, the bronchioles (air passages) in the lungs relax to accommodate greater air intake, and the arteries and veins constrict which raises blood pressure temporarily. Increased norepinephrine levels stimulated by nicotine result in even more arousal and alertness. This combined effect is interpreted by the smoker as having more "vim and vigor," greater mental awareness and improved ability to concentrate. Smokers feel "energized."

The neurochemicals affected by nicotine on the "down" side of energy and mood states include dopamine and beta-endorphine. Dopamine affects the brain's pleasure mechanism, causing smokers to experience greater and more intense feelings of enjoyment and well-being. Beta-endorphine reduces anxiety or pain. Nicotine stimulates higher levels of both of these neurochemicals. Smokers feel calmed and soothed, more able to tolerate pain, less responsive to stress and urgency, less "connected" to the outside world.

Think for a moment about the power the cigarette has for you. If you smoke one pack of cigarettes each day, you have twenty separate opportunities to recharge or energize yourself. And you have just as many opportunities to sedate or tranquillize yourself. That gives you a great deal of control over your moods. Think of it: with this ability to influence your own mood and physical energy states through smoking, do you really wonder why you have found cigarettes to be so indispensable? Do you see, now, why smoking is such a hard habit to break?

Why Quit?

There are numerous immediate positive rewards for smoking. The negative consequences of smoking are delayed and not so easily noticeable. Many of them are more probable than absolutely certain. Because you cannot easily visualize what the long-term damaging effects of smoking really are, you are likely to be less responsive to the threat of harm from tobacco smoke than to the immediate satisfaction of your own temporary psychological or emotional needs.

In other words, when you feel the need to ease, soothe, comfort, stimulate or otherwise manage your moods or energies, that need feels urgent. The potential physical problems from smoking don't seem urgent at those moments, so they are easier to shrug off in favor of an immediate solution for your present emotional needs. Actually, smoking offers an ever-present, inexpensive method for mood regulation which can be used in a wide variety of settings and situations.

Why, then, should you stop smoking? The answers to that question are varied and deeply personal. If you or someone close to you is experiencing any of the smoking-related diseases like emphysema, cancer of the lung or throat, or heart disease, you have a more visible or more urgent reason to quit. If you are not yet confronted with an obvious health threat, you may not be seeing the real impact of your smoking habit.

Tobacco smoke contains more than 4000 different compounds, many of which are toxic to the human body.[1] Arsenic, carbon monoxide, DDT, formaldehyde, hydrogen cyanide, methane, nitrous oxide and, of course, nicotine are just a few of the most significant ones.

Each one of these compounds impacts some area of the body. Irritating gases like ammonia, hydrogen sulfide and formaldehyde affect the eyes, nose and throat, while others, like nicotine, impact the central nervous system. Carbon monoxide reduces the oxygen carrying capacity of the blood, thereby starving the body of much needed energy. Carcinogenic (cancer causing) agents come into prolonged contact with vital organs and with the delicate linings of the nose, mouth, throat, lungs and airways. It is important that you realize how some of these compounds affect your body to help you fully appreciate the health risks of smoking.

To help you understand just how cigarette smoke affects your body, let's use a little visual imagery to take you through various parts of your body, the parts most affected by your smoking.

Your Lungs And Respiratory System

Dr. Anderson returned to Martha's room the next morning with some pictures and charts under his arm. "Martha," he said, "I want to explain what is happening in your lungs when you smoke. Here, look at this picture.

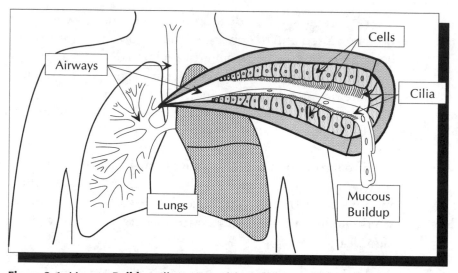

Figure 3-1, Mucous Buildup. Illustration of the lungs, with detail of an airway showing the cells lining the airway, normal and paralyzed cilia, and mucous buildup.

"*The function of your lungs and airways is to carry air into and out of your body. Follow along, on the picture (Figure 3-1) to see what happens when you take a deep drag on your cigarette. As you inhale tobacco smoke, it travels along your **airways** to your **lungs.** The **cells** which form the lining of your airways and lungs become irritated from the chemicals contained in the smoke. Because of this irritation, these cells become swollen and produce **mucous.***

"*The mucous then pools up in your airways where it combines with the tars and other substances from the tobacco smoke to form a thick, sticky substance. Bacteria and viruses which you take into your body normally through breathing, collect and breed in the mucous. This causes chronic infection and greater susceptibility to colds, flu, bronchitis and other respiratory infections.*"

"*Don't I cough up most of the mucous?*" *Martha asked.*

"Some of it," Dr. Anderson answered. "But as a smoker you have an addititional problem. Let's refer to the illustration again (Figure 3-1). Continued contact with tobacco smoke causes the tiny, hair-like projections called **cilia,** to become paralyzed. The cilia line the surface of the airways and the lungs. Their function is to sweep dust, mucous and other foreign particles upward. The motion of the cilia stimulates coughing which helps to remove the dust and mucous out of the airways. However, the smoke of one cigarette makes the cilia sluggish—inhaling tobacco smoke over long periods of time completely paralyzes them. When the cilia become immobilized, their sweeping action stops. Though you are coughing up some mucous, there is a great deal more still left in your airways and lungs.

"Mucous buildup is the factor underlying your chronic bronchitis. This is also why you have a harder time recovering from it. Your body's immune system is constantly having to fight the increased infection from bacteria-laden mucous that it cannot get rid of. The continuous contact of the tars on the delicate linings of the lungs and airways provides a constant irritant. This causes the cells of the linings to change, becoming precancerous—and potentially cancerous."

"Okay," Martha said impatiently. "I get the message. Smoking is an irritating habit as far as my lungs are concerned. What does all of that have to do with my emphysema?"

"Let's look at that next," Dr. Anderson replied calmly. "There is a protein substance produced by your body called elastin. You may have noticed that some of your face creams include elastin to help your skin remain soft and supple." Martha nodded.

"Elastin gives a springy or rubbery aspect to the tissue in your body like your skin, and your arteries and veins. Elastin allows these tissues to be pliable and resilient—like elastic," Dr. Anderson explained. "Elastin is a vital structural element of your lung tissue as well. Think of your lungs as a collection of tiny air sacs (little balloons) that expand and contract as you breathe. These air sacs need to remain pliable in order to fully function. Prolonged smoking reduces your body's normal production of elastin, causing a decrease in the pliability and resilience of your lungs and other tissues.

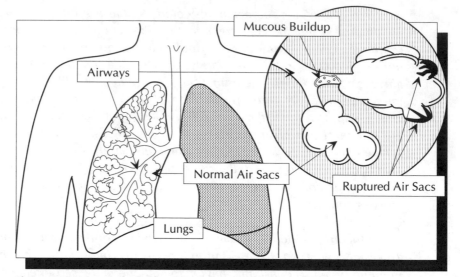

Figure 3-2, Ruptured Air Sacs. The lungs with details of airways and both normal and ruptured air sacs. Note mucous buildup in airway leading to ruptured air sacs.

"In terms of your lungs, specifically, two primary factors are at work. Look at this picture (Figure 3-2) while I explain. First, the **mucous buildup** in your airways obstructs the normal air flow into and out of your lungs, causing your lungs to work harder in order to force air around it. Your lungs cannot fully expel all of the air necessary because of the buildup. This and the mucous buildup in your lungs reduce your overall lung capacity.

"Second, decreased elastin in your lung tissue prevents the tiny **air sacs** from functioning normally as you breathe. They cannot expand or contract to their full capacity. Air that is not expelled by exhaling remains in the lungs, stretching the air sacs. This residual air increases pressure on the air sacs. This pressure, the force required to expel the air from the lungs, and the decreased pliability of the lung tissue may cause some of the **air sacs to rupture,** or break open. Once ruptured, these air sacs are no longer functional. The damage is irreversible!

"This condition is called emphysema. While nonsmokers can get emphysema, smokers have a greater susceptibility to it. This is due to the increased mucous buildup and decreased elasticity of the lung tissue.

While the ruptured air sacs cannot return to function, the good news is that by stopping smoking completely, your mucous buildup will diminish and your lung tissue pliability will improve. Your undamaged air sacs will once again be able to expand and contract normally. And your lung capacity will increase."

Martha thought for a moment, then looked up at her doctor. "Do you suppose that is why I feel tightness in my chest?" she asked.

"Yes, Martha," he replied. "That feeling should diminish once you stop smoking completely."

Emphysema may not be a reality in your life at this moment, but it is a possibility. It is one you should not ignore. Smoking affects the motion of your cilia and the stretchability of your lungs and other body tissues. The chemicals in tobacco smoke are causing changes in the cells that line the surface of your airways and lungs. You are undoubtedly experiencing buildup of fluid (mucous) and debris that affects your actual lung capacity. And your body is having to fight chronic infection every day. Your lungs and body cannot get out from under this burden without your active help. Are you willing to help?

Your Cardiovascular System

The function of your cardiovascular system is to carry oxygen and nutrients to all of the cells in your body and to transport the cells' waste products to the appropriate organs for elimination. The primary components of your cardiovascular system, your blood, blood vessels, and heart are greatly affected by elements contained in tobacco smoke. Read each of the following sections and review the illustrations carefully so you will fully understand the impact of smoking to each component of your cardiovascular system.

Your Blood

Smoking affects the blood in two ways: the carbon monoxide in cigarette smoke reduces the amount of oxygen carried in the blood; and nicotine causes the platelets to abnormally clump together which obstructs blood flow and may cause blood clots to travel in the blood. Let's look at these factors more closely.

Oxygen is vital to the body's cells to enable them to carry out all normal functions. Without oxygen the cells die. The primary function of the lungs is to bring oxygen into the body, and to remove carbon dioxide, the cells' waste product, from the body. The lung's air sacs are surrounded with tiny blood vessels so that oxygen and carbon dioxide can pass easily between the lungs and the blood. Oxygen and carbon dioxide are transported in the blood by the **red blood cells** which contain an oxygen-carrying protein called hemoglobin. Hemoglobin has a stronger affinity for **carbon monoxide** than oxygen. You probably remember carbon monoxide as the dangerous gas that comes out of your automobile's exhaust system. Smoking plays an important role in how much oxygen the body gets because of the carbon monoxide released from the burning tobacco. The illustration below will help you picture how smoking affects the red blood cells' ability to carry oxygen.

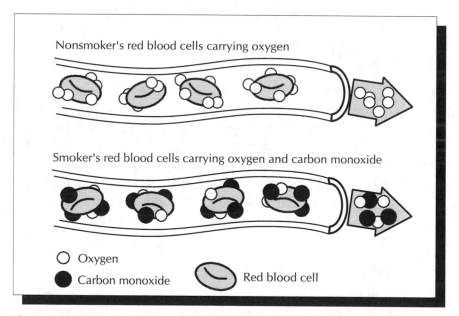

Figure 3-3, Blood vessels and red blood cells. Notice how the smoker's red blood cells attract carbon monoxide and are unable to carry as much oxygen.

No Ifs, Ands, or Butts

The hemoglobin in your red blood cells absorbs carbon monoxide 200 times faster than oxygen.[2] There isn't much room left for oxygen (Figure 3-3). Consequently, considerably more carbon monoxide than oxygen is carried to the brain, heart and other vital organs. The cells of these organs require oxygen for energy. **Less oxygen means less energy.**

Cigarette smoke contains one percent carbon monoxide (pipe smoke contains two percent carbon monoxide and cigar smoke contains six percent carbon monoxide). **The carbon monoxide concentration in cigarette smoke is more than 600 times the level considered to be safe in industrial plants!** [3]

A smoker's blood typically has four to fifteen times more carbon monoxide than that of a nonsmoker.[4] Carbon monoxide stays in the blood stream as long as six hours after the last inhalation of tobacco smoke, decreasing the available oxygen in the blood for six hours. This causes a feeling of energy depletion. Smokers looking for an energy boost light up a cigarette. This produces an interesting dichotomy.

The epinephrine stimulation from the nicotine lasts for twenty minutes. That's usually when a frequent smoker lights up another cigarette. This new cigarette produces carbon monoxide which continues to prevent the body from getting an increase of energy-producing oxygen for a full six-hour period. This is why heavy smokers frequently complain of having less energy, less vitality. While they do get brief stimulation from the epinephrine (adrenaline) response, the bigger picture is that they are also receiving less oxygen, a condition more important and longer lasting than the twenty-minute stimulation effect from each cigarette.

As much as ten percent of a smoker's hemoglobin is permanently bound to carbon monoxide, taking it out of circulation, so to speak, for normal oxygen-carbon dioxide exchange. The body tries to compensate for the lower oxygen level by producing an abnormally high number of red blood cells, a condition known as smoker's polycythemia.

The lower oxygen level contributes to the "shortness of breath" smokers experience with exertion. In addition to breathing more rapidly, smokers also breathe more shallowly than nonsmokers, a condition influenced by two additional factors. Nicotine stimulates the receptors in the carotid artery (in the neck) that regulate the brain's need for oxygen. Nicotine stimulation increases that need, but not the oxygen supply. The epinephrine response also triggered by nicotine increases the heart's need for oxygen, but again, not the oxygen supply. The result: faster, shallower breathing in an attempt to increase the blood oxygen level.

The risk of a stroke or heart attack is greatly increased by nicotine, which affects the blood in yet another way by impacting the **platelets** (see figure 3-4). Platelets are the tiny round or oval disks contained in the blood that enable the blood to clot. Nicotine causes the surface

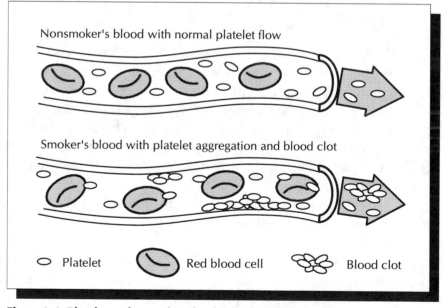

Figure 3-4, Blood vessels carrying platelets and red blood cells.

No Ifs, Ands, or Butts

of the platelets to become stickier, thereby increasing the platelets' ability to aggregate, or clump together. Thus, a **blood clot,** also called a thrombus, forms more easily.

Thrombosis is a term that refers to the formation of a blood clot. When a large clot forms and breaks away from its original site, it travels in the blood. If the arteries and veins which carry the blood are constricted or smaller in size than the clot, or if the clot is too large to pass through the blood vessel freely, it can become stuck, thereby restricting or preventing flow of blood through that vessel. If the blood supply is prevented from reaching a group of the body's cells, they die in a matter of minutes. For example, a thrombus in an artery of the heart results in a heart attack; in an artery of the brain it results in a stroke.

Your Blood Vessels

Smoking affects the blood vessels by restricting normal blood flow in four primary ways: clumping or aggregation of the platelets as explained above; constriction or narrowing of the diameter of the blood vessels; "hardening" of the vessel walls with resultant cholesterol buildup; and increase in total serum cholesterol. Refer to figure 3-5 on page 54 as you read through this section.

Nicotine triggers **increased levels of epinephrine,** as explained earlier, causing the blood vessels to constrict, or become narrower in diameter. This forces the heart to work harder in order to push the blood through smaller passageways, putting extra strain on the heart. Constricted arteries and veins also mean decreased circulation to the hands and feet, those parts of the body farthest away from the heart. This is why smokers frequently have cold hands and feet.

Nicotine has a particularly damaging affect on the arteries, resulting in thickening or "hardening." Nicotine causes little cracks or rough spots to appear along the inner lining of the arteries, making the otherwise smooth texture irregular. Cholesterol deposits itself on top of the cracks and rough spots, thickening the arterial wall and decreasing the internal diameter of the artery. If a blood clot forms in the area of a hardened, narrowed artery, the passage of blood may be blocked. This can result in a heart attack or stroke.

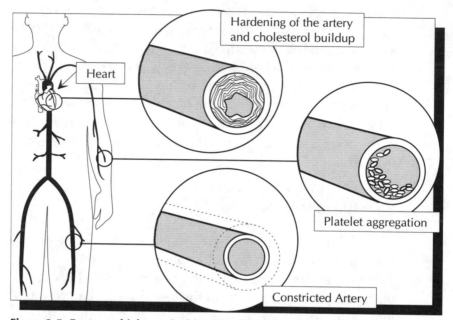

Figure 3-5, Factors which restrict blood flow. The heart and arteries with enlargements showing the effects of smoking.

Nicotine increases the amount of total serum cholesterol in the blood and adversely affects the ratio between "bad" and "good" cholesterol. Nicotine raises LDL ("bad") cholesterol, the form of cholesterol that adheres to artery walls. Each one percent *increase* in LDL cholesterol causes a one percent greater risk for heart disease. While nicotine raises LDL cholesterol, it lowers HDL ("good") cholesterol. The HDL form of cholesterol is actively removed from the artery walls. It floats freely in the blood and goes to the liver where it is processed. A higher ratio of HDL cholesterol diminishes the total cholesterol buildup on artery walls. Each one percent *decrease* in HDL cholesterol causes a two percent greater risk for heart disease. In fact,

No Ifs, Ands, or Butts

nicotine has been shown to lower HDL cholesterol as much as ten to twenty percent, which results in a twenty to forty percent increased risk for heart disease.

Your Heart

Now let's consider your heart. Nicotine increases epinephrine (adrenaline) output which causes an increase in heart rate of as many as ten to twenty-five extra beats per minute for twenty minutes following each cigarette smoked. **That could mean as many as 10,000 extra heartbeats for each pack of cigarettes smoked!** The epinephrine also causes constriction (narrowing) of the blood vessels. Platelet aggregation and cholesterol buildup restrict blood flow. Carbon monoxide reduces the oxygen level. Many of the chemicals in cigarette smoke cause irritation to the heart, resulting in arrhythmias or irregular heartbeats.

What does all of this mean to your heart? It means more beats, greater effort, less fuel, potential blockage of coronary arteries, and continual irritation from the chemicals contained in tobacco smoke. Is it any wonder why you face a greater threat of heart attack when you smoke? Like your lungs, **your heart is powerless to do anything about its situation.** You can do something about it, though. You can stop smoking.

Your Skin

Decreased blood circulation and lower levels of oxygen in the blood have adverse effects on the skin as well as the heart. Smokers frequently have a grayish tinge to the skin. Decreased elastin levels reduce the skin's elasticity, causing more excessive wrinkling in smokers skin. There is a medical syndrome called "smoker's face" which is characterized by gaunt facial features, deep lines around the eyes and mouth, a grayish tinge to the skin, and abnormalities of the complexion.

Dr. Anderson watched Martha carefully as he delivered this piece of information to her. "Smokers' skin ages faster and they tend to look older," he told her. "Maybe this will give you some extra incentive to quit smoking."

"Maybe I'll just opt for facial surgery," she exclaimed wryly. "All of this is pretty heavy stuff. I don't know what I think about it. I don't even know if I want to know what you're telling me. Remember, I'm the one who doesn't want to quit smoking!"

Dr. Anderson shook his head. "What will it take to get you to take this seriously?" he asked. "What will it take to get you to quit smoking?"

"I'm not sure," Martha answered. "Maybe a real medical emergency."

"Well, you're heading for one now!" Dr. Anderson retorted. "Let's look at how smoking affects your overall health."

How Smoking Affects Your Health

Dr. Anderson scowled as he fought to control his frustration. "You've smoked many cigarettes over many years. You smoke strong ones with weak filters. I'm going to give it to you straight and I want you to listen carefully. **The more you smoke, the greater the risk. The longer you've smoked, the greater the risk. The weaker the filter, the greater the risk.** But even one filter tip cigarette causes trouble," he warned.

"Do you realize, Martha, that **the 350,000 people who die prematurely each year because of smoking account for as many Americans as have been killed in all the wars fought in this century? Smoking related deaths outnumber the combined deaths from alcohol, illegal drugs, traffic accidents, suicide and homicide!** [5] **Smoking is the largest preventable cause of illness and premature death in the United States!**

"In 1983 alone, smoking-related deaths from coronary heart disease were estimated at 170,000, cancer deaths were 130,000 and more than 60,000 smokers died of chronic obstructive lung disease." [6]

"That's all very interesting but it really doesn't have much personal meaning for me," Martha replied with annoyance.

"Alright, Martha, let's look at the facts in a more personal way. [7]

- *"Each cigarette costs you, the smoker, five to twenty minutes of life. At two packs a day multiplied by 365 days, that could mean as many as 202 days (4,866 hours) of potential life lost in one year because of smoking. That's 2,020 days, or 5.5 years of potential life lost in just ten years as a smoker!*

- *"As a smoker, you are at twice the risk of dying before age 65 than is a nonsmoker.*

- *"Lung cancer is a very important issue for you. Your risk for lung cancer increases approximately 50 to 100 percent for each cigarette you smoke per day.*

- *"The risk of heart disease increases approximately 100 percent for each pack of cigarettes smoked per day, or 365 percent in one year for smoking only one pack daily.*

- *"If you switch to filter tip cigarettes, you can reduce the risk of lung cancer by about twenty percent. But filter tips do not change the risk for heart disease.*

- *"Smokers spend twenty-seven percent more time in the hospital and more than twice as much time in intensive care units than nonsmokers do.*

"It is entirely possible, Martha, that this very hospital stay could have been avoided if you had quit smoking when we first discussed it over a year ago."

"Maybe," Martha conceded. "But I didn't. And I am here in the hospital right now."

"And while you're here, I want you to use the time to think carefully and constructively about your health today and the implications for what that will mean to your health tomorrow.

"Each year since 1979, the United States Surgeon General has published a very lengthy, detailed report about the health consequences of smoking. I want to touch briefly on a few of the key points.

Heart Disease[8]

*"Cigarette smoking is a major cause of coronary heart disease in the United States for men and women. Thirty percent of all deaths from coronary heart disease are attributable to smoking. This means that **approximately 170,000 Americans will die prematurely of coronary heart disease every year due to their smoking habits!** Smokers are at a two to four times greater risk for sudden cardiac death than nonsmokers, and the risk increases with the number of cigarettes smoked per day. After ten years of stopping all smoking completely, the risk of heart attack for ex-smokers drops to a level just slightly higher than for people who have never smoked."*

"My problem isn't in my heart," Martha said wearily. "Why are you giving me all this information?"

"Because I want you to have the whole picture," Dr. Anderson replied. "Yes, your lungs are affected the most right now, but that doesn't mean your heart and your blood vessels are not being injured as well."

Cancer[9]

*"Let's look at cancer for a moment," Dr. Anderson suggested. "Since 1937, cancers have collectively become the second largest cause of death in the United States. In 1978 cancer accounted for 390,000 deaths, with 92,400 due to cancer of the lung. **For women, the incidence of lung cancer has increased 400 percent in the past twenty-five years due to the very big increase in the number of female smokers.***

*"This affects you, Martha, so listen carefully. Your risk is especially high because you began smoking so young, and because you smoke heavily, inhale deeply and use high-nicotine level cigarettes. Even if you had used a low-nicotine, strong-filter cigarette, you would be at a much higher risk than a nonsmoker would be. The good news is that **after approximately ten to fifteen years of complete abstinence from all tobacco smoke, the death rate from lung cancer drops close to that of nonsmokers.** What do you think about that?"*

"But I don't have lung cancer!" Martha wailed. "I just have emphysema."

"You mean you don't have lung cancer yet," Dr. Anderson retorted. "You are certainly not safe just because you do not have any spots on your lungs at this moment.

"Smokers who consume more than one pack of cigarettes a day have a three times higher overall cancer death rate than nonsmokers. Cigarette smoking is a major cause of cancer of the larynx, the esophagus and the oral cavity. By the way, alcohol consumption increases the risk of these cancers for smokers. Cigarette smoking is also a contributing factor in the development of cancer of the bladder, kidney and pancreas."

"Why is smoking such a big factor in cancer of the mouth and throat?" Martha asked.

"That is because there are so many cancer-causing chemicals contained in tobacco. Whether the tobacco is chewed, snuffed or inhaled, these chemicals come into prolonged contact with delicate tissues in the linings of the nose, mouth and throat. These chemicals irritate the gums and tongue, often causing severe dental problems and even cancerous lesions.

"The other cancers caused by smoking are due to the fact that these same chemicals are carried throughout the body in the blood. The parts of the body that are hardest hit by smoking are the ones that get the highest concentrations of these chemicals, like the kidneys and bladder, which filter and remove nicotine from the blood, and the pancreas which is a very vascular organ."

Lung Disease[10]

"You wanted to hear more about lung disease, so let's look at that now," Dr. Anderson continued. "The reasons for lung damage include direct contact with the more than thirty cancer-causing chemicals contained in the tars: loss of lung elasticity, paralysis of the cilia, and impaired immune system activity as a result of smoking.

"Of the 60,000 Americans who died in 1983 from chronic obstructive lung disease, which includes chronic bronchitis and emphysema, an estimated eighty to ninety percent were directly attributable to smoking.

"Smokers carry a thirty percent greater risk for chronic obstructive lung disease than nonsmokers do. As is true with the other diseases, the risk of death from lung disease increases with the number of years smoked, the number of cigarettes smoked each day, and the depth of inhalation. For you, Martha, this is serious. While the existing damage to your lungs caused by emphysema cannot be reversed, continuing damage can be reduced the moment you stop smoking. The sooner you quit, the better your chances are of reducing further disease and debilitation, and improving your health and quality of life. That should mean something to you, especially if you think about your kids."

Tears formed again in Martha's eyes at the mention of her children. She knew how worried she was that she might not be physically healthy enough to be as active as she wanted to be in their lives. Every once in a while, she wondered if she would be around to see her grandchildren. The truth is, Martha was scared. Too scared to smoke and much too scared to stop. This was the basis of her anger.

Dr. Anderson judged that Martha had enough input for one day. She had to remain in the hospital for one more night, so he told her that he would look in on her in the morning. He smiled at her as encouragingly as he could. "I have painted some very bleak health pictures for you," he said. "I did that to try to separate you from your fear of quitting. Your health picture will improve dramatically once you give up cigarettes. You have a lot to gain personally and physically from quitting smoking. Think carefully about it."

Women And Smoking[11,12]

Dr. Anderson returned to Martha's room the next morning. She looked as though she had had a restless night. They chatted for a few more minutes. Then Dr. Anderson opened discussion on his new topic.

"Smoking has some pretty specific risks for women, Martha, and because you are still in your childbearing years, I think there are some facts you should know."

Martha groaned. "Do I have to hear them now?"

Dr. Anderson laughed. "Definitely now. This is the only time I have you as a captive audience!"

Infertility

"**Women who smoke more than a pack a day may be considerably less fertile than nonsmokers. They are three times as likely to take more than a year to conceive than nonsmoking women. There is also a greater risk of ectopic pregnancy.**

"Estrogen hormone levels in women smokers are reduced, thus affecting normal ovulation and implantation of the embryo. Many research studies have shown that DNA, the carrier of our genetic patterns, is altered within the cells of a pregnant smoker's placenta. This genetic alteration of the embryo's DNA is one factor in the increased miscarriages among smoking couples, since miscarriage is nature's method for removing genetically defective embryos. Women who smoke have earlier menopause, a shorter reproductive life span, and even fewer opportunities to conceive successfully.

"**Smoking reduces men's sperm counts,** too. Their sperm tend to be more abnormally shaped and slower to move, both factors that affect normal conception."

"Interesting," Martha commented, "but what about pregnancy itself?"

Pregnancy

"**A pregnant woman who smokes faces increased risks of miscarriage, premature birth, stillbirth, infants with low birth weight, even retarded physical and mental development of the infant,**" Dr. Anderson explained. "Part of the risk to pregnancy stems from high carbon monoxide levels in the blood. This results in a decrease in oxygen going directly to the fetus from the mother through the placenta. A woman who smokes two packs of cigarettes a day reduces the available oxygen supply to the growing baby by twenty-five percent!" Dr. Anderson reported.

"**Nicotine has the same physiological affect on the fetus as it has on the mother.** Increases in heart rate and narrowing of the arteries and veins occur in the fetus each time the mother smokes. This decreases fetal blood flow and increases fetal blood pressure. Women who smoked throughout their pregnancies faced twenty-eight percent more stillbirths and infant deaths than did nonsmoking women. Smokers' babies averaged seven ounces less in weight and one inch less in length than nonsmokers' babies. The importance of low birth weight is that it increases the baby's chances of developing future health problems.

"Babies that weigh less than five and one-half pounds at birth are almost forty times more likely to die within the first month of life," Dr. Anderson continued. "And crib death occurs two and one-half times more often among babies of smoking mothers. Also, the newer research studies indicate a higher rate of birth defects among infants of smokers."

"That's pretty sobering information, Dr. Anderson," Martha replied. "I guess I'm pretty lucky to have three very healthy children. You said something earlier about smoking and birth control pills. I'd like to hear more about that."

Contraception

"After age thirty-five," Dr. Anderson began, "the combination of age and effects of smoking lead to higher risks of heart attack or stroke for women who take oral contraceptives. When your girls grow up, Martha, you should encourage them to stay away from smoking completely, especially if they plan to use birth control pills later on.

Let's look, now, at the final phase of the childbearing process: menopause."

Menopause

"A variety of recent studies suggest that **women who smoke cigarettes may reach menopause earlier than women who don't smoke,**" Dr. Anderson said. "The possible reasons, according to these studies, is that toxic chemicals in tobacco smoke may damage the hormone producing cells in the ovaries. These chemicals also cause the liver to speed up the chemical inactivation of the primary female hormone, estradiol. Nonsmoking women who live with smokers are also at risk because the toxic chemical level in passive smoke is sufficient to cause damage to the ovaries.

"Some women look at earlier menopause as a blessing, but it really isn't," Dr. Anderson warned. *"One of the biggest reasons has to do with osteoporosis, especially prevalent among post-menopausal women."*

Osteoporosis

"Post-menopausal women account for most of the 200,000 hip fractures in the United States each year. There is a 20 percent death rate for these women within three months. *Eighty percent of these women have pre-existing osteoporosis. What all of this has to do with smoking is that women smokers seem to lose bone in their bodies faster than nonsmoking women do, and **three-fourths of the women who have osteoporosis are smokers.***

"The reason for this seems to be caused by lower estrogen levels. Smoking is one factor in reducing estrogen levels for women. Estrogen appears to be particularly important to a woman's ability to absorb and retain calcium. The reduction of both estrogen and calcium cause a weakening of the bone structure that often leads to fractures that result in prolonged disability and possible death, as I explained earlier," Dr. Anderson said.

"Smoking also affects your liver function in ways that result in impairment of your body's ability to absorb calcium. That would affect you now," Dr. Anderson told Martha. *"You probably know how important calcium is to having strong bones and teeth. Quitting smoking can improve your calcium levels now, and that will be helpful to you later when you reach menopause."*

"Okay, okay," Martha reacted. *"You certainly do have a lot of ways to present me with the same message—quit smoking!"*

Summary

"Yes, Martha, you're right. I've been on a strong campaign to get you to change your mind about smoking. You are a strong-minded woman and you haven't made this easy for me. As your doctor, I am most concerned about your health. You obviously have other issues in your

mind that make you see things differently than I do. All I can do is present you with the facts about smoking. The rest is up to you."

It is true that the more you smoke, the greater the risks will be for all of the illnesses described earlier. This leads, however, to **a basic fallacy in some smokers' minds: one cigarette won't hurt.** In an effort to combat this rationalization, the American Lung Association and the American Cancer Society have concisely listed what happens to you, physiologically, from just one cigarette:

- It speeds up your heartbeat/rate by fifteen to fifty beats per minute for twenty minutes.

- It increases your blood pressure by ten to twenty points for twenty minutes.

- It increases the carbon monoxide level in your blood, robbing your body of oxygen for as long as eight to twelve hours after you finish a single cigarette.

- It increases your risk of a heart attack.

- It slows down the cleaning action of the cilia inside the bronchial tubes of your lungs, leaving you susceptible to infections.

- It clogs up the air sacs and thereby decreases your lung capacity.

- It decreases endurance and energy.

- It slows reflexes and impairs coordination.

- It coats your mouth, lips, teeth, tongue, lungs and throat with cancer-causing tars.

- It irritates and begins to destroy nerve endings.

- It promotes skin wrinkles and poor skin color.

Obviously smoking tobacco heightens your risk for a variety of very important and serious diseases. You probably knew that long before you picked up this book. Understanding what happens when you smoke is the important first step in understanding what happens when you stop smoking, and why the health picture improves so quickly once you've completely given it up.

If you're feeling discouraged or depressed by what you've just read, take a break for a bit and let the information settle in. The hazards of smoking are indeed real. Too real. The good news is that many of the immediate adverse physiological effects of smoking are relatively short-term, so the health picture improves quickly and dramatically.

What Happens When You Quit[13]

The outlook for health improves rather rapidly once you quit smoking. Here's the good news:

- Within **twenty minutes** of your last cigarette, your blood pressure, pulse rate and body temperature return to normal.

- Within **eight hours,** your body starts to heal itself; the carbon monoxide level in your blood drops to normal and the oxygen level in your blood increases to its normal level.

- Within **twenty-four hours,** your chance of heart attack decreases.

- Within **forty-eight hours,** nerve endings start regrowing, and your ability to smell and taste things is enhanced.

- Within **seventy-two hours,** your bronchial tubes relax, lung capacity increases, and breathing becomes easier.

- Within **two weeks to three months,** circulation improves, walking becomes easier and lung function increases up to thirty percent.

- Within **one to nine months,** cilia regrow in the lungs, increasing their ability to handle mucous, clean lungs and reduce infection. Coughing, sinus congestion, fatigue and shortness of breath decrease, and your body's overall energy level increases.

- Within **five years,** the lung cancer death rate for the average smoker (one pack a day) decreases from 137 per 100,000 people to 72 per 100,000 people.

- Within **ten years,** the lung cancer death rate for the average smoker drops to almost the rate of nonsmokers (12 deaths per 100,000 people). The risk for other cancers (mouth, larynx, esophagus, bladder, kidney, pancreas) also decrease.

Closing Thoughts

What you have seen in this chapter is how the body reacts to the presence of nicotine and carbon monoxide. You have also seen how quickly the body recovers once these chemicals are removed. Perhaps this will help you understand why cigarette smoking is considered to be the most important preventable cause of illness, disability and death in this country, and why the Surgeon General calls it the number one public health problem in the United States.

If you have promised yourself you will quit someday, the next step is to work within your own mind to effectively prepare yourself to do it. This will take some concentrated effort. For right now, take a break from reading. Get some fresh air or a little exercise, call someone on the phone, putter around the house. Let yourself unwind. Wait until you are mentally and physically rested before tackling the next chapter.

References

Much of the information presented was discussed by several references, but where passages or pieces of specific information were based upon particular sources, they are referenced in the text and cited below. Each of the cited publications contains a wealth of additional information if you want to read more about these subjects.

Technical Advisors:

Daniel Baker, Ph.D., Executive Director of Behavioral Health, Canyon Ranch Resort, Tucson, Arizona.

Philip Eichling, M.D., Medical Director, Canyon Ranch Resort, Tucson, Arizona.

Referenced Publications:

(1) U.S. Department of Health and Human Services. *The Health Consequences of Smoking: Cardiovascular Disease, A Report of the Surgeon General, 1983.* Office on Smoking and Health. Rockville, MD: DHHS (PHS) 84-50204, 1983, p. 8.

(2) Ray, O. *Drugs, Society and Human Behavior.* St Louis: C.F. Mosby Co., 1983, p. 201.

(3) Ferguson, T. *The Smoker's Book of Health.* New York: G.P. Putnam's Sons, 1987, p. 36.

(4) Ferguson, p. 36.

(5) American Cancer Society. *Fact Sheet on Smoking.*

(6) U.S. Department of Health and Human Services. *The Health Consequences of Smoking: Chronic Obstructive Lung Disease, A Report of the Surgeon General, 1984.* Office on Smoking and Health. Rockville, MD: DHHS (PHS) 84-50205, l984, pp. vii, viii.

(7) Based upon facts reported in Ferguson, p. 34.

(8) *A Report of the Surgeon General,* 1983, pp. 6-8.

(9) U.S. Department of Health and Human Services. *The Health Consequences of Smoking: Cancer, A Report of the Surgeon General, 1982.* Office on Smoking and Health. Rockville, MD: DHHS (PHS) 82-50179, 1982, pp. 5-8.

(10) *A Report of the Surgeon General,* 1984, pp. 9-14.

(11) Dorfman, S. "Tobacco, Women, and Health," *Not Far Enough: Women vs. Smoking.* Washington, D.C.: U.S. Department of Health and Human Services Publication No. (NIH) 87-2949, 1987.

(12) U.S. Department of Health and Human Services. *The Health Consequences of Smoking for Women, A Report of the Surgeon General,* 1980. Office on Smoking and Health. Rockville, MD: 1980, pp. 189-283.

(13) Arizona Lung Association. *Smoking: What Happens When You Quit, 1985.*

Changing Your Mind About Smoking

4

When you have to make a choice and don't make it, that in itself is a
choice.

... William James

A loving son stood among family and friends, reading the words
inscribed on a bronze plaque dedicated to the memory of his father,
"who in death, taught us the importance of making healthy choices
so we need never look back and wish we had lived our lives differently." This loving son is Mel Zuckerman, owner and founder of
Canyon Ranch Health and Fitness Resort. His father died of lung
cancer, regretting a smoking history of many years.

Each of us has had occasion to think about our health and about
the choices we make in support or opposition of that health. It is easy
to put off some decisions because there seems to be no pressing need
to take action. It is easy to delay taking action on some of the choices
we do make because of other inhibiting factors like time, money,
location, certain people and the like. We may comfort ourselves with
the assertion that our health is important and that we will do
something about it—soon. For some people, "soon" never comes.

Where smoking is the issue, it is especially easy to avoid making the choice to quit. On the surface, giving up cigarettes is painful and difficult, and the benefits to health seem less tangible and more distant. It is important, therefore, that you begin to change your viewpoint about smoking, to change how you think and feel about cigarettes and their control in your life.

The purpose of this chapter is to help you change your mind about smoking, to choose health for life. The topics covered include looking at cigarettes differently, your expectations about quitting and the self-talk you use to influence your thoughts and actions.

Looking At Cigarettes Differently

When you look at cigarettes themselves, what thoughts fill your mind? Do you think about the heady fragrance of the smoke when you first light up, or do you remember the rancid smell of stale cigarette smoke? Do you recall the wonderful feeling of the first few deep breaths of cigarette smoke or do you picture your lungs painted throughout with sticky, gooey tar? Do you think of the boost you get to sagging energy from the cigarette, or do you see your heart gasping and starving for oxygen? Do you see yourself as a powerful person with a cigarette in your hand, or do you see yourself as lost and alone without it?

Picturing the negative aspects of cigarettes in your mind may be a bit difficult for you to do in the beginning because, for all of your smoking life, you have carefully considered only the cigarettes' most endearing attributes. Shifting your point of focus to the negative features of cigarettes and of smoking requires some careful thought and consistent practice.

Let's look at a nonsmoking example to get a better idea of what this concept actually means.

Doughnuts are a particularly tasty but fattening item. When looking at a doughnut in the bakery case, the sugar is the most attracting aspect for most people. The gooey stuff next to the doughnut on the tray looks more like melted sugar than melted grease. The next time you drive to a bakery or doughnut shop in search of something sweet, park at the back of the shop. Get out of the car, breathing through your nose. The smell of liquid grease used for frying is more predominant at the back of the shop. By the time you walk around to the front of the shop and enter through the door, the melted sugar appearance of the doughnut will be transformed into its more appropriate reality, congealed grease mixed with sugar. If grease is not the attracting aspect of the doughnut for you, this tactic may help you steer yourself toward a sweet baked item instead. This analogy is not meant to be a special indictment against doughnuts. It is used here to illustrate the concept of picturing, or envisioning, the negative or harmful aspects of a particularly desirable object. This concept applies equally well to many items including cigarettes.

Your task for the next few weeks is to envision the negative attributes of cigarettes. Like stale coffee, stale cigarette smoke is not attracting. Sniff it often if it offends you. Mentally picture what happens to you physiologically from smoking. Review Chapter 3, What Happens When You Smoke, for concrete mental images. Picture a steel band around your chest preventing you from breathing. Compute how many extra heartbeats one cigarette causes (fifteen to twenty beats per minute for twenty minutes). Then multiply that number by the number of cigarettes you smoked per day, per week, per year. Picture your aging and weary heart, working so hard with so little help from you. Whose side are you on: your heart's or the cigarette's? Picture your aging skin, with tiny wrinkles and deep furrows increasing around your eyes and mouth.

Picture yourself being manipulated by the cigarette. Envision yourself rifling through ash trays and garbage cans looking for old butts. Remember the nights you were driven from the house in a frantic search for an open store or a vending machine so that you could buy cigarettes? Imagine an old-fashioned wild animal trap, the kind used to catch wolves, foxes, and other small animals. Picture that steel trap with its strong jaws clamped firmly over your foot. More specifically, picture the base of that trap as being a cigarette pack with your brand's name on it, and the steel jaws reaching out from the pack and over your foot to meet at your ankle.

Put these negative images into your mind often, especially during a craving. Get your anger up. How dare the cigarette do that to you! How dare you give the cigarette that kind of power! Get mad! Get tough! Use your best street language and direct it toward the cigarette. Some friend! True friends don't seduce you with the promise of pleasure and then knife you in the back. True friends don't continually undermine your vitality and your sense of control. True friends are not untrustworthy, keeping their shady attributes concealed from you.

You have given cigarettes their power over you. You have allowed cigarettes to bring you to your knees. You have let yourself be driven out of the house in the rain at 3:00 A.M. to buy more of them. You have stayed away from specific people or situations because they would not allow you to smoke. You have let cigarettes rob you of your pride. You have let cigarettes rob you of your independence. Take that power back! Ruthlessly shove cigarettes out of your way. They are not your friends. They are seductive. They try to control you. Fight their seduction. Turn your back on them. Push them out of your life. Take control into your own hands. You can manage yourself without cigarettes. Believe it! Practice it!

Your Expectations About Quitting

There is an old expression sometimes used to describe optimistic people: "They see the world through rose-colored glasses." This is most commonly used to imply that perhaps people aren't looking at things totally realistically. That phrase leads to an interesting viewpoint with which to examine the concept of expectations. Look at people who wear the latest fashion in colored eyeglass or contact lenses. What they actually see is filtered through the color of their lenses. People who wear yellow lenses see everything shaded in yellow; people who wear blue lenses see everything shaded in blue. People who wear particular definitions or expectations tend to look at everything filtered by those definitions or expectations.

People who have defined themselves as fat, for example, tend to view their reality through the filter of fatness. They deny certain foods to themselves on the basis of calories more than on the reality of whether or not they actually like or want to eat that particular food. When going through a buffet line, their typical internal conversation might sound more like, "You can't eat that because its fattening," rather than, "You don't like that anyway so look for something else," or even, "I eat potato salad all the time so I'm going to look for something more interesting."

Looking at another example, an overweight person who first begins an exercise program is more likely to attribute breathlessness and a low performance level to being heavy than he would to being sedentary or underfit. While excess weight is undoubtedly a factor, it isn't the only factor. The underlying viewpoint is that everything that is wrong in that situation is weight related. This is the "fat" person's reality.

Smokers also see their world in more limited fashion. They filter much of their reality through cigarettes. "I couldn't have gotten my act together without them (cigarettes)," is a common sentiment. "I couldn't imagine going through a day without them." "Cigarettes give me a lift." "Cigarettes keep me company." "When I get stressed, cigarettes are the only thing that keeps me going." "No cigarettes? I'd be so bored! I wouldn't know what to do with myself." This is the world through smokers' lenses. This is the smoker's reality.

Defining Your Own Reality

How you define your own reality is critical to your success as a nonsmoker. The viewpoint you adopt about why you do things or how you do things is very important. As a former smoker you may have resented "reformed" smokers who would no longer allow you to smoke in their presence. "I'll never act that way," you tell yourself. "I'll never make my friends smoke on the porch." You may have thought about that already if you've been thinking ahead about how you'll handle particular tough situations. If you have told yourself that you will never declare your house or office off-limits to smokers, perhaps you are still working with the old smokers' reality.

All of this is not meant to imply that in order for you to stop smoking successfully, you must become a zealot, or act in an obnoxious way. You will have to reinterpret your actions through a nonsmoking filter, though, and protect yourself from unnecessary hardship. If being in the presence of temptation (cigarettes) constitutes hardship for you, then you have to shift your viewpoint. You have chosen to stop smoking. What smokers choose to do for themselves is not your affair. Your concern is keeping yourself as comfortable and as controlled as possible.

The expectations you have for how successful you will be at quitting smoking will influence how you see your new nonsmoking reality. Some people who have recently quit smoking see themselves as smokers who have temporarily quit. They don't have confidence that they will remain nonsmokers. "Oh," they might say, "I'll stay away from cigarettes until things get rough." Or something like, "Everyone in my family's gotten cancer. If I get it I'm going back to smoking. There won't be any reason not to." Perhaps this last comment reflects an underlying problem in the person's motivation to quit smoking initially. Yet comments like this are heard fairly frequently. Some people with a temporary viewpoint have quit before and have gone back to smoking some time later. For them, another round of quitting may seem like only another attempt to do the impossible.

Other people expect to succeed. They don't question it. They don't look for signs of crumbling resolve. They accept that they will occasionally want a cigarette but they are prepared, psychologically, to handle that and not let temporary desires undermine their determination.

Your Expectations For Success

How people deal with other major tasks in their lives has some bearing on the development of their own expectations for success. When people view their success as a gift, they tend to take less responsibility for maintaining it. When people view their success as circumstantial, depending upon other people, events, or threats such as impending illness, then they tend to take a more temporary attitude toward the longevity of that success. When people take on a task on the basis of a bet or a dare, they expect a short-term success period, for the success was based on the achievement of something and once achieved, the motivation subsides. While these examples may seem more applicable to motivation than to expectation, a person's underlying motivation for doing something strongly influences the expectations for outcome.

If you expect to have trouble quitting smoking, you will undoubtedly pay attention to every craving, every challenge to your control, every moment of wavering commitment. Every one of them will assume more importance than they actually deserve. If, on the other hand, you expect to overcome all challenges and obstacles to living without cigarettes, you are more likely to minimize their importance, to spend less time dwelling on them.

What are your expectations for quitting smoking? Are you a smoker who is temporarily or hopefully quitting? Are you a ex-smoker who used to smoke but is not smoking anymore? Or are you a nonsmoker, a person who no longer thinks in smokers' terms? Do you expect to remain a nonsmoker? Do you expect to remain a nonsmoker unconditionally? It is very important that you think about your expectations early in the quitting process to help you plan ahead for potential pitfalls.

There are some dismal statistics being bandied about: that 75 percent of the people who quit smoking return to it within one year, that the average quitter requires three tries before achieving success in quitting smoking completely. If you have quit before and later returned to smoking, perhaps you see that there is some room for experimentation, for trial and error, for learning how you can change a habit, for exploration before you give up on yourself or your ability to achieve success in quitting for good.

Do You Need A "Trial Run"?

Some people need to "audit" a course before taking it for credit. This is a type of trial run in which people attend the classes, take some of the tests and read the material to help them become familiar and more comfortable with the information before submitting themselves to the stresses of grades and credits. This is a somewhat common practice for people who are afraid of difficult courses like statistics. One trip through the course to gain headway in understanding the concepts and processes can help immeasurably in preparing oneself for later success in the course when it is taken for actual credit.

Perhaps you would prefer to "audit" a stop smoking program before committing yourself to actually quit. This can be an important half-way step in preparing yourself emotionally and psychologically to overcome the fears, doubts and worries that might prevent you from taking on the challenge of actually quitting. Worry and fear have a way of masking a person's ability to think and to move ahead. Because most worries and fears are based upon emotion rather than actual information or happenings, perhaps some nonthreatening exposure to a stop smoking group or counseling session will help to relieve your fears.

If the idea of auditing a stop smoking program interests you, investigate your options. Your local office of the American Lung Association, the American Heart Association or the American Cancer Society is likely to have current information to help you. Most hospital and clinic wellness programs offer smoking cessation programs. You might even be able to find a weekly Smokers' Anonymous meeting to attend. Whatever your preference, begin exploring your options for observing first and then participating at a later time.

Another Option

Dr. Anderson thought a long time about Martha. He knew how critical it was for her to stop using cigarettes. It seemed to him that she blocked out the meaning of his words. He knew she was afraid of withdrawal and that she had very little confidence in her own abilities to do anything successfully except mothering her children. He knew his only option for helping Martha to stop smoking was to give her a tool she could feel confident about using, one that would give her some chance for success. He decided to try one last option.

*"I want you to consider something," Dr. Anderson said cautiously to Martha. "The biggest hazard to your health from smoking at this moment is in your lungs. I understand your worries about nicotine withdrawal. I can even understand your reliance upon nicotine for relaxation and stimulation. I'd like to suggest that you try using **nicotine gum** for a while to see if that will help you. My biggest concern is getting the cigarette smoke out of your lungs and airways. The nicotine gum allows you to still have the nicotine, but leaves your lungs free of the smoke. What do you think of that idea?"*

Martha said nothing for a few minutes. "I've heard it tastes awful, and that it can cause problems, too," she replied.

"You're right about one thing, Martha," Dr. Anderson answered. "Nicotine gum is not a permanent solution, but it is a very useful alternative for you for right now. You will have to limit your use to less than thirty pieces of gum a day for the first few months, and you will have to begin to taper that amount down after a few months until you are eventually able to go on without it. The gum is not meant to be a permanent solution, only a temporary helper to allow you to free yourself from the process or habit of smoking before tackling nicotine withdrawal."

"Does it work?" Martha asked. "I mean, will I feel anything from chewing the gum?"

"The nicotine effect isn't fast like it is with inhaling," Dr. Anderson answered, "but you will get a definite physical response from the nicotine. You will need to chew the gum slowly until you begin to taste the nicotine, and stop chewing it once you can fully taste the nicotine."

"What does the nicotine taste like?" Martha asked.

"A little like metal," Dr. Anderson laughed. "Some people feel it in their mouths as a tingling sensation, rather than a definite taste. Once you feel or taste the nicotine, you should stop chewing the gum until the taste or sensation subsides. Then chew it some more until the taste or sensation returns. When it does, stop chewing again. This will help you regulate the amount of nicotine released from the gum. If you get too much nicotine at once, you might feel lightheaded or a little nauseated. You might have some mouth or throat irritation, just like you did when you first began smoking. You had to experiment with cigarettes in the beginning, too, to see how deeply you could drag on them without feeling sick."

Martha smiled as she listened. She couldn't help picturing her very first smoking adventures. She remembered being very lightheaded and sick to her stomach at first. She looked thoughtful for a few minutes, then asked, "Do you think the gum will work for me?"

"We'll just have to try it and see," Dr. Anderson answered. "I'd be willing to give you the prescription for it, but I want to work out a deal with you first."

"Oh, here comes the bad news!" Martha exploded.

"No bad news, Martha," Dr. Anderson said. "Just a little deal for the long run. I'd like you to visit the smoking cessation program given here in the hospital to see what it is all about. You don't have to join it right now. Just meet the instructor, go to one session and see what you think about it. Are you willing to do that in exchange for the prescription?"

"Let me think about it," Martha answered.

"Fair enough," Dr. Anderson replied. "I'll check back with you after lunch when I sign your discharge papers."

Taking Your Next Step

There are certainly a variety of ways to approach quitting smoking. You can read and study on your own; audit or attend classes, groups, or counseling sessions; get acupuncture treatments; use hypnosis; exercise a lot; or use nicotine gum. You can cut down the frequency of your smoking, reduce the nicotine and tar levels of your cigarettes, and inhale shallowly. You can quit "cold turkey".

There are no easy, magical cures for quitting smoking. Nicotine gum, acupuncture and hypnosis all provide assistance to help you through the initial stages of withdrawal from smoking. Some people experience more difficulty withdrawing from their smoking habits than from nicotine itself. For this reason, some people prefer to deal with their smoking habits first, then tackle the nicotine withdrawal after the habit patterns are broken.

Remember that smoking has been a tool that you have used to manage your moods and energies; that smoking alleviated certain discomforts for you. Make certain that you take sufficient time to study and practice with alternative tools. Release from cigarettes is one thing; effective self-management is another. Don't short-change yourself. Do it all.

Learn to COPE. No matter what method you choose for quitting smoking, there is a plan of action that will help you prepare yourself to do it successfully. The plan is called COPE and it is intended to help you do just that! The letters stand for:

C ommitment
O bservation
P lanning
E xperimentation & Evaluation

Let's look at each of these components in more detail.

Commitment

The commitment to stop smoking is the single most important ingredient to your ultimate success as a nonsmoker. Without it, nothing substantial or long-lasting happens. Commitment is the subject of Section I, Chapters 1 through 4 of this book. By this time you should be feeling some of that commitment as you prepare for Section II: Taking Action to Quit. If you feel no sense of commitment to quit at this time, go back through Section I for further reflection and study. Continue to explore your options for reducing your daily cigarette consumption. Talk to former smokers. Listen to their suggestions. Think about your personal goals. Talk with people who have the medical or psychological expertise to help you find and establish your commitment. Then, when you feel ready, decide upon your method for quitting. Enroll in a program or make appointments with people who can help you accomplish your goal. Use this book as a continuing reference and resource, or as a self-help guide. If you are ready to continue at this time, move on to the next item below.

Observation

Self-observation is a component that many people choose to eliminate, thinking that it isn't important or that it requires too much time. When you remember that cigarette use underscores important needs and functions in your life, the more you know about your smoking habits and patterns, the easier it will be for you to satisfy those needs and functions successfully without smoking. If you have attempted to quit smoking at other times, taking the time to observe and track your patterns now may provide some important clues to why you have failed in the past. Few scientists begin their experiments without collecting data first. This is equally important for anyone preparing to change firmly established habits like smoking.

Observe your smoking habits and patterns for a few days. The Tracking Your Smoking Patterns exercise on page 305 contains eight simple log sheets for daily use in observing your smoking patterns.

Remove them from the book, or copy them, and carry them with you. Instructions for using the log sheets are on page 308.

Perhaps you feel that you already have sufficient information to be able to analyze the meaning, role and function of your smoking habits. You may find, however, that two or three days of tracking your smoking patterns will bring forth some new information.

Analyze and synthesize the information you have collected. Much the same way that chemical assays, gram stains and data analysis sheets aid the investigator in making sense of the information collected, the Smoking Profile Questionnaire on page 320 will help you examine and synthesize the information you have gathered on your log sheets. Whether you complete the log sheets first or choose to answer the questions based upon your impressions, the Smoking Profile Questionnaire is especially important for helping you anticipate your areas of potential strength and weakness during the first few weeks without smoking. Take a few minutes right now to look over the exercise and be sure to complete it before proceeding on to Taking Action To Quit, the next section of this book.

Think also about your actions and reactions in the more general arena of self-management. What "sets you up" for undesirable action (i.e., smoking, overeating, drinking too much alcohol)? How do you react when you do it? Do you give in to your urges, or do you punish yourself? Then what happens? Do you settle down and return to your desired behavior patterns? Or do you balk and resist, or do you sabotage your efforts, thus driving yourself further out of control? These are questions for self-reflection. The answers can be included on the last page of the Smoking Profile Questionnaire. Recognizing how you handle yourself in other areas of personal habits like overeating, will give you a very realistic picture of how you are likely to handle yourself when it comes to quitting smoking.

People who are on the "fast track" to quitting smoking tend to eliminate the investigative and analytical exercises. The majority of these people also return to smoking because they didn't learn enough about themselves, their habits and their needs to enable themselves to establish appropriate and effective action plans. Don't fall into the trap of exchanging thoroughness for speed. **The time spent in learning about yourself will pay greater dividends in the permanence of the changes you seek.**

Planning

Once you have identified when you smoke most, why and in what circumstances, you can move ahead to the issue of what to do about it. In Section II, Taking Action To Quit, you will encounter lists of tools. You will learn to use these tools and how to use Cue Cards for designing and implementing specific action plans. These cards provide a simple and effective method for planning.

Another aspect to planning is the purchase and storage of the necessary supplies required to help you manage yourself successfully without cigarettes. If you are depending upon the presence of certain items and they aren't readily and easily available, you may grab a cigarette instead. Setting yourself up for the desired outcome (not smoking) requires some diligence and attention to detail, especially during the first few weeks without cigarettes. Chapters 5 through 9 will help you develop plans for daily use and plans for control recovery should you ever have a temporary slip-up.

Experimentation and Evaluation

What follows next is experimentation, the "trying on for size" to see which plans and tools fit best. Evaluate each of them. Is it practical? liveable? achievable? likeable? Are you willing to do it for a lengthy period of time? Yes? Then continue using it. No? Change or replace it. Much more will be said about all of this in later chapters. For now, keep in mind that you will be developing and evaluating plans that will cause you to respond in the desired ways. You will be experimenting and evaluating the tools you select for their "fit". Those that don't fit well can be exchanged, modified or eliminated

No Ifs, Ands, or Butts

as required in your search for the handful of tools you will rely on most for your control, those that will help you "COPE" the best.

Your Attitude Affects Your Actions

Think about your expectations for quitting smoking and listen to your internal self-talk. Picture someone saying, "Congratulations. I heard you stopped smoking." If your outward response is, "Yeah, at least for now," how strong is your expectation for long-term success? If your outward response is "Yes. I've gone two weeks without smoking," but your inward message is, "We'll see how long I can keep this up!" perhaps your underlying expectation for success is shaky.

All day, every day, we give ourselves internal messages. "Yes, I can," or "No, I can't." Often these messages are more subtle. "Two days without cigarettes doesn't make a lifetime." "I quit twice before and then went back to smoking." "I know all kinds of people who smoked and still lived until their seventies or eighties." "I'm always good for a while. We'll just have to wait and see." "When I'm good, I'm very, very good; when I'm bad, I'm horrible."

What kind of messages are you giving yourself? What do you think when people comment upon your good behavior, or your success in general? Do you mentally put down the compliment, reminding yourself that you are far from perfect, or that the success was due to someone else or to some particular circumstance? Do you view your recent withdrawal from smoking as just a lucky break?

Your self-talk reflects your attitude, and your attitude directly affects the way you act or behave. By changing your self-talk, the conversations and messages you give yourself, you can change your attitude, shaping it in the direction of your choice. Instead of the earlier comment, "Two days without cigarettes doesn't make a lifetime," shift it. Say, *"I've gone two days without smoking and I'm doing all right."* Or you might say to yourself, *"Two days without smoking* *means I've survived 57 cravings. That's a lot!"* Or you could even say, *"Today makes two days without smoking; tomorrow makes three. In four more days I'll have gone a week without smoking."* All of these examples reflect recognition and support of your continuing efforts to quit smoking. They are positive and encouraging. Develop some similar phrases of your own. Write them down. Read them. Say the words aloud as you read them. Practice using these positive, encouraging words until you feel comfortable saying them to yourself.

Changing your self-talk may seem like a superficial task, something you can't relate to very seriously. But your language does reflect your attitudes, and your attitudes do direct and shape your behavior. You can get a head start on changing your behavior by first changing your attitudes—and you can change those attitudes by making your daily messages to yourself positive and encouraging. Listen to your self-talk. Think about the meaning behind the words. Then commit yourself to programming your thinking for success. Remember these words from author James Allen: *"You are today where your thoughts have brought you; you will be tomorrow where your thoughts take you."*

Closing Thoughts

Keep this message in mind: no matter what sequence, procedure or speed you use, **the ultimate goal is to stop smoking completely and successfully.** Explore your options. Talk to people who have quit smoking. Talk to people who lead smoking cessation programs. Learn what is involved. Read the next three chapters of this book. Learn what to expect when you go through withdrawal. A little factual information may go a long way toward reducing some of your fears. Reading and talking with other people who are knowledgeable about quitting smoking might make you feel less edgy about the whole process.

Don't think of yourself as being a weak person because you want to check things out first. Thoughtful consumers research their options before making a commitment or a purchase. Didn't you shop around for your last automobile? Didn't you look at several houses before buying the one you're living in now? Didn't you do a little investigation before selecting a doctor or dentist when you relocated to a new city? This is the same process, just a different item.

Find an approach that feels good to you. Once you've found it, get going with it! Let yourself think about it. Talk about it with others. Get yourself fired up about it. Make some positive self-affirmation statements about how you know you can be successful. Remind yourself that significant changes require study, and practice; time and effort. Allow for that. Don't get too concerned about the little mistakes or setbacks. They happen to everyone with just about everything they are learning to do. You've needed a lot of time and practice to get your smoking habits to their current position of stability and importance in your life. Give yourself some time to insert the new, nonsmoking routines you will be learning into your life, and to practice them long enough that they will become stable— and automatic.

For right now, take another reading break. Change your activity, get out of the house for a while, get together with a friend. Give your mind some time to absorb and deal with all the information you have been reading. Then, when you feel ready, turn to the self-study exercises which follow.

Recommended Self-Study Exercises

Tracking Your Smoking Patterns, page 305.

Your Smoking Profile, page 317.

No Ifs, Ands, or Butts

Taking Action
To Quit

II

Father and son climbed into the family car and headed for the electronics store. **Jeremy** squirmed impatiently in his seat, barely able to contain his excitement. He had finally accumulated the personal fortune needed to purchase the HAM radio kit he had been dreaming about for nearly a year and he could hardly wait to get started on his building project.

Jeremy sat proudly on his seat on the return drive home, holding the heavy box on his lap. The moment the car came to rest in the garage, Jeremy opened the door and carried his precious cargo to the dining room table which his mother had graciously set aside for his project. Both parents smiled indulgently as Jeremy busied himself unpacking and arranging the component pieces of his kit. He worked quickly and methodically until he reached the first hurdle: he had the general plan and the components, but no tools. He forgot about the tools! Jeremy dashed through the house looking for his father. "Dad!" he shouted. "I haven't got any tools for my radio kit!"

Together, Jeremy and his father made a list of the tools that would be needed and went out to the garage to collect them from his father's big red tool chest. Jeremy was back in business. He had the plans, the components and the tools. He started reading over the directions. The first steps were easy and he completed them without difficulty. He was so absorbed in his project that he barely heard his mother summon him for dinner. Immediately following dinner Jeremy returned to his project, *diligently working on each task in the sequence given on the direction sheet.*

Jeremy worked on his radio kit until forced to go to bed, and was back at the dining room table by 7:00 the next morning. By midmorning, Jeremy showed signs of frustration. "Anything wrong, Son?" his father asked. "No," Jeremy answered, ending the conversation.

Shortly before noon, Jeremy took a long break to watch a movie on TV. He returned to his project later that afternoon, but couldn't seem to concentrate. He fidgeted, left the table often, and was irritable when spoken to. By dinner time, the radio kit had become "a dumb project".

Jeremy's father understood the problem: Jeremy was stuck and wouldn't ask for help. With some hard coaxing, Jeremy's dad was able to lead his son back into the dining room. "Let's see how far you've gotten," he said to Jeremy.

Together they solved the problem. Jeremy's enthusiasm, and diligence, returned. A day or two later, the picture changed again. Jeremy became irritable; work on his project was sporadic and of short duration. Jeremy's father interpreted the problem correctly: his son was stuck once more. A pattern emerged. When Jeremy understood what to do and how to do it, his excitement and his performance were high. When uncertain or when something didn't go together correctly, Jeremy became frustrated and unhappy. He figured that he should be able to do everything absolutely right the first time he tried. He had little patience for trial and error, for taking time to actually understand how things worked. He just wanted to get his project done in a hurry so he could begin using it.

For adults as well as children, initial enthusiasm for a project is highest at the beginning. Then, as setbacks, lapses in understanding, mistakes in technique and the like occur, that enthusiasm dims. Impatience and frustration may block the normal ability to think clearly. This is why intellectual understanding of how things work must precede blind selection of a few tools or techniques for a hit-and-miss approach to achieving a goal. This is also why the extra time spent in advance mental preparation is so important in enabling a project to run smoothly.

No Ifs, Ands, or Butts

The focus of Section II is to help you successfully complete your own building project: your nonsmoking lifestyle. Like Jeremy, you will need plans, tools, and component pieces for the completed project. You will also need to understand *how* and *why* things work as they do, *why* you respond as you do, *what* you actually need to complete the job of managing yourself successfully and comfortably without smoking. You also need to observe your own patterns and note when your enthusiasm and resolve waiver. Work with the chapters in this section in their existing sequence: tools for change, withdrawal, self-management without smoking, application and problem-solving.

Tools For Change

5

Give a man a fish and he will eat for a day. Teach him how to fish and he will eat for a lifetime.

... Japanese Proverb

The lesson of this proverb is especially important for smokers. If a magic wand could be waved to take away your desire for a cigarette, that might work for the short run. But think, once again, about how you have used cigarettes to answer specific needs in your life. You have used them for reward, pleasure, stimulation, relaxation, companionship, and so on. In this respect, **the cigarette has become an all-purpose tool or implement which you use in a variety of ways to help you manage your daily moods and energy levels.** When you look at the cigarette as a tool, and the craving for the cigarette as the need to use that tool, the process of quitting smoking becomes one of learning to use *new* self-management tools rather than simply removing cigarettes from your life.

If you have quit smoking before and then gone back to it, or if you have not fully explored a variety of methods for replacing the role and function of cigarettes in your life, then plan to take some time with this entire section of the book. If you are committed to not

---

smoking ever again, you will need this time to learn to use other tools and establish other methods for meeting the needs cigarettes once answered for you. Don't fool yourself: **stopping smoking is more than a matter of not ever picking up a cigarette again.** Cigarettes were tools that helped you function more effectively in specific ways and at specific times. You need to replace your old smoking tools with effective new nonsmoking tools.

As commonly defined, a *tool* is an implement or instrument used to accomplish a particular task or operation. Whether used by mechanics, surgeons, gardeners, seamstresses or teachers, the proper tools are critical to the performance of their occupational or professional tasks. The tools of the author's trade are words. The tools of the ex-smoker's trade are contained in this and the next four chapters.

The "Magical" Tool Box

Have you ever experienced the magic of the big red tool box? That red metal chest of numerous drawers, filled with row upon row of fascinating shiny tools? Fathers, grandfathers, big brothers and mechanics rummage in the boxes' depths, looking for the perfect instrument with which to "magically" fix or create something. To have such a tool box is the dream of many young boys... and many young apprentices too. With the proper tool and the proper technique, it seems that almost anything can be built, repaired or improved.

Whether the tool box is a red metal chest, sewing chest, set of surgical instruments, tackle box, camera bag or set of writing or drafting instruments, most people have their favorite tools. These are the ones that feel good in their hands, the ones with the proper weight or balance, the proper size for gripping—the ones that "fit" them. Don't you have a favorite implement of some kind? A pen or pencil that you prefer to write with, a favorite gardening tool that feels most comfortable to you, a set of words or phrases that seems to best express your thoughts or feelings?

You have most likely experimented a bit before identifying your favorite tools. Perhaps you held a variety of tools in the store, testing the feel of each in your hand before purchasing it. Perhaps a particular tool became your favorite because of familiarity, for it was the one you used most often and its feel was well-known to you. Another tool may have become a favorite because it had some prior special meaning for you. Perhaps it was given to you by a loved one, or a highly respected person in your field of occupation.

Whatever the reason, favorite tools are known to nearly everyone. Because they are favorites, these tools are regarded highly and used often. They are familiar and comfortable to use. The more you use them, the better they feel to you. The better they feel, the more secure you feel when using them.

As a new nonsmoker, you will have to exchange your all-purpose tool, your old cigarette pack, for a set of new nonsmoking self-management tools. These are the instruments you will use to gain the same benefits or outcomes you used to get by smoking. They are the "wrenches", "hammers", and "screwdrivers" you will use to manage yourself daily without smoking. Each of these general tools can be adapted to handle individual needs and problems more specifically, much the same way as one particular wrench is more suitable for a specific job than another wrench of slightly different design.

Swapping Cigarettes For Other Tools

Betheny was actively preparing herself to quit smoking. Too proud to join a group, and too conscious of her image to tell anyone she worked with that she was going to quit, Betheny decided that she could do it alone with a little long distance help on the telephone from *Bob.*

Bob had asked Betheny to make a list of her smoking triggers, the objects, actions or people that made her want to light up. Betheny was reading her list to him on the telephone.

"Getting into the car, opening the mail, talking on the telephone, having a drink with people after work," she said. "And when I hear people shouting at each other, that's when I really want to light a cigarette!"

Bob chuckled. "Any more triggers?"

"I think that just waiting for something to happen is the worst," she continued. "Waiting for the water to boil or the food to cook, even waiting for a friend to arrive makes me crazy. I have to do something. So I smoke."

"Why don't you get a deck of cards and play solitaire or do a crossword puzzle while you wait?" Bob asked.

"I can't sit still," Betheny answered. "Besides, I don't have much patience. If I have to look around to find something to do, it just won't happen. I almost never have to hunt for cigarettes."

*"This is an important point," Bob told Betheny. "I've discovered that one of the classic 'quirks' of human nature is that **what gets done is what is easiest, and what gets used the most is whatever is most easily seen.**"*

"What do you mean by that?" Betheny asked.

"I'll try to explain," Bob replied. "Think about what happens with smokers. Cigarettes go wherever the smoker goes. They are carried around in pockets and purses, or rolled up in shirt sleeves. They are so easy to carry and so easy to use. Smokers leave them lying around every place they spend time, whether it is the desk at work, the car, the kitchen, the easy chair or the bathroom."

Betheny laughed. "How did you know I smoke in the bathroom?"

"I didn't," Bob answered. "But a lot of smokers do. I did. I smoked absolutely everywhere, and I left cigarettes everywhere. I never had a chance to forget about them. They were the very easiest thing to find in my life and the very easiest thing to use whenever I was bored or restless. When I stopped smoking I didn't know what to do with my hands. I was so used to playing with cigarettes."

No Ifs, Ands, or Butts

"I do that," Betheny said thoughtfully. "It seems that I use cigarettes for lots of other things too. They calm me down. They take the edge off of my nervousness at work. You know what? If someone asks me something and I don't have an answer, I can use up two or three minutes trying to light my cigarette while I fumble around in my head for the answer. It works every time!"

Bob laughed. "I did that too," he admitted. "Betheny," he said more seriously, "what you are describing to me is something that is critically important. **You are using cigarettes as a 'coping tool,' a method for helping you deal with some personal need.** What I mean is this. You and I began smoking mostly for pleasure, and also because it looked so sophisticated. But now you, like I once did, use it for lots of other reasons. You use it to help you manage or deal with things that bother you."

"I still don't understand," Betheny said.

"I'll try to explain it," Bob replied. "I like to fish. It's one of my favorite hobbies. I spend hundreds of dollars, it seems, on line, lures, weights, reels, rods, nets and tackle boxes. I can spend hours playing with the stuff in my tackle box. Then I can go off by myself to fish. Most men go through all the bother of buying gear and fishing licenses so that they can bring home some fish. I occasionally bring home some fish too, but my real reason for fishing is to get away from things that have to be done, to think or to just let my mind wander."

"I'm confused," Betheny said. "How does fishing relate to smoking?"

"Like the fishing gear, cigarettes are 'tools'. The intended outcome of smoking might be similar to the ones I experience when I go fishing: time out, time off, tension release, pleasure, relaxation. The fishing gear is important to me for its play value, and because it gives me something to do with my restless hands. This may sound a little crazy to you, but I keep a few lures in my desk to play with while I'm on the phone. I keep a fly tying kit in my car and whenever we go to my folk's house for the day, I take it inside to give me something to do so I can sit still and be pleasant company."

"A lot of women do that with knitting," Betheny said. "I've never been one to work with needles and thread. I don't even sew on my own buttons. But I know what you mean about having something to do with your hands.

I've always had cigarettes so I never thought much about other ways to keep my hands busy."

"That's what I mean about a coping tool," Bob explained. "You will definitely need something to keep your hands busy now that you're quitting smoking. **You can't remove one coping tool without replacing it with another one that will accomplish the same purpose.** Otherwise, you'll just go back to your original tool: smoking.

"Cigarettes have helped you settle yourself emotionally and physically," Bob continued. "The cigarettes were the only tool in your self-management 'tool box', and you've become psychologically dependent upon them. If you pull the cigarettes out of there, your tool box will be empty. If you don't find some new tools to get the same job done that the cigarettes once did, you will go back to smoking. At the time you feel a need for calming, soothing, comforting, gearing up or gearing down, companionship, time out, even putting off someone's question until you've thought out the answer, you may also experience a cigarette craving. This is because you trained yourself to smoke whenever you feel these needs.

"Just because you decided you aren't going to smoke anymore doesn't mean that the learned associations between your emotional or physical needs and smoking will suddenly disappear," Bob cautioned. "You will need to train yourself to use other tools that will also calm, soothe and comfort you—tools that will allow you to gear up or down, take a break or keep you company. The sooner you find new tools and practice using them, the sooner your cigarette cravings will go away."

"I'm still not sure I understand," Betheny said. "Do you mean that when I'm stressed and craving a cigarette, it's not the cigarette I really want?"

"That's correct, once you've gotten past physical withdrawal," Bob answered. "You feel tension and you think, 'cigarette' because that's what you've always used to release the tension. Cigarettes are associated in your mind with tension and tension release. Once you have found some alternative ways of achieving tension release and have some practice using them, the cigarette cravings during tense moments will begin to fade in intensity and in frequency. The more you use your new tools for tension release, the sooner you will build new learned associations. In time, when you feel tension increase, you'll automatically think of your new tools instead of the cigarette."

"Okay," Betheny sighed. "I guess it all makes sense. It's just hard to imagine that the cigarette cravings will go away. Besides, I don't have a clue about where to find new tools."

"There's one real easy one," Bob said encouragingly. "When tension builds, take a few long, deep breaths. Mimic how you breathed when you smoked. The long, slow inhalations physically feel good, and it is a familiar pattern for you. The deep breathing is settling, too, so you will get some relaxation benefit from doing it.

"I've got one more for you, Betheny," Bob said after a few moments. "I've noticed that you sometimes wear eyeglasses. The next time someone wants an answer to a question and you need to stall for time, pick up your glasses, making sure to put at least one fingerprint on the glass. Then take as much time as you need to slowly clean that fingerprint off the glass."

Betheny laughed. "I'll remember that one!"

Like Betheny, **you will need to understand and identify the ways you use cigarettes to manage your own moods and to accomplish specific purposes in your daily life.** Unless you have ideas of what else you can use to get the job done and actually use it, you will be pulled very strongly toward cigarettes. That will not be an issue of nicotine addiction, once nicotine has cleared your system. It will be an issue of "psychological addiction", or dependency upon cigarettes to meet your personal needs.

Your first objective is to stop smoking. Your second objective is to learn about the alternative tools you can use instead of cigarettes to meet your specific needs—to develop a practical, usable tool kit for managing yourself daily as a nonsmoker. This chapter contains the general tools you will use to quit smoking. Many of these general tools are adapted specifically for withdrawal (Chapter 6), and for meeting your particular individual needs (Chapter 7).

Assembling Your Nonsmoking Tool Kit

Imagine that you are assembling a nonsmoking tool kit—a chest or special bag that contains all of the essential equipment and instruction sheets you will need to become a nonsmoker. Consider making an actual tool box or bag to use for keeping and carrying your nonsmoking gear. You will be preparing lists, writing Cue Cards and storing specific items you will need. An identified nonsmoking box or bag is a handy way to keep everything together. The essential components of your nonsmoking tool kit are these (the chapters where specific instructions are given for their use are in parentheses):

- List of general tools for quitting smoking (Chapter 5)
- Cue Cards with tools for withdrawal (Chapter 6)
- Cue Cards with tools for meeting specific needs (Chapter 7)
- Specific items necessary for implementing the tools (Chapter 6 and Chapter 7)
- Resource List (Chapter 8)
- Control Recovery Card (Chapter 9)

You will learn about each of these components as you study Chapters 5 through 9.

General Tools For Quitting Smoking

Your answers and scores on the Smoking Profile Questionnaire have undoubtedly helped you crystallize the needs and triggers that influence your smoking habits. There are many general tools available to help you respond differently to those needs and triggers. They include: **R**elaxation, **E**nvironmental control, **D**elay, **R**eward, **E**scape, **S**ubstitution, **S**upport, **E**ncouragement and **D**istraction. The first letter of each tool collectively spells the word: REDRESSED. In the singular form, *redress* means to remedy or correct; to make amends;

to adjust. These general tools give you a means for making your own corrections or adjustments to remedy an unhealthful practice in your life, and to make amends by eliminating your smoking habits—and put them in your past. Hence the past tense, REDRESS-ED.

You will use these tools in more specific form when developing your action plans for quitting smoking. Read about each of them, thinking of ways they apply to you. Remember that these general tools represent the big picture or the *how* of quitting smoking. In more common terms, they are the "hammers" and "wrenches" in your nonsmoking tool kit. In Chapter 6 and Chapter 7 you will get to the more specific hammers and wrenches needed to get a particular job done.

Use of these tools in various situations will appear to overlap in certain respects. The important thing to keep in mind is what each tool specifically means to you, the images that each of them makes in your mind as you think about them. Make margin notes in the book whenever important thoughts or additional ideas for their use occur to you. Let's examine each of the general REDRESSED tools so you can get a "feel" for them and begin to evaluate whether they will work for you.

Relaxation

Short, brief spikes of tension create strong demands for lighting up. Slow, deep breathing is most helpful in alleviating the urgency you feel to have a cigarette. It calms tension physically while giving you the necessary time to emotionally settle yourself.

Cigarette smoking has most probably been your primary means for taking time off or time out of your busy schedule to relax. Brief concentration breaks can be accomplished by getting up and doing something different for a few minutes; or by letting your mind wander a bit while staring out of a window, watching children or pets move about, watching firelight or candle flame, or gazing into a photograph of a landscape or harbor.

Longer relaxation breaks usually mean that you will need to give yourself permission to have time off for doing nonproductive, fun or relaxing things. This means permission to just sit and do nothing, if that appeals to you. It means permission to play, to work on hobbies or crafts, to putter, to curl up with an absorbing book or magazine, to watch old movies or do anything else that helps you unwind. It does not mean taking your office work home with you, and it does not mean housework.

Whether for a whole evening or part of an evening, a whole weekend day or part of that day, you need periodic rest and relaxation. Smoking provided one method for meeting that need with frequent cigarette breaks. Make certain you don't inadvertently push yourself back into smoking because you have neglected to take bigger or smaller relaxation breaks when you need them.

Environmental Control

While the concept of a nonsmoking environment is readily understood as a helpful factor in reducing and controlling the urge to smoke, you have been used to providing a smoking environment for yourself. The availability and visibility of cigarettes or smoking-related objects continually reminded, and even "triggered" you to think about smoking.

The tasks in preparing a nonsmoking environment are two: keeping absolutely no reminders of smoking or cigarettes anywhere, and keeping a continual supply of nonsmoking items visible and available to use in place of cigarettes. Though the subject of substitution is covered later, this concept applies to environmental control. You will need to change your immediate environment in such a way that you are naturally lead to use nonsmoking items or methods to handle the needs you once met by smoking.

You can't use what isn't available, whether that refers to cigarettes or alternative nonsmoking items. Combine the substitution and environmental control concepts to successfully prepare your home and office surroundings to support your nonsmoking objectives.

It is surprising how many people believe they have truly not succeeded in quitting smoking until they can place themselves in the presence of smokers and cigarettes without having a single urge to smoke. With this in mind, they continually play the temptation game, telling themselves that the tougher it is to control themselves, the stronger they will eventually become.

There is indeed some fun in pitting your strength against that of the opposition. If you lose one battle though, you may set yourself up to lose the whole war. If you have one cigarette in a moment of weakness, it is possible that you will start smoking once again.

Don't look for trouble. There will be many times when you will have to be tough and will need to rely on your personal strength. Don't wear yourself out needlessly. Protect yourself. Keep cigarettes and smokers out of your way as often as possible. Keep nonsmokers and nonsmoking items around as much as possible.

Delay

Ease and availability of cigarettes were undoubtedly strong factors in establishing your smoking habits. Because cigarettes were always with you, there was very little time between the urge for a cigarette and the actual lighting up. Most people reach for whatever is most readily and most easily available to satisfy their needs. If you reach for things that aren't there or if it is awkward or difficult to obtain the things you want, a delay of time between the thought and the getting of the items takes place.

This delay between thought and action provides an opportunity for reconsideration of what you are about to do. Since much behavior is automatic, happening quickly without thought, there is typically little time between impulse (thought, craving) and response (lighting a cigarette). If more time is needed to find or prepare the desired items, there is greater opportunity to notice what you are doing and consciously do something different instead.

This strategy is similar to environmental control, but it extends beyond your immediate environment to encompass how you handle yourself in any setting. You will not always be able to control the environment in which you find yourself. The presence of other smokers, vending machines and all-night stores provide an avenue for obtaining cigarettes.

If you carry dollar bills of higher value and few coins, vending machines are less convenient. There is a delay while you find the proper change. If you shove something in your mouth as soon as you have a craving, like gum or mints, you might obtain a few minutes of precious time to gather control of yourself before grabbing a cigarette from someone else. The point of all this is to delay your impulsive dash for a cigarette long enough for you to control that impulse and settle yourself in another way.

Reward

What happens to all those nice little rewards you once got as a result of smoking? Will you have to give up your moments of idleness, relaxation, tension release, pleasure, companionship and so on just because you are no longer smoking? Of course not! But you do have to find other ways to obtain them.

Relaxation and reward seem to go together in the sense that time away from projects and deadlines can be both relaxing and pleasurable. Like Bob who used fishing as one method for providing time off, relaxation and fun in his life, you will need to discover the little things as well as the bigger, more involved things that help you meet your continual needs for reward and pleasure throughout the day. Some of them will not be daily things, like moments of solitude. They will be weekly, perhaps, like a day off to yourself with enjoyable things to do, or an evening or two for fun activities like movies or dancing.

The concept of reward may have another meaning for you, as in purchasing little presents or trinkets for yourself. Many people don't give themselves permission to spend money in frivolous ways. Cigarettes are often an exception to this rule for many people, and when they quit smoking, they lose their principle means for spending money indulgently on themselves. Spend the money you save from smoking on indulgences: books, magazines, audio or video tapes, video games, flowers, fragrances, tickets to the ballet or theater, restaurant meals, the circus or carnival, and so on. You are saving money by not smoking. You are not used to having that extra money in your pocket yet, so spend it on pleasure. Enjoy!

Escape

Do you remember how, during difficult conversations or quarrelsome gatherings of people, you used to slip away from the group to have a cigarette? You probably thought you were responding to a need to smoke. You were, but you were responding to something else as well: the need to escape from the discomfort or from the people themselves. As long as you smoked, people didn't question your periodic absences. They knew you'd be back. The cigarettes provided a much needed avenue of escape for you.

Now that you are quitting smoking, you will still need to escape from tense situations. You may also need to escape from smokers at times, especially when you are tired or emotionally upset. Getting away from the source of the discomfort for a few minutes will help you establish control of yourself and reduce your tension. Excuse yourself, perhaps, to go to the bathroom; get a glass of water; take the dog for a quick walk outside; help the host or hostess with some task during a cocktail party; do anything that seems reasonable to back away from the stressful situation and clear your mind.

Substitution

As Pavlov discovered in his famous laboratory experiments with the dogs, the food and the bell, it takes longer to "unlearn" something than it takes to learn it initially. For this reason, a logical strategy for breaking old learned smoking habits is to *learn a new response* to replace the old, undesired response. Thus, if you can teach yourself to grab pens and pencils for doodling at the sound of the telephone ring, the new response will substitute for (replace) the old, grab-a-cigarette response. As the new response is practiced, it will eventually become habit.

Perhaps substituting your morning cup of coffee with another beverage that is not associated with cigarettes, or even using a new activity like an early morning walk can break up your old cigarette-and-coffee routine. Perhaps leaving the dinner table immediately after finishing the meal and relaxing on the sofa with a cup of herb tea can serve as your after-dinner relaxant. Or, maybe a piece of sugarless candy or gum while driving will ease your longing for a cigarette. Fill the ash tray with gum and mints and teach yourself to use them. In time you will be able to get into your car without a sharp cigarette craving.

The value of this strategy stems, in part, from the fact that it is physically and psychologically easier to do something different than it is to rigidly contain your impulse to do something you prefer not to do. To remain immobile and steel yourself against doing something requires tremendous energy. You will be asking yourself to exert a tremendous force of will power (or "won't" power as it is often called) to prevent yourself from grabbing at cigarettes. You will have a much easier time if you train yourself to reach for alternative things in place of the cigarettes. You will be learning about a variety of substitutions in the next chapter.

Support

Most people look for the acceptance and approval of other people to help them feel good about the changes they are making. Many people will be delighted to know you have quit smoking. Some of them will help you feel genuinely good about yourself. Others, with an "I told you so" attitude, may lead you to feel angry or frustrated. There may even be a few people who aren't altogether happy to see you succeed with a difficult challenge while they are unable to overcome difficult challenges of their own. These people may actually be positive about your not smoking, but feeling so negative about themselves or their own performance that they transmit their negativity to you.

Look for people who share your challenge, others who are quitting also. There is considerable support from working along with others who are doing the same things. Join a smoking cessation group or a self-help support group. Look for support from people who have quit smoking and enjoy watching the success of others. Find one or two people in your family, work environment or social network with whom you feel comfortable and secure. Once you have identified your supporters, stay in contact with them regularly. Suggest getting together for dinner or fun activities. Call one of them at times or on days when you feel upset or lonely. These would have been smoking times. Even a few minutes of contact with someone who makes you feel good can help to improve your mood and outlook.

Encouragement

Do you remember how good it feels when someone cheers you on, or when you read or hear an inspiring message? It seems to provide added strength, a little burst of stimulation to help overcome fatigue, frustration or discouragement. It provides renewed hope and belief in your ability to reach the goal you have set for yourself.

Does your own internal dialogue, the messages you tell yourself all day long, sound encouraging? Or do those messages make you feel tired and disheartened? If you are self-critical you may not be used to giving yourself any "pats on the back" until you have achieved your goal. The problem is that most people respond poorly to continual criticism, to personal reminders of their inability to perform well or perfectly. In short, messages of this type destroy enthusiasm. They drain the personal energy reserve needed to fight tough battles like quitting smoking.

In this critical time of learning to live without smoking, you will need all the encouragement and enthusiasm you can find. Make absolutely certain that you can find it within yourself. Train yourself to use phrases like, *"I can do it!"*, *"I will do it!"*, *"I am doing it!"*

Praise yourself for every craving you handle without smoking, no matter how trivial you may think it is. Every urge to light up that is denied makes you one notch stronger in your ability to overcome the power of cigarettes in your life. Just as children blossom with the approval and praise of their parents, you will blossom with daily encouragement from yourself.

Distraction

Since most cravings or desires for a cigarette are relatively short term, distracting yourself for a few moments can be especially effective in shifting your attention away from thoughts of cigarettes. Suppose, for example, you have just received notice that your charge account payment is past due. Before you can reach for a cigarette, your daughter bursts into the room with some exciting news. You jump up to hug her. For a few moments, your attention is distracted away from the cigarettes. The craving momentarily passes.

Little things work well for distraction: talking to someone, filing a few papers, writing a couple of checks, doing some stretching exercises, playing a game of solitaire, putting a few jigsaw puzzle pieces in place, watering a plant, putting a load of clothes into the washing machine. This strategy is increasingly effective, the farther away you get from withdrawal. As the intensity of your physical need for nicotine diminishes, it will become progressively easier to shift your attention away from cigarettes to something else.

The HALT! Technique

There will be times when you will not be able to get up and move about, and times when your thoughts will be more difficult to control. Sometimes you will have to break into your cigarette cravings in a forcible way and consciously redirect your thinking pattern.

In Alcoholics Anonymous, recovering drinkers are taught to thrust their hand straight forward, palm facing away from the body in a 'halt' position and accompany the motion by saying the word, "HALT!" when experiencing a craving for a drink. The abrupt hand motion attracts the person's attention. Next, the person asks himself, *"Am I Hungry, Angry, Lonely or Tired?"* The question is intended to redirect the person's thinking away from the craving itself and focus it on the reasons that caused the craving. The next step, of course, is to meet the emotional or psychological needs in an alternative fashion. You might try the "HALT!" technique on yourself the next time you experience a cigarette craving.

Tools Summary

The general tools for changing habits that are discussed in this chapter are:

R elaxation
E nvironmental control
D elay
R eward
E scape
S ubstitution
S upport
E ncouragement
D istraction

Keep them in mind by remembering **REDRESSED**—and your smoking habits will become part of your past.

To Do:

Copy the general **REDRESSED** tools from page 107 onto a 3x5 index card and use the card for reference as you work with the next two chapters. You may also want to include the **HALT!** technique on the card. Carry the card with you for general reference to help you handle cigarette cravings and other smoking-related situations successfully.

Test Yourself

Once you have read and thought about the tools presented in this chapter, the next step is to apply the information to some imaginary situations. This provides a type of rehearsal, or practice session, to help you fix the concepts more firmly in your mind so they'll be there when you need them.

A shrill sound disturbs the morning stillness. "Um," **Louise** *grunts to herself as she fumbles for the alarm button. 5:45 A.M. Louise yawns and stretches sleepily. Momentary thoughts of a cigarette fill her mind. "Nope," she says to herself, "no more." Rolling onto her back she breathes in and out, filling her lungs satisfyingly with the cool air drifting in through the open window. Two weeks since her last cigarette. She still has occasional moments of strong desire, especially in the early morning, but even they are beginning to fade with time. This is Louise's third attempt to quit smoking and she is determined to be successful this time.*

Louise gets up and moves toward the closet, stopping briefly to bury her nose in the fragrant flower bouquet she keeps on her bedroom vanity. "They smell so good," she thinks to herself. Donning a sweatsuit, she heads off to the kitchen for a quick glass of juice before her new morning ritual: a brisk walk with her new puppy, a honey-colored cocker spaniel.

Louise lives a busy life and her morning cigarette offered her the only time she had in the day for unstructured thinking, the only time she had alone with herself. She realized that as soon as she gave up cigarettes. Her therapist wisely suggested that she buy the dog as a gift to herself for quitting smoking, and also to help her get away from the old morning

---

smoking pattern. Louise fell in love with the dog immediately. Her new morning activity pattern was turning into the highlight of her day!

Louise rinses her glass and grabs the leash from the counter where she left it the night before. Calling to the dog, she takes one more deep breath, noticing again how much easier it is to breathe these days. She fastens the leash to her dog's collar and they move quickly through the door and off for a pleasant walk in the gathering dawn.

Can you see yourself in this picture? Perhaps your home setting doesn't lend itself to the very same pattern as Louise's. Perhaps you are not a morning person. Perhaps you are allergic to dogs. The specifics of the pattern matter less than the concept. If you, like Louise, need some morning time off to yourself to think, to slowly get into your day, to leisurely read the paper before the mad scramble of the rest of your day, and if the cigarette was a part of that morning ritual, then you need to develop a new pattern. Let's go back over Louise's new morning pattern to identify the general tools she used.

Louise turns off the alarm, stretches, and encounters her first thought of cigarette. The "Nope, no more," is an *encouragement* technique, rapidly followed by deep breathing which is a *distraction* from her old "grab the cigarette immediately" pattern. Next, she smells the flowers, *rewarding* herself for quitting smoking which increased her ability to smell. The morning walk is clearly a *substitution* for her cigarette at the kitchen table which had originally served her underlying need for time to herself. The juice, in Louise's case, is a *substitution* for the coffee, which had always been a trigger for a cigarette. The puppy is an important source of *support* and a wonderful enhancement to an already planned change in routine. Without a dog, Louise could have looked for a human walking buddy, walked on a treadmill or used any one of a wide variety of other exercise possibilities.

This scenario illustrates the kinds of tools a person can actually use to change a habit pattern. This chapter sets the stage for the more specialized tools given in the following chapters, the specific tools you will use to develop some alternative plans for the establishment of new habits and habit patterns. Let's take one more scenario for practice.

*The moment of decision is over. Only one dissenting vote among the seven managers present. Everyone gets up to stretch and pour a cup of coffee. **Tim** is conscious of the tension in his neck and shoulders. This had been an unpopular proposal when he first introduced it more than a month ago, and Tim is relieved that his managers accepted it this time. Automatically he reaches for his shirt pocket. No cigarettes. "Damn!" he mutters irritably. Then, a little sheepishly, he reaches into his jacket pocket for a mint.*

Tim hasn't smoked for eight days. He doesn't miss it most of the time, only at moments like these when he's under extreme tension. "Only ninety seconds," he reminds himself. "Cravings only last for ninety seconds." Breathing deeply, Tim moves to the refreshment table for a glass of water, and then looks for his friend, Neil, a former smoker. Neil looks up as Tim approaches, and smiles. "Some meeting!" he exclaims. "Cliff hangers like that one make me nervous." Noticing Tim's shaky hand holding the glass of water, Neil comments, "You're doing great. Meetings like that could make a smoker out of anyone and you're not smoking. Just hang in there a little longer and you'll be over the hump. Trust me. I've been there."

What general tools can you identify in this scenario? You should be able to find *encouragement, relaxation, substitution, distraction, environmental control and support.* There is nothing magical about the tools used in either of the two situations described. They represent basic coping tools carefully selected to meet the underlying needs that the cigarettes once met.

Closing Thoughts

In the days ahead you will have your own scenarios, your own need for effective, usable tools for dealing with your own smoking urges. "Easier said than done," you may be thinking to yourself. Remember that all learning takes time and that it begins with some very obvious, concrete first steps.

Pay attention to your smoking patterns during the next week or two. Try to understand more about the role smoking plays in your life and anticipate the situations you think will give you trouble now that you are stopping smoking completely.

Be aware of your needs for reward and pleasure during the next week or so. Make notes about the nature of those needs: whether they involve a few moments or several hours, whether they need to be met daily or at some less frequent interval, whether they require idleness or some type of activity, whether they are best handled in solitude or with the companionship of others. Add that information to your Smoking Profile Questionnaire.

Recommended Self-Study Exercises

List the general REDRESSED tools and HALT! technique on an index card for quick reference.

Update your Smoking Profile Questionnaire, page 320, with additional information (insights, needs, triggers, etc.).

Withdrawal

6

The only thing we have to fear is fear itself.

... Franklin Delano Roosevelt

These words, quoted from President Roosevelt's First Inaugural Address, March 4, 1933, weren't directed specifically toward smokers facing a fearsome challenge. They were aimed at thousands of people who were confronting fear on other fronts. Yet there are some important commonalities to fear, no matter what the underlying reason. Perhaps the uncertainty of what to expect, of how to adequately prepare ourselves to handle the unexpected, the pervasive feeling of loss of control are each factors that give rise to the emotion we frequently call *fear*.

Among smokers, withdrawal can be an alarming word. In the extreme, it conjures up images of people writhing in pain, of severe mental and physical debilitation, of hospital rooms and straight jackets. **Many people fear the process so greatly that the major symptoms they experience are more attributable to the fear than to the actual withdrawal.** The more you understand about nicotine withdrawal and how to cope with it, the less unsettling the whole process will be for you.

The intent of this chapter is to help you prepare for and deal successfully with nicotine withdrawal. The topics include: withdrawal symptoms; nicotine cravings; preparation for quitting; gradual, progressive withdrawal ("cut down"); and abrupt, immediate withdrawal ("cold turkey"). Read the entire chapter first; then lay out your action plan.

Facing The Challenge

Whether you choose gradual or abrupt withdrawal; whether you use nicotine gum for a while; whether you seek instruction, therapy, hypnosis or acupuncture; or whether you choose to simply "tough it out" on your own, the time for action has arrived. Pay attention to your feelings as you read the narrative and the information which follows. They will help you anticipate what to expect during withdrawal, and will help you identify what you might need in order to get yourself through the withdrawal process most comfortably.

*True to his word, **Dr. Anderson** met **Martha** in her hospital room after signing her discharge papers. "I'm willing to go along with the nicotine gum idea," Martha told him. "I just hope it will work for me."*

"It will certainly give you some time to deal with your smoking habits and get them out of your way first. I think that the Quit Smoking Program in the hospital here will offer a great deal of help to you in dealing with those habits. That's why I'm being so insistent about taking you down there to meet the instructors."

"I'm not so sure about the program," Martha answered. "I'm still a long way from making permanent decisions about all of this."

"I understand," Dr. Anderson replied. "I'm just glad you're willing to check it out."

Dr. Anderson led Martha into the cheery conference room near the first floor cafeteria. She looked around cautiously. Five people were seated, two were standing, three were pacing back and forth. A few others were talking quietly among themselves. Everyone appeared to be nervous; a few seemed outright edgy.

*"**Tim!**" Martha exclaimed. "What are you doing here?"*

Tim looked a little sheepish. "My wife doesn't smoke," he told Martha, "and she gets all upset whenever I smoke at home. We haven't been married long and I want to try to quit smoking if I possibly can."

"But why here?" Martha asked. "You don't live in town, do you?"

"Just thirty miles away," Tim answered. "I know I can't do this alone. I've tried before and failed. I don't want to fail again. Not this time."

The group fell silent as a man and a woman entered the room and took their places at the front of the group. "Good afternoon," said the woman. "Welcome to the first session of our Quit Smoking Program."

"That's Sue Burns," Dr. Anderson whispered to Martha. "She's one of the best community health nurses I know. Her assistant's name is Steve." They listened quietly for a few moments, then Dr. Anderson waved a silent good-bye. Martha moved closer to Tim and they took seats at the back of the room.

Scenes like this are repeated daily as people seek help for separating themselves from nicotine, and from the process of smoking. Many are repeaters. That is, they have quit at least once before. Some are novices, about to experience withdrawal for the first time. Most are nervous, some are sad, others are angry. More than a few are uncertain about how much they really do want to quit now that the moment for action has finally arrived.

The concept of withdrawal is frightening for many people. It implies a sense of submersion into a process over which the person has no apparent control. In some ways it feels akin to jumping into a swift-flowing river, of giving oneself up to the current and hoping to survive the imbedded rocks to later be washed up gently on a sandy bank, tired but unharmed. The worries are many. "Can I do it?" "How awful will it be?" "Will I be miserable?" "What if I don't succeed?"

The instructors had completed their introductions and opening statements, and were now proceeding on to the main topic of concern: withdrawal.

"This program will give you all the help and support you need to stop smoking completely," Sue Burns announced. "Our goal is to get you off of nicotine, and away from smoking by the time our one-week program is over. There may be a few of you who want to use nicotine gum. You will have to consult with a physician first, but you can certainly attend all of our sessions and do all of the homework assignments."

"That's what I'm going to do," Martha whispered to Tim.

"Not me," Tim whispered back. "I want to get it all over with at one time."

Sue continued. "Some smokers experience little difficulty in the withdrawal stage while others have a much tougher time. **Most of the withdrawal symptoms peak in the second or third day and then drop off rapidly.** There is a smaller, milder peak somewhere around the seventh day for some smokers. It is not likely that you will experience all of the symptoms we'll talk about. The important point to remember is that all of the symptoms you do experience will fade away quickly with time. **Usually by the eighth day, and often by the fifth day, most of the strong physical symptoms are gone."**

Withdrawal Symptoms

Steve stepped forward and switched on the overhead projector. "Let's look at specifically what happens during withdrawal," he said. "The nicotine in tobacco smoke causes stimulation to the smoker's central nervous system, and a lot of irritation to the smoker's body. Many of the physical symptoms smokers have during withdrawal are the result of the body and the nervous system returning to their normal state."

Steve smiled at the group. "Look at the symptoms of withdrawal as the milestones of progress along the path of quitting smoking." He pointed to the list of physical withdrawal symptoms on the screen.

Physical Withdrawal Symptoms	
• Fatigue	• Sleeplessness
• Drowsiness	• Excess saliva in the mouth
• Sweating	• Warmer hands and feet
• Headaches	• Runny nose
• Muscle aches and cramps	• Cough
• Nausea	• Weight gain
• Dizziness	• Constipation or diarrhea
• Sensory changes in nose & mouth	

"Sounds like a blast!" Martha hissed at Tim.

"Yeah," Tim agreed. "I'm not looking forward to it."

"People rarely experience all of these symptoms," Steve explained. "You may be lucky and not feel much of anything at all. The number, frequency and severity of symptoms vary with each person. Some of these symptoms are actually good signs, signs that the body is recovering. For example, greater warmth in the hands and feet mean that circulation is improving. An increased sense of smell and taste means that the irritation to delicate membranes in the nose and mouth is subsiding. Increased coughing shows recovery of the cilia which are returning to their work of sweeping dust and debris from the lungs and airways."

Steve paused while Sue added a few words. "In the very early days of tobacco use," she told the group, "tobacco was considered to be a cure for just about everything, including bronchitis! Olden-day doctors treated colds, flu and coughing spasms by enclosing the poor patient in an unventilated room filled with tobacco smoke. The effect of the nicotine from the tobacco caused paralysis of the cilia, whose real purpose is to cause the person to cough up dust, debris and phlegm. The patient stopped coughing, and the doctor thought he had worked a real cure. Later on, when the cilia recovered and began their cleansing action once again, coughing resumed and the doctor again treated the patient with tobacco smoke."

A few people laughed, some smiled. Steve exchanged transparencies, then continued. "When you stop using nicotine completely, your body will respond in very positive ways. Most smokers see these physical benefits within the first few days:

Physical Benefits Of Withdrawal
• *Decrease in blood pressure*
• *Decrease in heart rate*
• *Decrease in metabolic rate*
• *Improvement in breathing*

"The decrease in heart rate, blood pressure and metabolic rate all mean much less added stress on the heart. That comes from eliminating nicotine. By eliminating burning tobacco, you will not be getting high levels of carbon monoxide from the smoke. You will be getting normal levels of oxygen, which might cause you to feel a little light headed due to the higher levels of oxygen reaching the brain.

"Smokers in early withdrawal from nicotine are often scattered in their thinking," Steve explained further. "They appear to be fuzzy-minded and forgetful." He changed transparencies again, then pointed to the list of psychological effects.

Psychological Withdrawal Symptoms	
• *Irritability*	• *Sadness*
• *Jumpiness or nervousness*	• *Weepiness*
• *Restlessness*	• *Listlessness*
• *Anxiety*	• *Inability to cope with stress*
• *Anger*	• *Intense cigarette cravings*
• *Depression*	

"Increased appetite is also common for people during withdrawal," Steve said. "For some people this comes from their need to have something

in the mouth to chew or suck on. For others this comes from a very improved ability to taste and enjoy food."

"That'll be great for weight gain!" Martha groaned.

Sue heard Martha's comment and smiled. "Yes, that could be a problem. We'll be giving many suggestions for eating control later on." Sue glanced at her notes, then stepped forward to pick up the discussion.

"The number and intensity of your withdrawal symptoms may vary from one day to the next," she said, "but they should ease up considerably after five days of complete abstention from all nicotine in any form, including nicotine gum."

Nicotine Cravings

"Nicotine is the addictive substance in cigarettes," Sue told the group. "Every inhalation is a drug 'hit.' Each smoker has an optimum nicotine dose level which is specific for that person. Smokers are able to regulate and maintain those levels by how deeply and how often they smoke, and by the nicotine level of the cigarettes they use."

"In research studies of smokers who were unknowingly given cigarettes of varying nicotine levels, the smokers automatically adjusted their smoking style to increase or decrease the nicotine level according to their own optimum dose level. Smokers given low-nicotine cigarettes dragged harder, inhaled deeper and longer, and smoked the cigarettes right up to the filters. When given higher nicotine levels in their cigarettes, the smokers inhaled more shallowly and smoked less of the cigarette."

"How do smokers know what their dose level is?" asked a woman in the front row.

"Smokers don't consciously know what that optimum level is," Sue answered. "They just smoke in ways that allow them to reach the desired level. Once the level is reached, the smoker stops smoking.

"This information is important to you if you choose to cut down your cigarette consumption prior to quitting," Sue explained. "If you use cigarettes that are progressively weaker in nicotine levels than your *current brand, make absolutely certain to keep yourself from dragging harder, inhaling longer or deeper, and from lighting up more often. Otherwise, you'll defeat the purpose of using lower nicotine cigarettes.*

"Nicotine reaches the brain approximately seven seconds after the first inhalation. High levels of nicotine remain in the brain for twenty to thirty minutes after the last inhalation. This is the time when heavy smokers reach for another cigarette. This is a physiological craving resulting from the body's demand for more nicotine. There are psychological cravings for cigarettes also, but we will cover that later on."

Handling The Cravings

"In the very early days of nicotine withdrawal," Sue continued, "you will be most conscious of the cigarette cravings themselves. The actual cravings are brief: only thirty to ninety seconds in length. In the beginning your body will be very demanding, so you may experience what we call 'rapid fire' cravings: one craving followed in rapid succession by another, and yet another. In a relatively short period of time, the cravings will get farther and farther apart. Instead of two or three cravings hooked together, you will experience only one followed by a brief period of relief, then another craving again followed by a period of relief."

"That's a relief!" quipped someone from the back of the room.

Everyone laughed. The humor relieved a little of the tension in the room.

"Think about this," Sue suggested positively. "Individual cravings only last thirty to ninety seconds. You can probably get yourself through ninety seconds of anything. Right? Here's what I want you to do when you feel a strong craving for a cigarette."

"Deep Breathe!"

"Stop for a minute, breathe slowly and deeply, filling your lungs with oxygen. Hold your breath, then slowly exhale. Repeat the process slowly, several times in succession.

"Do it with me right now...

Inhale slowly......hold your breath......exhale slowly.
Again, slowly inhale......hold......exhale.
Once again, inhale......hold......exhale.
One more time, inhale......hold......exhale."

Sue paused, watching the group intently. "Let's try it once again," she suggested. "This time I want you to purse your lips when you exhale so that you feel a little more resistance. This will help you exhale more slowly."

Sue guided the group through another round of deep breathing, lasting ninety seconds.

"That was one craving's worth of deep breathing," Sue said. "You did that for ninety seconds. I want you to follow this breathing procedure through every craving. The deep breathing mimics what you did with cigarettes. It feels physically good to deep breathe. It is one of the aspects of smoking that probably felt especially good to you. Nonsmokers don't often think to deep breathe. You are used to deep breathing. Keep on doing it to relax, to oxygenate, to get your mind off of the craving. You may be surprised at how quickly the cravings will subside when you deep breathe. And if another craving comes along quickly, deep breathe a few times, stretch, shift your body position a little and deep breathe once again.

"In time only a few deep breaths will be needed to ease any cigarette craving," Sue said encouragingly. "In time there will be no cravings, only desire."

"What do you mean about no cravings, only desire?" a man called out from the back of the room.

Sue answered. "Cravings are a strong, intense, more urgent form of want or desire. They come on hard. They dominate your thinking for a few moments. They might even make you feel like they are controlling you. Desire, as I meant it, is a much weaker form of the same thought. It's more like saying to yourself, 'I wish I could have,' or 'I would really love to have'."

Someone else in the group responded. "I know people who have quit who say they never lose their desire for a cigarette."

"Many people do say that," Steve agreed. "I'll bet if you asked them about it, they'd tell you that it usually bothers them mostly when they are in the presence of cigarettes or smokers, when they are tired or upset, when they are wound up and overstressed, or when something specific triggers their memories."

Steve smiled. "Look at it this way. Do you ever completely lose your desire for a good old-fashioned talk with a very dear friend who moved away many years ago? You may not think about it much, only occasionally when something reminds you about him or her, or when you are feeling emotionally needy yourself. That's much the same kind of dynamic that happens with cigarettes. They've been a part of your everyday life for a long, long time. You won't suddenly just forget them. You won't suddenly be immune to their charms. But **their importance will fade with time, and with good alternatives to use in their place.** You'll be learning about them in this program."

Sue shifted position, then picked up the thread of her original message. "In just a little more time, desire for the cigarette will diminish to want, want will diminish to thought, and thoughts about cigarettes will fade altogether until someone, something or an emotional trigger like a burst of extreme tension cause a momentary feeling of need. Remember:

CRAVING →➤ DESIRE →➤ WANT →➤ THOUGHT

"That momentary feeling of need," she continued, "will most likely feel like a sudden cigarette craving, particularly if cigarettes had once been used to satisfy the type of need that is triggering the craving: time out, time off, tension release, and so on.

"Reassure yourself that **cravings of this type are very momentary, and very circumstantial.** They are psychological more than physical in origin. They will subside quickly. Deep breathe once, twice, three times. Get up. Move about. Distract yourself for a few minutes, then get back to what you were doing."

Tim and Martha walked out together at the conclusion of the orienta-
tion. "What did you think of it?" Martha asked Tim.

*"It sounded okay to me," he answered. "I'm going to stick with it. I've
got one more night to smoke so I'm going to take a long ride and enjoy
it. Then I've got all this stuff to read." He nodded toward the sheaf of
papers in his hand. "What about you?" he asked. "What did you think?"*

*"I'm not completely sure," Martha replied. "I've got to do something
soon. My emphysema is worse. I'm really scared of quitting, but I'm not
really sure why. Maybe it's because I think I'll crack up, or that everybody
will hate being around me. I've always felt so out of control without
cigarettes!"*

"Is that why you're going to use the gum?" Tim asked.

*"Yes," Martha said. "It feels like a coward's way out, but I know it's
not. I also know that I'll still have to go through nicotine withdrawal
someday. I just think that if maybe I can get control of myself without
actually smoking, then it won't be so awful to give up the nicotine later.
The lady said it isn't all that bad, and that the worst is over in a week or
so."*

*"I hope I'll see you in the program," Tim said earnestly. "I'd love to
have your company. More than that, though, I think you'd learn a lot to
help you get that control you're looking for."*

*"I'm sure you're right about that," Martha replied. "I've got a lot of
thinking to do first."*

Tim and Martha went their separate ways, each lost in private
thoughts. You may be having your own private thoughts right now
about what all of this means to you, and how you want to proceed
with your objective of quitting smoking.

Whether you use nicotine gum or leave nicotine completely, you
will have to address your smoking habits. You will have to learn to
forge ahead without cigarettes' presence in your life. You may prefer
to move quickly through the process from smoking to quitting, to
abstain completely and irrevocably as soon as possible. Or, you may

prefer to proceed more cautiously, to move ahead at a pace that feels more acceptable to you.

Before moving ahead, though, take some time to review the section entitled, "What Happens When You Quit", beginning on page 65. Review the withdrawal symptoms described earlier in this chapter. Remember that the severity and number of the symptoms vary with each person and that with most everyone, the worst is over in a very few days. The cravings will be intense and frequent at first, but even they will subside relatively quickly after the first few days.

Preparing To Quit

In Chapter 5 you were introduced to the concept of general tools. In this chapter you will be learning about a variety of *specific* tools for withdrawal. You will notice that many of the general tools from Chapter 5 appear directly or in some more specific way throughout this chapter. **The tools in this section are organized into a sequential number of steps to follow for preparing to withdraw from cigarettes. Follow the steps in the recommended sequence,** taking whatever time is necessary to use each of the individual tools. It is important that you **experiment with each tool in this section.** When you have done so, place a check mark in the box provided alongside each tool. This will help you keep track of your overall progress.

1.   **Track Your Current Smoking Patterns**

   ❏   **Track and analyze your current smoking patterns for a week.** This tool was offered in Chapter 5 and if you have already tracked your smoking patterns, page 305, and completed the Smoking Profile Questionnaire, page 320, place a check mark alongside this tool and move on to the next one. If you have not yet tracked your patterns or completed the Smoking Profile Questionnaire, please do that before moving ahead. The insights and information will be particularly valuable later when you have finished withdrawal and are in the retraining phase of developing your nonsmoking patterns.

2. **Establish A Quit Date**

   ❏ **Pick a definite date.** Make it within one or at most two weeks from today. Circle it on every calendar and write it in every appointment book (including your secretary's). Write it down on pieces of paper and tape it everywhere you can to keep it constantly visible to you.

   ❏ **Tell others about your quit date.** The very strongest level of commitment is when you tell others about the decision and the date. You are visible when you tell others and thus, more likely to actually do what you said you will do. Perhaps pride is the underlying issue in sticking to goals you have told others about. Whatever the reason, let the people who live, work and socialize with you know that you are quitting smoking. This helps them prepare to be supportive, and it helps you stick to your goals.

3. **Prepare a Nonsmoking Environment**

   This particular step applies to the time period just before you intend to stop smoking completely. **Make certain that you have used each of these specific tools before you extinguish your very last cigarette.** You will need all the extra help you can get during early withdrawal, and removing temptation is certainly a most powerful tool.

   ❏ **Remove all trace of cigarettes, ash trays, lighters, matches,** etc. from your home, car, office, gym bag, or anywhere else you stashed them—**all of them!** Do this immediately. To leave any hidden opportunity to return to old habits is a potential sabotage to your success. If you remember a few more hiding places later on and need some help to get the last of the cigarettes out of your way, call and ask a family member, secretary, cleaning lady, friend or even an older child to do it for you.

❑ **Wash and dry clean a supply of clothing** so you will have fresh smelling clothes and undergarments to wear.

❑ **Clean and freshen your bedding, closet, house, car, office and desk so they will smell fresh.** Small deodorizers and fragrant drawer linings can be helpful.

❑ If you smoke in your car, **have your car detailed to thoroughly clean and deodorize the inside.** Fill the ash trays with sugarless gum and mints.

❑ **Make a dental appointment for cleaning your teeth some time during your first or second week after quitting.**

❑ **Prepare one or more people to be your support system—** preferably someone who has already successfully quit smoking. You will need someone to discuss your stop smoking project with, someone you can do social or recreational things with whose presence will help you become strong and sociable without cigarettes.

❑ **Set some dates on your calendar before quitting for socializing and for regular exercise (with nonsmokers whenever possible).**

❑ **Make reservations in the nonsmoking section of the airplane for all flights; sit in the nonsmoking sections of restaurants.**

❑ If you live or work closely with someone who smokes, you will not be able to physically erase all evidence of cigarettes or smoking in your living and/or working environment. **Establish some agreed upon "no smoking" areas in your home. And make your office a nonsmoking place.** You may be reluctant to take these steps, remembering how you once felt about prohibitions against your smoking in certain places. Keep this in mind: *your mission is not to reform others.* Your intent is to have some places you can go to escape the presence of cigarettes. You need to be free of cigarettes' influence in your own office, your car, and in specific rooms of your home.

4. **Develop a Social Support System**

❑ **Let other people know what you are doing.** New nonsmokers worry excessively about offending other smokers. They also worry about failing in the eyes of their nonsmoking friends. This worry could lead you to be secretive about quitting. When other people understand what you are doing, they are more likely to be supportive of you and less likely to take offense at some of your actions or remarks.

❑ **Be pleasant but firm in saying "no" to the offer of a cigarette, or when reminding someone about not smoking in your car, office, or home.** Let others know that you need to do this to help yourself out for a while. Make use of the many tasteful "please do not smoke here" signs available for doors, table tops, even automobile dashboards. Ask other smokers to please not offer you a cigarette, nor let you borrow one from them at some possible future moment of weak resolve.

❑ **Pick a former smoker to act as resource person and reinforcer for you.** Ask that person for some ideas about how to handle yourself with smokers. Check in with that person daily for a while. It is especially important to have a nonsmoking support person at work if smoking is still allowable at your job site.

❑ If you have a number of smoking friends, **you may either need to spend a few weeks away from them until you are past the acute withdrawal stage, or to socialize with them only in the presence of other nonsmokers or in nonsmoking places.** This may seem a little harsh to you right now, but when you are going through nicotine withdrawal and even for several weeks afterward, you will take comfort in the control that a nonsmoking environment offers you. Believe it.

5. **Choose your method of withdrawal.**

Your alternatives are to "cut down" gradually, page 129, or to withdraw abruptly and completely by quitting "cold turkey", page 134. Choose the approach that meets *your* needs and follow the directions for doing it "to the letter"!

6. **Prepare a Cue Card.**

Whether you use the "cut down" or "cold turkey" method of withdrawal, follow the procedure suggested next for selecting and using specific withdrawal tools. These tools are described in the Gradual, Progressive Withdrawal ("Cut Down") and Abrupt, Immediate Withdrawal ("Cold Turkey") sections of this chapter.

This same procedure will also be used for selecting and using the self-management tools when you get to Chapter 7.

❑ **Carefully read about all of the tools presented.** Take time to think about them and how they fit into your needs and lifestyle.

❑ **Place a check mark (✔) alongside the tools you want to experiment with,** to use on a daily basis.

❑ **Prepare a Cue Card from the carefully selected list of tools.**

• Use a 3x5 index card for your Cue Card.

• Write a title across the top of the card (for example, Withdrawal, Quit, etc.).

• Go back to the tools you have checked and write up to seven of them on the index card.

You may prefer to work with the tools in only one or two of the categories, or you may decide to include tools from several categories. Whatever method you choose, the important thing to keep in mind is that working with too many tools at one time may overwhelm and confuse you. It is far more effective to concentrate your time, attention and energy on just a few items. For this reason, do not include more than seven tools on your Cue Card. If you prefer to work with fewer than seven, that is all right.

As you work with the tools on your Cue Card, you may find that one or more of them doesn't fit or isn't useful. You may find that you don't like using one or another of them. If so, remove it from the Cue Card and replace it with another tool you have checked but are not yet using.

❑ **Carry the Cue Card with you.** Make a copy and tape it to your bathroom mirror. Use the card as a **guide** for what to do, and as a **daily reminder** to do what is listed on the card.

Gradual, Progressive Withdrawal ("Cut Down")

Some people, when getting into a swimming pool, move excruciatingly slowly. First the toes, then the heel, ankle, shin. Then they shriek, "It's cold!!" before they scramble out and have to start all over again. Perhaps this is your method. Other people know the water will be cold and just plunge in to get it all over with in a hurry. Either way the ultimate result is the same: they get into the water.

With smoking cessation there is a final day of reckoning when the last good-byes to cigarettes are said. For a great many people, easing themselves into the withdrawal process gradually is more appealing and less harsh than abrupt change. If this applies to you, use the "cut down" methods explained in this section to get yourself started. Use them for one to two weeks, then quit completely. At that time, you will need to follow the guidelines in the "cold turkey" section of this chapter, beginning on page 134.

The intent of the "cut down" approach is to gradually reduce the amount of nicotine you take into your body daily—to wean yourself away from nicotine a little more each day. The first four categories of gradual withdrawal tools are directed toward the objective of smoking less by smoking differently.

1. **Delay lighting up.**

   ❏ **Do something else first.** Get up and move about, take a trip to the bathroom, run an errand, climb a flight of stairs, go to the mailbox. Movement of any kind has a calming influence. If you're concerned about weight gain, though, don't move toward the refrigerator or cupboard!

   This tactic teaches you the process of slowing down cigarette consumption by inserting something between *impulse* (craving) and *action* (lighting up).

   ❏ **Take ten slow, measured deep breaths before lighting up.** Give the cigarette craving a chance to subside before taking action. Refer to the Deep Breathe! on page 120.

   ❏ **Each day, postpone lighting each cigarette for ten minutes.** This means a ten-minute delay per cigarette the first day, a twenty-minute delay per cigarette the second day, a thirty-minute delay the third day, and so on. Over time, the frequency of your smoking is reduced considerably.

   ❏ **Smoke at only odd or even hours of the day** to help strengthen your ability to delay lighting up immediately. Similar to the suggestion above, this is simply another way to decrease the number of cigarettes smoked. This will help you become accustomed to denying yourself a cigarette, and will make it easier for you to say "no" to yourself later on when you are not smoking at all.

2. **Put something else in your mouth instead of cigarettes.**

   ❏ **Drink a glass of water or citrus juice.** Nicotine depletes your vitamin C level so having a glass of juice first is a particularly useful alternative.

   ❏ **Use something else to suck or chew on:** gum, sugarless mints, cloves, flavored toothpicks, cinnamon sticks or vegetable sticks. Oftentimes anything in the mouth decreases the urge for a cigarette.

3. **Smoke less of each cigarette.**

   ❏ **Inhale less.** Use shallow breaths at a slower pace.

   ❏ **Smoke only half of each cigarette.** Cut the length of all cigarettes in your pack ahead of time. Begin by cutting off one-quarter of the original length. Once you are adjusted to that, begin cutting off half of the original length. Be careful not to inhale too deeply or to smoke right up to the filter.

   ❏ **Take fewer puffs per cigarette.** Let it burn in the ashtray. While this will not reduce carbon monoxide levels from the burning cigarette itself, it will reduce the amount of tar and nicotine you inhale.

4. **Reduce the tar, nicotine, and carbon monoxide levels of your cigarettes.**

   ❏ **Change to a brand of cigarettes that is lower in tar and nicotine than the one you now smoke.** If you are smoking a brand very high in tar and nicotine, change brands a couple of times, gradually bringing down the tar and nicotine levels. Be aware that you may want to smoke more cigarettes to make up for the lower nicotine levels. *Do not increase the number of cigarettes!* If you are unable to reduce the tar and nicotine levels without increasing the number of cigarettes you now smoke, then stick with your original brand until your quit date.

   Smokers with lower nicotine cigarettes tend to smoke them right up to the filters, thereby getting the higher levels of tar and nicotine that are concentrated in the last one-third of the cigarette. In addition, these same smokers tend to inhale more deeply and hold the smoke in their lungs for a longer period of time which enhances the absorption of smoke products into the blood stream. *If you find yourself doing either of these practices as a result of the lower nicotine levels, return to your original brand of cigarettes until your quit date.*

❑ **To help reduce carbon monoxide levels, select a brand with perforated paper and/or a perforated filter.** This dissipates some of the carbon monoxide into the air around the cigarette, resulting in slightly lower levels of carbon monoxide getting into the lungs. Because carbon monoxide is an important risk factor in cardiovascular disease, there is a definite additional benefit from using a low carbon monoxide cigarette.

❑ Overall, the **gradual reduction of nicotine, tar and carbon monoxide levels is the most beneficial.** If you are heavily dependent upon nicotine, it may be easier for you to use a cigarette with higher levels of nicotine but lower levels of tar and carbon monoxide. Since tar is the most important risk factor of the three elements for cancer, and carbon monoxide is such a high risk factor for cardiovascular disease, using a cigarette lower in these two elements will make a positive difference for you.

The job of the next group of tools is to make smoking less automatic or habitual. If you frequently light up without even thinking about it, you may discover that by keeping cigarettes out of your immediate reach you will not smoke as often. You may also discover that by removing the environmental reminders or "triggers" of specific objects, locations or actions, you will not think about smoking as often.

5. **Make smoking less automatic.**

❑ **Buy cigarettes by the pack, not by the carton.** This makes it more difficult to get to the next pack. This will also help you become more aware of what you are doing.

❑ **Stop carrying cigarettes with you** at home and at work. Cigarette smokers are never without cigarettes, so little thought is needed between craving them and lighting them. Make it more difficult to automatically smoke.

❏ If you always light up when first getting to your desk in the morning, **try doing something else instead.** Brew a cup of tea, get a glass of water, arrange some fresh flowers in a vase for your desk, water your office plants, file a few papers, and so on. You may simply be needing a bridging activity to get yourself mentally ready to work.

❏ If you always smoke when you sit in a particular chair, **sit somewhere else for a while.** Better yet, sit somewhere that is not normally associated with cigarettes. For example, instead of that relaxing cigarette in the living room before bed, settle into a tub of hot water. See if that relaxes you, if it reduces your craving for a cigarette.

❏ If your coffee cup is a trigger to think of a cigarette, **change your cup** and see what happens. This sounds a bit simplistic but you'll be surprised by how many urges to smoke are created by the visibility of an object always associated with smoking. Remember Pavlov and his dogs?

❏ If you always smoke at the end of a meal, **start carrying cinnamon sticks** to use as stirrers for your coffee or tea. This will give you something to suck on and to play with.

Smokers find a great deal of pleasure and relaxation in smoking. This is one of the strongest reasons why people are reluctant to give up smoking. To increase your determination not to smoke, find ways to erase the pleasure and relaxation from smoking. You will need to be equally conscientious about having alternative enjoyable and relaxing things to do each day, ones not associated with smoking.

6. **Make smoking less comfortable.**

❏ If you are accustomed to smoking outside or with the windows open, **sit in an enclosed room or car,** no windows open, to smoke. The resulting smoke build up will help you put the cigarette out sooner.

❏ **If you always sit when smoking, stand up instead.** Make the whole process less relaxing. This may increase your impatience with the entire smoking habit.

❏ **Before lighting up, go wash your mouth out with a strong flavored mouthwash or brush your teeth with a strong flavored toothpaste.** Cigarettes won't taste the same after that. See if it helps.

❏ **Choose a cigarette brand you don't like.** Smoke that or nothing. Sound unfair? Remember, the objective here is to reduce the pleasure of smoking.

❏ **Let cigarettes pile up in your ashtrays.** This will help you see how many cigarettes you have smoked at each location. If the smell and appearance is offensive, so much the better for reinforcing your commitment to quitting.

To repeat a caution stated earlier, if you use the nicotine reduction approach and find yourself inhaling more deeply or smoking more often, return to your original brand of cigarettes and work with the other tools on your Cue Card. If you are still not reducing your cigarette consumption, then your next option is to quit "cold turkey".

The "cut down" approach is designed to get you going. You will eventually have to quit smoking completely. Set your date for quitting now, if you haven't already done so. Don't procrastinate. It is very easy to put off quitting smoking forever. That's not the objective. **The real goal is to get the job done as quickly and as painlessly as possible.** Now it's time to go "cold turkey".

Abrupt, Immediate Withdrawal ("Cold Turkey")

The best way to approach abrupt cessation of all cigarettes is to **give yourself a week away from your usual stressors:** work, school, major responsibilities. Whether accomplished at home, at a mountain cabin, a residential smoking cessation program, or a resort, give yourself a period of time in which you can allow yourself to slow down, be a little thick-headed or ill-tempered, and be able to do nothing or to do something as the mood suits you. Maintaining a "performance edge" as you must do at work, and dealing with daily stress and tension may only serve to undermine your overall ability to handle yourself successfully during withdrawal.

If you are unable to take time away, **remove as much added stress as possible.** Take a break from extra voluntary jobs; put off working on extra projects; stay away from stressful social or family situations whenever possible. Join a stop-smoking support group or instructional program. Team up with someone else who wants to quit "cold turkey" and do it together.

Read through the list of new tools that follows, placing a check mark (✔) alongside each one that appeals to you. Then **follow the directions for preparing a Cue Card** (described under item 6 on page 128). List no more than seven tools presented below on your card. Make a copy of the card, carrying one with you and taping one to the bathroom mirror. Use it as a daily guide and reminder to help you get through abrupt withdrawal successfully.

❑ In the early days of withdrawal, **drink as much fluid as you possibly can.** One of the best methods for removing excess nicotine from the system is to literally flush it out. Pouring fluid in while promoting fluid release through sweating and urination help to flush nicotine out faster. Use hot baths, the steam room, sauna, or jacuzzi, if your physician approves. **If you have high blood pressure, you should not use excessive heat or steam.**

❑ **Exercise as much as you reasonably can.** It will not only cause you to sweat, the exercise will also help to relax tensions and force you to breathe deeply.

❑ **Use high-chew or crunchy low-calorie foods for snacking. If you need to suck on something, use sugar-free mints or low-calorie hard candies.** The tendency, when leaving cigarettes, is to turn to something else for comfort and for something to do. People commonly choose food since it involves both the hands and the mouth, and can be extremely comforting. Chapter 10 has many additional ideas for eating and weight control.

❏ Remember once again that **cigarette cravings last only thirty to ninety seconds.** In the very beginning of complete withdrawal you will probably experience "rapid fire" cravings: one craving immediately followed by another. Remember, **slow, measured deep breathing will help to get you through them more comfortably.**

❏ **Keep yourself busy. Distract yourself.** If you can't sit still, walk, swim, play tennis or racquetball, go dancing, play with a musical instrument, do a handwork project, set up a jigsaw puzzle, take your garden clippers or your fishing pole and head for the outdoors. **Tire yourself out, then relax** with a book, magazine or TV if you can.

❏ **Talk with other people.** Let them know you are quitting smoking. Companionship, extra help and encouragement are vitally important at this time.

❏ **Give yourself permission to be self-indulgent.** Take some time off for pleasure. Go to a movie, go out for dinner with nonsmoking friends. Invite someone to go somewhere with you for fun: skiing, skating, horseback riding or a walk; shopping, gallery-looking or a visit to a museum. If you enjoy playing cards or table games, invite some of your friends to join you. If you are able, get a back rub or massage, a facial, a manicure or pedicure. Soak in a hot tub, stretch out with an interesting book, or rent a favorite movie. Whatever you choose, give yourself plenty of permission to enjoy it.

❏ You may find yourself craving cigarettes less when you are in **an environment which doesn't allow smoking:** public buildings, libraries, theatres, exercise and health clubs, and the like. It feels so good to be able to leave the "burden of control" at the entrance of the building and know that for several minutes or several hours, smoking urges will not be as intense. After all, you didn't smoke in those places before so why will you miss cigarettes now in places where you never smoked?

❏ **Spend your time with nonsmoking friends, co-workers and family members.** This is especially important during the first few weeks without cigarettes. Their added strength will help you keep yourself in line more comfortably. In time your smoking friends will not represent such a big threat to your control, although later on, on days when you feel tempted to smoke, being with nonsmokers will be very helpful.

Prepare yourself for battle for about a week. Then plan for a two to three week period of vigilance over yourself and your "automatic" reaches for a cigarette. By the end of this period the worst of the withdrawal process will be behind you. The cravings and the difficulties that lie ahead will be far more attributable to your level of psychological dependence upon cigarettes than to physical addiction itself.

Reaffirm this message to yourself every day and with every craving: **"Giving up smoking is the single most important good thing I can do for myself, for now and for the rest of my life!"**

Changing Your Diet

Research has shown that smokers are very dose specific when it comes to nicotine, which means that their bodies attempt to maintain a consistent, specific nicotine level. When the level drops, the smoker is triggered to want another cigarette. In gradual withdrawal this information is of particular importance since the nicotine level in the blood can determine how often and how many cigarettes the person smokes.

Nicotine is filtered out of your blood by your kidneys and eliminated from your body through your urine. Urinary pH, or the relative acidity or alkalinity of your urine, determines whether nicotine is eliminated or reabsorbed. When the urine is more acidic (pH of 5.5 or less) more nicotine is eliminated. When the urine is more alkaline, more nicotine is reabsorbed.

If you are using the "cut down" approach to withdrawal, you will want to retain as much serum nicotine as possible to reduce the number of cigarettes you need to smoke in a day. A more alkaline urine will help you retain a higher serum nicotine level in your body for a longer time period, thus reducing the number and severity of your cigarette cravings.

Conversely, if you are quitting "cold turkey" you will want to bring your serum nicotine level down quickly. A more acidic urine will cause nicotine to be eliminated faster, bringing you into and through the withdrawal stage faster. You can adjust the alkalinity or acidity of your urine by the foods you eat.

High-Alkaline Diet for Gradual Withdrawal

Foods containing potassium, calcium, magnesium and sodium produce a more alkaline urine. To bring your serum nicotine level down more gradually, increase the amount of alkaline-forming foods and decrease the amount of acid-forming foods in your daily diet.

Increase the use of these alkaline-forming foods: shrimp; dairy products; fruits, vegetables and grains other than those listed below; almonds, brazil nuts, chestnuts and filberts; water and mineral water.

Decrease the use of these acid-forming foods: meat, poultry, fish, eggs; cranberries, plums, prunes and prune juice; asparagus and corn; rice and lentils; peanuts, pecans and walnuts; alcohol.

High-Acid Diet for Abrupt Withdrawal

In abrupt, immediate withdrawal, where the objective is to get the nicotine out of the body as quickly as possible, the nutritional strategy is to decrease the alkaline-forming foods and increase the acid-forming foods. Foods containing high levels of phosphorus, sulfur and chlorine produce a more acidic urine.

Increase the use of these acid-forming foods: meat, poultry, fish, eggs; cranberries, plums, prunes and prune juice; asparagus and corn; rice and lentils; peanuts, pecans and walnuts.

Decrease the use of these alkaline-forming foods: shrimp; dairy products; all other fruits, vegetables and grains; almonds, brazil nuts, chestnuts and filberts; water and mineral water.

If you wish to use a more specific set of dietary guidelines to help you in withdrawing from nicotine more comfortably, a Seven-Day High-Alkaline Diet for gradual withdrawal, and a Seven-Day High-Acid Diet for immediate withdrawal are included in the Appendix, beginning on page 333. These well-balanced, nutritional diets were developed by a registered dietitian and are simple and easy to follow.

One word of caution: **if you are currently following a medically prescribed diet, consult your physician or dietitian before changing your diet in any way.**

Steps For Withdrawal—A Review

For quick reference and review, three summarized lists are presented below. Each list contains the basic tools for successful withdrawal. Put them on Cue Cards and carry them with you for easy reference and daily guidance.

Preparing To Quit

- Track your usual smoking patterns for a week before changing them.

- Establish a definite quit date. Notify everyone.

- Prepare a nonsmoking environment prior to quitting smoking completely.

- Develop a social support system.

- Choose your initial method of withdrawal and follow the directions as written.

- Prepare a Cue Card with a list of the specific tools you intend to use. Use it as a daily guide and reminder. Carry it everywhere with you.

Gradual, Progressive Withdrawal

- Delay lighting up.

- Put something else in your mouth instead of cigarettes.

- Smoke fewer cigarettes.

- Smoke less of each cigarette.

- Reduce the tar, nicotine, and carbon monoxide levels of your cigarettes.

- Make smoking less automatic.

- Make smoking less comfortable.

- Use a high-alkaline, low-acid diet.

> ### Abrupt, Immediate Withdrawal
>
> - Free yourself from added stressors as much as possible.
> - Drink as much fluid as possible.
> - Exercise as much as you reasonably can.
> - Use high-chew or crunchy low-calorie foods, sugar-free mints or candies.
> - Change to a high-acid, low-alkaline diet.
> - Slowly deep breathe during cravings.
> - Distract yourself; keep busy; talk with other people; be self-indulgent.
> - Spend as much time as possible in nonsmoking places and with nonsmoking people.

Closing Thoughts

Remind yourself daily that **withdrawal symptoms are temporary.** What you are feeling during withdrawal is also temporary. You will survive it. Consider that any eight-hour period without cigarettes in the past put you into the very beginning stages of withdrawal. If you used to go without smoking for a couple of days at a time, you have already had some experience with withdrawal. You may not have looked at it this way before. Perhaps this viewpoint will help you to relax a bit if the notion of withdrawal is unsettling to you.

If, after two or three weeks, you are still struggling to stay away from cigarettes, if the cravings are too strong to manage on your own or if you are unable to go through one or two whole days without a cigarette, you will need to consult your physician for some extra assistance. Nicotine gum is an acceptable short-term remedy to help you stop smoking. You will eventually need to physically withdraw from the nicotine gum but until that time, the gum will ease the nicotine cravings so that you can break your smoking habits. Your physician can guide you in the use of the gum or direct you to community smoking cessation programs that use nicotine gum as part of their treatment plan for quitting smoking.

An alternative method of short-term drug therapy using Clonidine is also available under a physician's care and guidance. Clonidine is a prescription drug frequently used for management of high blood pressure and is also used for Methadone drug detoxification. Recent studies have indicated that Clonidine is helpful in the reduction of discomfort during nicotine withdrawal. Your physician is your best advisor about whether or not Clonidine will be appropriate for you.

Whether you gradually cut down your cigarette consumption first or quit "cold turkey", whether you use only the guidelines in this book or use nicotine gum or Clonidine to help you temporarily, quitting smoking is one of most important steps you can take to improve your health.

Keep in mind that **quitting smoking is a process, not a single act.** This applies to everyone who quits smoking, no matter what method is used to do it. The simple act of throwing a pack of cigarettes away does not necessarily create a long-term nonsmoker. If you have quit before and then restarted, you probably understand that concept readily. The act of throwing away the pack begins a process which starts with the decision to quit. And once you've quit, the retraining begins.

If you experience resistance to following some or many of the guidelines laid out for you in this chapter, don't despair. This is normal. You are, after all, attempting to cut down and eventually discontinue cigarettes in your life. Until now, cigarettes have represented pleasure, comfort and reward, consolation and companionship. It is natural that you would not want to give these nice benefits up. You won't have to. You'll only have to acquire the same benefits by other means. That's what the rest of this book is about.

Recommended Self-Study Exercises

The Self-Study exercises listed below have been mentioned earlier. If you have not completed them, please consider doing it now. These exercises will aid you in acquiring the information and understandings necessary for quitting smoking successfully.

Tracking Your Smoking Patterns, page 305.

Your Smoking Profile, page 317.

Cue Cards, number 6 on page 128.

Seven-Day Diet Plans for Withdrawal, page 333.

References

A wealth of material exists about how to quit smoking successfully. The following sources were particularly helpful for this chapter on Withdrawal.

Technical Advisors:

Daniel Baker, Ph.D., Executive Director of Behavioral Health, Canyon Ranch Resort, Tucson, Arizona.

Philip Eichling, M.D., Medical Director, Canyon Ranch Resort, Tucson, Arizona.

Linda Connell Hadfield, R.D., former Director of Nutrition, Canyon Ranch Resort, Tucson, Arizona, now practicing in Houston, Texas.

History

Brooks, J.E. *The Mighty Leaf*. Boston: Little, Brown & Co., 1952.

Nutrition

Ogle, J. *The Stop Smoking Diet*. New York: M. Evans & Co., 1981.

Canyon Ranch Nutrition Department. *"Tips to Help Quit Smoking."* Tucson, AZ: Canyon Ranch Resort, 1986.

Nicotine Withdrawal

Fact sheets from the American Cancer Society, American Heart Association, and American Lung Association.

Ferguson, T. *The Smoker's Book of Health*. New York: G.P. Putnam's Sons, 1987.

Ray, O. *Drugs, Society and Human Behavior*. St Louis: C.F. Mosby Co., 1983.

Witters, W. and Jones-Witters, P. *Drugs & Society*. Monterey, CA: Wadsworth Health Sciences, 1983.

Clearing the Air: A Guide to Quitting Smoking. Washington, D.C.: U.S. Department of Health and Human Services Publication No. (NIH) 85-1647, 1985.

Self-Management Tools
For Non-Smokers

7

Free peoples can escape being mastered by others only by being able to master themselves.

... Theodore Roosevelt

If you apply the concept of self-mastery to smoking, the objective is to free yourself from cigarettes' control in the daily management of your moods and energies by developing a set of strong nonsmoking self-management tools that meet the same needs. In other words, if you can satisfy your daily needs for physical pleasure, psychological support, stimulation, and relaxation and tension release by nonsmoking means, the importance and usefulness of cigarettes will fade quickly. And you will once again be in the driver's seat of your own self-control.

In Chapter 5 you were introduced to the nonsmoker's tool kit, and learned about some general nonsmoking tools. In Chapter 6 you used a combination of those tools proven successful for nicotine withdrawal. In this chapter you will learn to use specialized tools for managing yourself without cigarettes, for maintaining yourself as a nonsmoker. These are the specific implements with which you will explore and experiment in your search for the handful of practical, usable, comfortable tools you will turn to daily—the ones with the correct feel and fit for you.

You will recognize many of the general REDRESSED tools discussed in Chapter 5 as you read through the entire list of tools in this chapter. Notice how some tools are geared toward *delay*, *distraction* and *escape*, while others deal with *substitution* and *environmental control*. Some of the tools will show you ways to *relax*, *reward*, *support* and *encourage* yourself. All of the tools are important, some more so than others. Some of the tools will be more appropriate and meaningful to you than others. You are not expected to like and use everything. The ultimate objective is for you to identify the tools that best meet your needs and fit most comfortably into your daily routines.

Smoking Patterns Determine Tools Selection

Before proceeding further, you need to identify some of your predominant reasons, needs or benefits derived from smoking: *habit*, *physical pleasure*, *psychological support*, *stimulation*, and *relaxation and tension release*. Each of these categories appears later as a heading in this chapter. Knowing *why* you smoke will help you select the appropriate tools to help you quit smoking and remain a nonsmoker.

Now, get your pencil and 3x5 cards. Begin with step one of the instructions which follow. Do each step in sequence.

1. **Complete the "Smoking Patterns" section of the Smoking Profile Questionnaire,** page 320.

2. **Score questions 4 a-b and 5 a-c of the Smoking Profile Questionnaire.** Enter your score for each pattern category alongside the section heading as indicated on pages 151 through 157. Scores of 12 or more for any category suggests that you will need to study the tools listed within that category.

3. **Read about all of the tools listed under each category first. Then go back and place check marks (✔) alongside the tools that seem most interesting and important to you.** Keep your mind as open as you can to the message of each tool, taking care not to automatically discard something as unworkable or too simplistic before you've had a chance to experiment with it. Sometimes the simplest tools are the most effective.

4. **Prepare a Cue Card for each category where you have a score of 12 or more points.** Take a 3x5 index card and write the category name across the top (i.e., Habit, Physical Pleasure, Stimulation, etc.). Then list up to a maximum of seven tools you have selected for use within that category on the index card. That index card becomes a Cue Card to be used as a daily guide and reminder. This is the same procedure you followed for preparing Cue Cards in Chapter 6, item 6 on page 128. For example:

Cue Card: Habit
• **Change where I sit.** Sit on sofa instead of reclining chair, read paper on sofa instead of kitchen table, watch TV on bed where I never smoked.
• **Use a cordless telephone** so I can roam around while I talk. Leave a copy of the Yellow Pages and pens for doodling by the office telephone.
• **Remove all cigarettes, lighters, ash trays, cigarette cases.** Replace with gum, mints, deck of cards, decorative trinkets, flowers, photos, things to fiddle with.
• **Avoid coffee in the morning and alcohol in the evening.** Replace with tea, flavored mineral water with lemon or lime, nonalcoholic mixed drinks.
• **Socialize with nonsmoking friends as much as possible:** Karl, Kevin, Jim, Sue, Laurie, Bev and Judy.
• **Insist on nonsmoking sections in restaurants and airplanes.** If none are available, wait for a nonsmoking table or sit with nonsmoking people only.

Note that the presentation style used for preparing the Cue Cards in the preceeding example gives the tool first, followed by specific suggestions for what to do. This eliminates confusion later when you need to refer to your Cue Cards. These Cards will be especially important to you during the times when you are agitated, having a tough day, desperately wanting a cigarette, or any one of the other social, emotional, or psychological situations that can block your ability to think clearly.

5. **Concentrate on one Cue Card at a time.** Work with the tools on that one card until you feel comfortable and secure with them. If you checked only five to seven tools in total for all five Smoking Patterns categories, you may prefer to prepare only one Cue Card and list all of the tools on that one Card.

6. **Eliminate, modify or add tools to your Cue Card as appropriate.** When you feel ready, select a new Cue Card and follow the same procedure: list the tools, experiment with them, evaluate them and modify or eliminate them as needed. Slowly, over time, you will acquire a number of important and effective tools for your long-term use.

7. **Consolidate all of your tools onto a Resource List,** page 329. The Resource List will provide a simple, easy to use method for summarizing all of the nonsmoking tools you eventually want to use into a single resource. Used for reference and guidance, the Resource List will enable you to set a sequential plan of action for using your nonsmoking tools. Specific instructions for preparation and use of the Resource List are given in Chapter 9. For now, you only need to transcribe the tools you wish to use on a long-term basis from your individual Cue Cards to the Resource List.

Setting The Stage For Change

Randy, the high-school football coach who stepped forward to lead his school's Smoke Out Campaign, was preparing a series of information sheets for the parents' "Butt Kickers Club". Spurred on by the kids who followed Randy's example and "trashed" their cigarettes three weeks earlier, a group of parents gathered together to tackle their own smoking habits. Impressed by what Randy was able to do with himself and their children, the parents regarded him as a role model for themselves as well as the kids. They asked him to give some lectures to help them learn how to live successfully without cigarettes.

Randy collected the information sheets for this evening's parents' meeting and headed off for the copy machine. Twenty minutes later he was standing in front of thirteen parents, reviewing the Smoking Profile Questionnaire they had worked on the day before. Scores for each of the categories in questions 4 and 5 of the questionnaire varied from person to person, but a few patterns emerged. Scores tended to be highest in the areas of Habit, Psychological Support and Relaxation. Stimulation received high scores for some people, while Physical Pleasure seemed to be low for almost everyone.

As Randy discussed the implications of the various scores, he noticed a tall, stocky man sitting at the back of the room, casually fingering the leaves of the large plant sitting to the right of his chair. Randy called out to the man, "Jim, what was your score in Physical Pleasure?"

"Just Four," Jim answered. "The only part of that question that fit me was inhaling deeply. I miss that the most."

Jim shifted his position in the chair. After a few moments he began fondling the silk flowers in a basket on the table at the left side of his chair. Silk flower heads piled up on the table top as the discussion progressed. "Jim," Randy called out again, "look at your left hand."

Jim wore a blank expression for a moment, then smiled sheepishly. "I guess having something to play with is more important than I thought," he said.

"That's exactly what I'm trying to get across," Randy responded. "Sometimes we don't realize how deep some of our patterns go, or even *that we do certain things. Physical pleasure is a good example. Most people don't realize they have restless hands until they quit smoking and no longer have the cigarettes to play with. I certainly didn't. I discovered that I like to hold and touch things. I enjoyed the feel of something smooth in my hand. The same was true for having something in my mouth. I never realized how much I would miss sucking on something."*

Several people nodded in agreement. A few laughed.

"I want each of you to think about your scores and about the things you do," Randy continued. "The questionnaire is helpful to get your thinking started. Watch yourself for a few days and think about your cigarette cravings. Try to understand what you're really missing when you think you're missing the cigarette. You'll miss the cigarette too, believe me. But you'll notice other things. Restlessness. Boredom. Anxiety. Not knowing what to do with yourself. Lots of things."

"I've put together some information sheets that match the Smoking Pattern categories used in questions 4 and 5," Randy told the group. "You will find several tools listed for each category. After you read it over you'll probably want to try too many of the tools at one time. At least that's what usually happens. You'll have to have a plan for what to do with all of the information but first, just read the information sheets with an open mind. Check off the ideas that appeal to you. Add ideas of your own. That's all I want you to do for right now. Tomorrow I'll teach you how to work with the information."

Just as Randy instructed his class, **you need to follow these steps:**

- Note your score for each Smoking Patterns category: *habit, physical pleasure, psychological support, stimulation, and relaxation and tension release.* These categories begin on page 320 of the Smoking Profile Questionnaire.

- Read about each category on the following pages (151-157). Focus on the ones with scores of twelve or more.

- Check (✔) the tools that appeal or apply to you and your needs.

- Write ideas of your own in the margins alongside the listed tools (or write them on a separate piece of paper).

Smoking Pattern Categories

Habit   (Score: _____)

Smokers with scores higher than 12 in this area are typically less dependent upon the chemical action of the nicotine, than upon the continuation of their daily smoking routine. Many strong habit smokers, for example, are less aware of their smoking and of the actual cigarette itself than is true for other types of smokers. Habit smokers typically light their cigarettes and place them in ash trays, often forgetting that they are there. They rarely smoke an entire cigarette. Habit smokers tend to light up more often in response to particular people or activities, being in particular places, even experiencing particular emotions, than in response to cigarette cravings. The issue is *awareness*.

If you are a habit smoker, you can interrupt your automatic response pattern by increasing awareness, changing routines, or replacing smoking and cigarettes with other alternatives. Your smoking habits can be effectively broken with these tools!

❏ **Break the patterns!** Look at where and with what activities (drinking coffee, sitting at the table at the end of the meal, etc.) smoking most often occurred. Then change whatever is necessary: the places you sit, the cup you drink from, where you sit to read or relax at home. The idea here is to break up paired associations.

❏ **Sit in different places at home and at work.** This sounds simplistic, but frequently particular places are so deeply paired with smoking that just being there triggers a desire to smoke.

❏ **If you smoke while talking on the telephone, move the phone to a new location; give yourself a new object to play with.** Keep a hand grip or rubber ball to squeeze, Rubic's cubes or other "hands on" types of puzzles to play with. Look up some of the tools given in the Physical Pleasure section on page 153. Once you decide on the other things you intend to use, buy them and set them in the places cigarettes used to rest. You will automatically reach for something; make certain it can't be cigarettes.

❑ **Remove all suggestion to smoke:** cigarettes, lighters, matches, cases, ash trays—everything connected in your mind with smoking, everything leading you to automatically pick up or think of picking up a cigarette. Don't leave a few favorite smoking items around for sentimentality. You need to remove all smoking items. EVERY ONE!!

❑ **Change the scent of everything around you.** Everything used to smell like tobacco, fresh or stale. That kept you more susceptible to lighting up. Clean and launder all clothing and bedclothes; have your car thoroughly cleaned to remove all smell of tobacco smoke.

❑ **Avoid alcohol, "pot", cocaine and other substances which have a disinhibiting effect,** because each of them lowers control. The best way to handle this issue is to keep yourself alert, and to avoid situations normally associated with smoking.

❑ **In the early days of quitting smoking, visit with your old smoking buddies only in the presence of someone with whom you would not allow yourself to smoke, or in places where you cannot smoke.** Your old smoking pals may provide strong temptation for you to smoke. This will be hard for you to handle when you first quit smoking. By having someone around whose presence is a deterrent for you to smoke comfortably, you will be able to be in the presence of other smokers without losing control. Do this for as long as it takes for you to gather sufficient strength and security with yourself as a nonsmoker to enable you to be in the presence of smokers without feeling uneasy.

❏ **Find new restaurants and other places for social gathering that are not associated in your mind with smoking.**

❏ **Especially on hard-to-control days, spend your time with non-smokers, and in a nonsmoking environment.** Go to a health club, for example. The environment there will help you to reconnect with healthy living and to reassert or reestablish control. Libraries, public buildings and the homes or offices of nonsmokers are all good places to spend time.

Physical Pleasure (Score: _____)

Many smokers don't realize how much physical pleasure they derive from smoking until they stop using cigarettes. The feel of the cigarette in the mouth, the sensation of breathing deeply, the comfort of holding the cigarette all underscore the importance of physical touch. When you are at a low-energy point, either emotionally or physically, your need for touch and even for something to suck on may be stronger than usual. This is when thoughts of cigarettes and of food come to mind. The issue is *comfort*. Physical touch is comforting and soothing. The objective is to find nonsmoking methods of comforting and soothing yourself. If weight gain is a worry, these tools should be nonedible as well!

❏ **Use slow, measured deep breathing.** Whatever the effects of nicotine as a tranquilizer to your central nervous system, the practice of sitting back in your chair and breathing deeply, as you do when dragging hard on cigarettes, will serve to relax and soothe you. Slow, measured deep breathing is a frequently used tool by many nonsmokers to calm and soothe themselves.

❏ **Grooming and polishing activities provide soothing emotional and physical touch.** Facials, manicures, pedicures and massages (do your own or share with a partner) allow for a more intimate type of touch and can be healing to the spirit as well as the body. Grooming a pet, brushing a child's hair, polishing indoor plant leaves, polishing a well-loved piece of furniture are each effective at keeping the hands busy and providing emotional and physical comfort.

❑ **Hot baths, whirlpools, saunas and steam rooms provide comforting, soothing relaxation.** Even soaking your feet in a basin of warm water feels physically good. Allow yourself time to indulge in these activities.

❑ **At the end of a meal, use cinnamon sticks to suck on or to stir your coffee or tea.** This will provide something to keep your hands and mouth busy, helping to reduce the longing for a cigarette.

❑ When sitting down to read, watch TV or work at your desk, **sucking or chewing on a flavored toothpick, popsicle stick, or any other smooth, hard object** will provide temporary relaxation and comfort.

❑ **Keep little objects around to hold or play with when sitting.** Something to hold while driving will ease the longing for cigarettes in the early weeks without them. Cinnamon sticks, swizzle sticks, popsicle sticks and the like can substitute for cigarettes as objects for holding. Interesting items like coins, tiny figurines, puzzles, souvenirs from special places, highly polished or wood objects, are only a few of the possible items that are useful for holding or playing with in idle fashion. If they are favorite items, their presence provides an important sense of comfort. This may sound superficial to you until you watch someone "play" with the items in a much-cherished collection or touch an item given by a loved one. Look for such items of your own and keep them on tables or desks where you sit.

Psychological Support   (Score: _____)

Many smokers believe they can't function without cigarettes during moments of stress or discomfort. They believe it is the cigarette itself that gets them through the crisis. In actuality, the cigarette provides something to psychologically "hold on to", a rallying tool which enables the smoker to bring his or her own internal resources into play. The issue here is *belief*.

If you, the smoker, believe you cannot handle your uncomfortable feelings without the aid of the cigarette, you will not be open to exploring new options. Further, it will be easier for you to revert to smoking when things are not going well, despite the fact that you can abstain from smoking under normal circumstances. Most new nonsmokers say they would prefer to handle their stresses without the aid of cigarettes, but don't have good ideas for coping effectively with their emotions. Here are some tools to try. Open your mind to experimenting with them before determining whether they will or will not work for you.

❏ **When emptiness or loneliness are the issues, call a friend who is important to you, or put yourself in the presence of other people if you are physically alone.** This means that if you work by yourself in an office, take a break and seek the company of someone else. If you are alone at home, call someone and plan a meal or an activity together for the same day or evening. Seek out the companionship of a child, a pet or even a good book.

❏ **Put an old favorite movie on the VCR, or go to a movie theatre.** Oftentimes the distraction of something that is visually and auditorily compelling removes the burdensome thoughts for a while, and can lift your spirits.

❏ **Talk to someone who used to smoke when you are feeling discouraged or burdened with the project of quitting smoking.** They can be excellent resources for good ideas, and they can provide much needed support and encouragement.

❏ **Allow yourself to get plenty of rest, especially right now.** Fatigue often paves the way for low-energy moods like depression, emptiness and loneliness. Take an occasional day off when you need to and sit by a lake or waterfront, watch a fire or the flame from a candle, go to a park and watch the people, or to a zoo and watch the animals. This provides some inward contemplation time which you will need in some measure to get yourself "centered", to renew your balance and perspective.

❑ **Keep a journal for your thoughts, feelings and experiences. Note your emotional needs at those times. Think about what else you could do to meet those needs.** Write your ideas down in the journal or list them on a piece of paper. Tape the piece of paper to the inside of a cupboard or closet door, or somewhere easy to find and easy to see. Keep an identical list in your pocket or purse for reference when you are away from home. **Consult the list during times of need.** Select an idea and try it out.

Stimulation (Score: _____)

A score of 12 or higher in this category indicates that you are *energized or stimulated* in some way by the cigarette. Perhaps the cigarette helps you to feel more alert, better able to organize your thoughts, more animated, better able to keep going. This is probably due, in part, to the action of the nicotine on your central nervous system. Some smokers look for the oral stimulation that comes from the acrid bite of the cigarette on the tongue. If you have turned to smoking to meet these needs, read the suggestions that follow.

❑ **Get up and move around:** run an errand, wash a dish, go up and down the stairs, take a brisk walk, jump rope for a few minutes, do a few stretching exercises from your chair or on the floor, do some filing. If you feel sleepy, do something active. Motion of almost any kind will wake you up, help you to feel more alert. Don't deliberate about it—just get up and move!

❑ **Have a brief conversation with someone in person or on the telephone.** The motion of dialing the telephone or going to find someone to talk with and the change of focus provided by the conversation itself will help to charge you up a bit.

❑ **Peppy or fast-paced music can energize you.** People who exercise to music will probably tell you that they get a harder and longer workout when using high-energy music. Use it in the car, at home, with earphones in the office for brief periods when you want to get yourself moving.

❑ **Strongly or very definitely flavored items are effective for oral stimulation.** Use a sharp or spicy flavored tooth paste; an astringent mouthwash; highly flavored sugarless mints or gum; whole cloves or Sen Sen to put in your mouth; toothpicks soaked in oil of clove, cinnamon or mint to suck on; or vegetables marinated in a strong vinaigrette for nibbling. Strongly flavored seeds like fennel, caraway, anise, and dill can be used a little at a time for that feeling of stimulation on the tongue that the cigarette once provided. Breath sprays are also good for this purpose.

❑ **Pungent flavors** like grapefruit, lemon, cloves, and vinegar all **spoil the taste for a cigarette.** This is a very helpful substitution strategy.

❑ **For a quick refresher or energizer, drink juice, ice water, carbonated beverages, caffeinated tea, or strongly flavored herb teas** (Red Zinger, Ruby Mist, Cinnamon Rose, Orange Spice).

❑ **Eating something can act as a quick stimulant.** Chew on rice cakes, popcorn, Lavosh or bran-a-crisp crackers, shredded wheat biscuits, raw vegetables or fruit. These are all low-calorie items, especially helpful if weight gain is a concern.

Relaxation And Tension Release   (Score: _____)

This is a high score area for many people, primarily for two reasons: *nonproductive time* and *stress reduction.* Smoking once gave you a method for unwinding, for time off, for letting go of stress. Perhaps smoking provided the only nonproductive time you allowed for yourself. If this is true for you, then you will need to find other alternatives for pleasure and relaxation.

Not so long ago people used hobbies, musical instruments, puzzles, games and many other distraction activities to achieve time out from more productive activities. Their use brought rest and relaxation. They also offered a means for settling surface tension, the tension seen in restless hands when you are feeling stressed or anxious. These needs will seem more prominent when you are no longer smoking. Which of the following tools appeals to you:

❏ **Keep objects to play with in constant reach** at your sitting places at home and at work, and in your pockets or purse. "Executive" puzzles, Rubic's cubes, paperweights with luminescent colors or things that move inside when they are tipped over, hand grips, rosary beads, worry stones or beads, paper clips, key chains, trinkets, pens, pencils, eyeglasses frames and charm bracelets represent a few small, easy-to-carry, distracting items. The range of objects is limited only by your imagination. Explore and experiment.

❏ **Have little activities to keep your hands busy while talking on the telephone, watching TV, listening to music.** These can include hand work projects like hooked rugs, stitchery, needlepoint, crafts, model building. They can also include coin, stamp, photography or other collections. Polishing silver, cleaning jewelry, and sanding, staining or painting wood are useful household activities that are small enough to provide something to keep your hands occupied.

❏ **Take time out for nonproductive play,** particularly when you don't feel like doing anything important or are trying to put off doing something you don't particularly want to do. Each cigarette provided up to two minutes of "time out". Gardening, crafts, playing around with a musical instrument, computer games, playing solitaire, coloring in design books or posters, jigsaw puzzles, crossword puzzles, pencil and paper games (mazes, word searches, etc.), playing with the word dice in games like Spill and Spell, looking at old photos and home movies and so on all provide relaxation, diversion and refreshment.

❏ **In restaurants, order foods that have extra "play value":** foods that require cutting, peeling, or cracking; foods that have bones to chew on; vegetables like corn on the cob and artichokes; foods you cook as you eat like fondue; foods you eat with chopsticks, and so on. The extra time and effort taken to eat these foods will reduce the time available for smoking as well as the need for holding a cigarette.

❏ **Give yourself permission to daydream, to get lost in your own thoughts.** Cigarettes used to give you those mental concentration breaks. You can accomplish this by finding ways to slip away from concentrated thought. Watching water, firelight, people, birds, tropical fish in a tank are all helpful for mental escape. Candlelight sets a nice mood and is easy to use. Photographs of roads, paths, harbors—whatever lets your eye travel into the picture will also let your mind travel as well. Prisoners of war talk at length about how their ability to emotionally cope with confinement stemmed from being able to go places in their mind's eye. The pictures, the firelight, the water can "grease the wheels" of your ability to step away from the cares of the world, to get lost in your own thoughts.

❏ **Social or recreational activities are very important for fun and relaxation.** Dancing, movies, sporting events, games like tennis or miniature golf, table games, scenic drives, walks or hikes with others, are examples. Everyone needs some of this kind of time. If you have been unable to give yourself permission to indulge yourself in activities like these, no doubt smoking was a critically necessary refuge. Use activities like these as part of your anti-smoking project and give yourself permission for some much-needed rest and relaxation.

❏ **Use meditation, yoga or relaxation techniques to help you unwind and calm yourself.** If you have never explored these avenues, get some instruction and experience them for yourself. People in the Eastern cultures learn early in life how to create peace from within. Our Western culture teaches us to rely more heavily upon outside resources. Proficiency in any of these techniques will help significantly during stressful times.

❏ **Hot baths and herbal teas help to soothe and relax.** Mint and chamomile teas are particularly relaxing. Chewing on licorice root (available in health food stores) can also help to relax and soothe the emotions.

❏ **Exercise, mild to strenuous, is an excellent tool for stress reduction, anxiety release, even for gearing up to face a difficult task.** Take your dog for a walk, do a few stretches, use your exercycle for ten minutes, or go for a real workout. You will find the motion to be anxiety reducing. Hard workouts have the added benefit of endorphin release, thereby giving you an emotional "upper". Any way you look at it, exercise in some form and at any level of intensity is beneficial.

Finding The Tools That Fit You

The objective, now, is to find the tools and techniques that appeal to you. Explore. Experiment. Find out what fits you, and what is effective for you. If you try something and it doesn't work, remember that it is not you who failed. The idea (tool or technique) failed for you. Toss out that idea and try another. If that one fails, discard it and try another. No idea is a bad idea. Some tools simply work more effectively in some situations than others. Some tools fit some personality types better than others.

Handling Cigarette Cravings

If cigarette cravings seem a little more intense or more frequent on some days, keep these few simple tools in mind. Write them on a Cue Card for quick reference.

- **Cigarette cravings last only thirty to ninety seconds and then they go away for increasingly longer periods of time.** Tell that to yourself repeatedly. **Use deep breathing exercises to get you through the ninety seconds.** In the beginning, you may experience "rapid fire" cravings, ones which follow each other in rapid succession. As time, and abstinence, progresses, the distance between the cravings increases. The intensity of the craving will always be strong, but less and less frequent. Deep breathing works. It is a tool that is always with you.

- **Use the "HALT!" technique** described on page 107 to pinpoint your cravings as **Hunger, Anger, Loneliness or Tiredness.** It will help you move your thoughts away from the cravings and onto a different topic.

- **Distract yourself.** Get on the telephone, run an errand or do a household chore, exercise intensely but briefly, or pound your pillow. Floss and brush your teeth. Play around with a musical instrument. Do something active. Don't just sit and think about how much you want to smoke.

- **If you need something in your mouth, use very definite things** like licorice root for chewing, strongly flavored foods like oven-crisped tortilla chips in hot salsa or vegetables marinated in vinaigrette. Suck on whole cloves or mint leaves, or toothpicks soaked in strongly flavored extracts like those used in flavoring frosting.

The Next Step

Randy met with the parents' group the following evening, as promised. Voices were animated as people traded ideas and opinions about the nonsmoking self-management tools Randy had given them. One woman stood up and addressed Randy directly. "I read everything," she said, "but I don't see how these little tricks will work for me. I can't see that doodling in the Yellow Pages will keep me from wanting a cigarette while I'm talking on the telephone."

"This all sounds very superficial to me!" the man next to her exclaimed.

"I understand why you might feel that way," Randy responded. "I have thought that myself at times. But, if you really stop to think about it, smoking is a pretty superficial tool, too. Smoking doesn't solve problems, it just makes you feel better temporarily. Playing with the cigarette pack is no different, is it, than doodling in the telephone book? Both activities calm you down a little. Both activities let you sit still long enough to finish your conversation."

A few people laughed. Randy smiled and continued. "What I'm trying to say is that smoking and doodling are both tools we use to cope with certain situations. They are simple, convenient, pretty superficial things to do, but they do meet a need. Smoking is harmful; doodling is not. Which makes the most sense to you?"

No one spoke for a few moments. Randy took a deep breath, then plunged into the heart of the matter, as he saw it. "The hardest thing for me to do, sometimes, is to keep an open mind. I see or hear something and I immediately evaluate it. This will work, this won't work. This is a good idea, this is a stupid idea. This is deep, this is superficial.

"The other thing I do," Randy continued, "is tell myself that I know all about that information already. I convince myself how knowledgeable I am and then put aside everything I hear as being old information. I get so caught up in being so smart that I miss all the important stuff. I don't try anything. I stay stuck in the same rut that created the problem in the first place."

Randy looked earnestly at the group. "I'm sure I sound like every other quit-smoking crusader you've heard. I don't know how to say this any other way. **Please take this seriously. You need to open your mind to try everything, even the simple, superficial things. Sometimes the simpler and more superficial something is, the better it works.** Honestly."

No one said anything. Randy riffled through the papers on the desk in front of him. He wondered what everyone else was thinking. He hoped he had made sense to them, but he knew that most of them would have *to think about what he had said for a while before they would have any real opinions. He sighed. This is the hardest part of quitting smoking, he thought to himself. Getting and keeping an open mind is so hard to do!*

"Are you ready to hear about what to do with all this information I've given you?" Randy asked. People nodded. "OK, let's go.

*"Once you've read everything and had a little time to play with the different tools, you'll probably want to start choosing the ones that feel or work the best for you. Some of you may find only a few that you want to spend a lot of time on. Most of you will pick too many tools to work with all at once. **The goal, here, is to work your way down to maybe five to seven tools, and then practice them daily until they take root and become habits."***

Your Action Plan

The best way for you to handle a big job like this is to break it down into smaller steps. Here's the overall plan to follow for selecting and using the tools in this chapter.

Discovery

1. **Complete the Smoking Patterns section of your Smoking Profile Questionnaire** (begins on page 320).

2. **Score questions 4 a-b and 5 a-c.** Enter your scores alongside the corresponding Smoking Pattern categories in this chapter, pages 151 through 157.

3. **Read about all of the tools in each category first.** Put check marks alongside the tools you wish to use.

Exploration and Evaluation

4. **Prepare a Cue Card for each Smoking Pattern category having a score of twelve or more.** If there are no scores as high as twelve,

prepare Cue Cards for your highest scoring categories. List no more than seven tools per Card.

5. **Use one Cue Card at a time.** (Note: if you marked fewer than seven tools in total for all five categories, list them all on one Cue Card.)

6. **Eliminate, modify or add tools to your Cue Card as appropriate.**

7. **When finished with one Cue Card, begin working with the next, following the same procedure.** Do this until you have worked with each Cue Card you have prepared.

8. **Prepare a special, emergency Cue Card to handle cigarette cravings, page** 160.

Consolidation

9. **Retain only the tools that are effective** (they make a positive difference to you), **practical** (they are do-able within your lifestyle and time availability), and **likeable** (you like them well enough to keep using them). Eliminate all others.

10. Look at all of the tools remaining on all of your Cue Cards. **Consolidate them on one single Resource List** (see page 329). The Resource List becomes a master list of all selected tools. It will ultimately serve as a guide for giving order and sequence for using the individual tools written on it.

Closing Thoughts

This is a critically important chapter so please take the time you need to work with the information in it. **You cannot hurry the learning process too much without short-changing yourself.** Discovery, experimentation and evaluation all take time. This is the learning process in action.

The identification, selection, evaluation and modification of the tools and techniques for retraining yourself to function without cigarettes is the objective of this chapter. This is a big task and you may choose to spend a few weeks working with this chapter. Perhaps this sounds like an unnecessary investment of time and energy. It isn't, especially if you have struggled to quit before and have been unable to stay away from cigarettes permanently. For now, the task is to find out what works for you, what meets your needs and what feels good to use in place of cigarettes. In later chapters you will learn how to integrate the tools more effectively and to build flexibility into your daily plan.

Watch your behavior. No matter what you say to yourself in your mind, if your actions show that you are not consistently using a particular tool, that behavior presents a truer picture of your commitment and willingness to use that tool than any words you might say. Poor follow-through, not getting around to using the tool, and making excuses are all signs that the particular tool needs to be eliminated, modified or exchanged for something more workable.

Keep in mind that there is nothing magical about any particular tool. **The magic resides in you,** not in the specific tools. It resides in your ability to tap your own commitment, identify your own needs effectively, evaluate the tools honestly, and select only those you are truly willing to work with and to practice consistently.

Use whatever reinforcement and help you can get for yourself. Review the Potential Resources section of your Smoking Profile Questionnaire, page 323, for ideas about where to gather support. Praise, approval, attention and achievement are all effective for maintaining motivation. Whether you have to join a group, seek help from a professional, join a Smokers Anonymous chapter, spend your time with nonsmoking friends who support your quitting smoking, keep charts and graphs of your progress, or reward yourself with little gifts for reaching milestones (for example, two weeks without cigarettes), do it.

Don't be too proud or too independent to take advantage of the many reinforcers for your desired behavior. Your agenda is to find effective alternatives to meet your needs in other ways, and to gradually kick nicotine out of your life completely. This is a real challenge, especially if you are doing it alone. Look for aid and reinforcement wherever you can find it, whether from an instructor, a physician, a counselor, former smokers, even your children.

Keep this thought from Henry Ward Beecher, noted American clergyman and orator, in mind during the next few weeks:

"The difference between perseverance and obstinacy is, that one often comes from a strong will, and the other from a strong won't."

Recommended Self-Study Exercises

The Smoking Profile Questionnaire, especially questions 4a-b and 5a-c on page 320.

Cue Cards, beginning with item 4 page 147, and item 4 on page 163.

Resource List, page 325.

Application And Practice

8

Practice is the best of all instructors

... Publilius

The time has come to apply what you have learned, to test your ability to use your nonsmoking tools for solving specific problems associated with smoking. This chapter is designed to help you do that. By using a combination of imagination, visual imagery and applied knowledge, you will have opportunities to develop solutions to challenging hypothetical practice situations. This is meant to prepare you for the potential difficult-to-control circumstances or high- and low-energy moods that can occur in your own life.

You will be doing a great deal of writing in this chapter to develop specific action plans for managing yourself *without* smoking. The more practice you have in problem solving, the more skilled you will be in guiding yourself safely through the anticipated obstacles or hazards in your path toward smoke-free living.

The key to this chapter is your *imagination*. Defined as the ability of the human mind to form a mental image or concept of something that is unreal or not present, imagination allows you to use the creative ability of your mind to confront and cope with anticipated problems or worries. In terms of not smoking, you can use your imagination to prepare yourself in advance for situations or circumstances that worry you as a new nonsmoker.

Your imagination allows you to mentally rehearse the actions you will need to take in each specific situation to produce the desired result, to mentally see yourself taking those actions. This mental imagery is similar to what actors do to visualize each aspect of their on-stage performance prior to actual rehearsal. Behavioral psychologists have coined the term "role rehearsal" to refer to the imaginative process of mentally practicing, or rehearsing, your coping skills in advance of needing to use them.

The "Check Yourself" section of this chapter will help you practice your application skills with some carefully planned scenarios. Each scenario is followed by the question, *"What will you do?"* Write your answers on the lines provided before reading the practical discussion that follows your answers. The second section, "Write Your Own Scenarios", takes you one step further by asking you to write new nonsmoking scenarios to replace your old smoking ones. And, because mood management without cigarettes is of concern to most former smokers, the last section will help you prepare for handling your high- and low-energy moods without smoking.

Keep the Cue Cards that you prepared readily available when you read and develop solutions for the imaginary situations that follow. This will enable you to easily remember and apply the tools you have selected. A quick review of the general REDRESSED tools will be helpful to you before beginning to check yourself.

R elaxation
E nvironmental Control
D elay
R eward
E scape
S ubstitution
S upport
E ncouragement
D istraction

Check Yourself

✍ *Imagine that you are on the last leg of a long nighttime drive home.* About forty miles out of town your engine overheats and you are forced to stop. It's late, you are tired, and you have no flashlight. In exasperation, but with hope, you raise the hood of the car and pray for a trucker to come by and help you. One does. He adds fluid to your dry radiator and gently lowers the hood. What relief! Both of you take a deep breath and chat for a minute. The trucker reaches into his shirt pocket for a pack of cigarettes. He offers a cigarette to you...

What will you do?

_____

_____

_____

_____

When people offer something they usually lean forward, hand extended. The most typical response from the other person in that situation is to lean forward also, almost in an attitude of acceptance. Without thinking, a cigarette could be in your hand, even in your mouth. What kind of strategy will help you in that situation? You can teach yourself to lean back when something is offered to you, providing a moment to collect your thoughts and decide whether or not to accept the item. This is a *delay* tool. You can shove your hands in your pockets to prevent yourself from automatically grabbing everything that is offered to you. Another *delay* tool. You can reach, instead, for a pack of mints and offer one to the other person and take one for yourself. This is a *substitution* tool. You can take a deep breath and simply say, "No, thanks. I don't smoke."

✍ *You and your friends have been cross-country skiing for the day.* You have all returned to the mountain cabin owned by one member of the group.

Everybody settles down in front of a roaring fire, each with a steaming cup of hot buttered rum. Everyone in the group smokes, except you. Everyone lights up a cigarette as they relax and begin reliving the wonderful day of skiing. What about you?...

What will you do?

_____

_____

_____

_____

For years you have protected your ability to smoke. Going away for a long weekend with all nonsmokers would have been difficult for you, maybe even unthinkable. Perhaps even riding in a car filled with nonsmokers would have been impossible. If that has been true for you in the past, why do you think you would find the opposite situation any less difficult? Remember, too, that alcohol destroys the nonsmoker's resolve even more because it lowers inhibitions, thereby relaxing the person's self-control. Visualizing the social consequences of an event or outing can help you prepare for it in advance so that you can enjoy it—and not smoke.

When you are planning a long drive or a long weekend in the close companionship of others, make certain there are nonsmokers in the group. You will find it much easier to handle yourself in the presence of other nonsmokers, and their strength will help you during moments of desire for a cigarette. If you are worried about the possibility of smoking, go on long excursions with nonsmokers only. Use *social support* and *environmental control* to help you. *Substitution, distraction* and *escape* will also be useful. Take nonalcoholic beverages with you. Situations like these involve some careful pre-planning. Don't leave your success up to chance, or fate or blind circumstance. Take time to think about each situation in advance and **plan ahead.**

✍ ***Your weekly bridge group has just left.*** *It's been a pleasant evening. You even won a little money. As you pick up the dishes from the refreshments you served, you notice a pack of cigarettes on the low coffee table in front of the couch. "That's odd," you think to yourself. "I don't allow smoking in my house anymore. I wonder who left them?" As you busy yourself with cleaning up, your thoughts keep wandering back to the cigarettes. You look at the pack on the table. Finally you reach out and pick it up...*

What will you do?

_____

_____

_____

_____

The temptation here is to play a quick but potentially dangerous game of seduction with the cigarettes. First you pick up the pack and turn it around in your hand, just to see how it feels. You examine it carefully. *"This doesn't look so dangerous,"* you tell yourself. Next, you peer into the pack. *"No problem yet,"* you think. So you take one cigarette out and sniff it cautiously. *"It smells pretty good. I wonder how it will feel to just put it in my mouth..."*

Will you light it? How will you feel about yourself if you do? Will that little experiment lead you to become a smoker once again? "Play with fire and you'll get burned," wise people often say. Do you see this example as playing with fire? Hopefully you do because seduction and temptation games might be playable when the conditions are favorable and your energy is high, but when you are alone and in moments of low energy or poor self-esteem, these games can backfire.

What happens to someone who plays with temptation and actually lights the cigarette? Sometimes the person smokes the one cigarette and never picks up another. More often he "borrows" other peoples' cigarettes for awhile, telling himself that he is not a smoker as long as he never buys a pack for himself. Then one day he starts feeling guilty about all of the cigarettes he's borrowed and so he buys a pack for each person he's borrowed from and, finally, one for himself.

How about this alternative? Picture yourself doing something really bizarre with the cigarettes on the coffee table. First, get angry that someone would leave cigarettes in your house, knowing that you have quit smoking. Then get mad at the cigarettes for continuing to try to seduce you. Open the front door, then walk over to that low coffee table. After removing all of the other objects from the table, kick the cigarette pack off the table and onto the floor. Then kick the pack across the room, out the door, down the steps and into the nearest puddle where you can then proceed to trample it. Turn on your heels and march back into the house and slam the door.

This strange approach allows you to build anger against the real foe: the pack of cigarettes. Anger is one emotion that creates energy, the very energy you will need to cope with the overwhelming temptation you are feeling. Kicking the cigarettes off the table and out of the house gives you a way to express your anger, and it gets the temptation out of the house. The next morning you can scoop up the soggy pack with a trowel and dump it into the garbage. If you never put your hands on another pack of cigarettes ever again, you are certainly less likely to smoke ever again. Will a strategy like this work for you?

✍ *You have just concluded a very complicated and very lengthy contract involving seven other people and two other firms. A feeling of exhaustion overtakes you. As the whole group steps out of the building together, one man reaches into his pocket for a pack of cigarettes and holds it out for others to take one. Two men extract cigarettes from the pack. It is offered to you next…*

What will you do?

_____

_____

_____

_____

This is the "offering and receiving" ritual once again, in a different setting. The tricky part here is blocking yourself from automatically grabbing the cigarette before you are aware of what you are doing. A little *delay* is the best first step. Lean back, step back, shove your hands in your pockets. Try a new routine. Whenever you leave a room or building, or when you complete a task or meeting, get into the habit of deep breathing, putting a tooth pick or a tiny sugarfree candy in your mouth or getting a drink of water. You may find that a *substitution* object or action to fill in the end-of-the-meeting relaxation need will block your tendency to think of cigarettes.

✍ *You and your partner have just finished a set of mixed doubles in a local tennis tournament. You played well but not as well as you needed to. Other contestants are moving toward the refreshment area for something to drink. A few are smoking. Soon you are surrounded by smokers. "Oh," you think to yourself, "a cigarette would taste so good right now..."*

What will you do?

_____

_____

_____

_____

How will you keep control of yourself? Will you *substitute* a glass of water, a mint or a stick of gum? Will you take a few deep breaths to *relax* yourself? Will you back away from the group and find some *supportive* nonsmokers to talk with? Will you *escape* by excusing yourself to take a restroom break? Sometimes escape is the very best tool when you are struggling for control. Relocation to a group of nonsmokers will also help to stabilize you.

✍ *Your mother has been taken to the hospital suddenly. A neighbor calls to let you know. You dash out of the office and head quickly for the car, all the worst thoughts racing through your mind. You arrive breathless at the hospital. You are asked to wait outside. Other family members are there. Some are smoking. You are anxious and upset...*

What will you do?

_____

_____

_____

_____

More than a few people have returned to smoking in a situation such as this. When emotions are strong, thinking is clouded. Tension drives people to seek relief in some way. Something quick, easy and available. The common options are food and cigarettes. You will want the comfort of both. There are some other options, though. One is to wait in a nonsmoking area of the hospital, using *environmental control* to help you. If you are a person who does handwork like knitting, or who finds comfort in prayer or holding rosary beads, or who needs overt physical motion like running up and down several flights of stairs, do it. Look for *social support*. Call a nonsmoking friend who can understand your worry about your mother and also your struggle not to smoke. Talk about it to help you recommit yourself to not smoking. Keep something in your mouth. Deep breathe. In situations like these, the urge to smoke, if it comes at all, is not a sign of nicotine need if you have not been smoking for several weeks. It is a sign of anxiety and of need for comfort. How can you calm, soothe, comfort or distract yourself?

✍ *Another Thanksgiving meal. Another long, drawn-out after-dinner family chat at the table. Trapped. You can't leave the table without offending others; you can't sit still without driving yourself crazy. Cigarettes used to give you something to do. You're feeling nervous just thinking about it...*

What will you do this year?

_____

_____

_____

_____

Perhaps you will offer to clear the table this year, giving yourself something constructive to do. Maybe you will bring along a jigsaw puzzle or some kind of interesting game to play immediately after dinner. Perhaps you will bring some kind of handwork project to do, or something to put in your mouth. Maybe you will leave the table to brush and floss your teeth, or to make a telephone call to someone for extra *distraction* and *support*. Whatever appeals to you, plan ahead for it, bring the necessary items along and use them.

Each of these scenarios portrays a set of circumstances that create some level of personal need. These are some of the common situations that lead many people back to smoking. They are situations that can happen to you in some way, at some time in the future. No one likes to feel helpless or hovering on the edge of losing control. People who truly believe they will never smoke again will do something to actively settle themselves in unsettling situations. Many people believe, though, that the only way they were able to get through tough situations like these in the past was with the aid of cigarettes. These same people, under pressure, can give up control too quickly and return to smoking. This is not nicotine dependence. This is *psychological dependence.*

In earlier chapters cigarettes were presented as a coping or self-management tool that helped you handle a particular situation or need. Because of the very general nature of cigarette use, it became a broad spectrum, universal, all-purpose tool for helping you manage your various moods and energy levels. The removal of cigarettes may cause you to feel like a piece of swiss cheese, with lots of holes in your ability to manage yourself successfully. Nonsmokers have to manage their moods and energy levels without cigarettes. You can do it too.

Write Your Own Scenarios

Study the scenarios presented in this chapter and browse through earlier chapters for potential solutions or alternatives to smoking. When you feel ready, **think about the difficult-to-handle scenarios in your own life,** the ones that make you nervous to think about now. These scenarios can be related to particular people, events, obligations, actions or moods. They can be influenced by location, time of day, your stress level or other factors. Use a sheet of paper to jot down some general notes about the ones that first come to mind. Then **select one and picture it in your mind's eye.** Mentally observe yourself in the picture. What are you doing, saying, feeling? What bothers you about the picture as you are envisioning it? Open your eyes and **write the scenario on the lines below.**

_____

_____

_____

_____

No Ifs, Ands, or Butts

Now **plan your strategy for how you want to deal with it as a nonsmoker.** Put the scene back into your imagination. **Envision yourself doing and saying the desirable things.** See yourself going through the motions. What are you feeling? If you are not comfortable with the picture as you envision it, change the action around until you feel comfortable with what you see yourself doing and what you hear yourself saying.

Write the improved version of the original scenario on the lines below, making sure you include the specific actions or solutions in your write-up. Ask yourself if there are any props you need such as sugarless mints, gum, _____, _____, (fill in your own) or your Cue Card to get you through the scenario successfully. Note each of the necessary items as part of the solution.

_____

_____

_____

_____

This is a *rehearsal* technique, using visual imagery to help you see yourself in desired ways. This is a very powerful tool for helping you plan ahead for potentially difficult situations. By rehearsing it mentally you begin preparing yourself at the deeper levels of consciousness for managing yourself in nonsmoking ways.

Think back to when you were first learning to smoke. Did you ever practice smoking in the mirror so you could learn to hold it in just the right way and inhale it in just the right way? Did you picture yourself in a variety of situations, holding or smoking the cigarette and feeling sophisticated or in control, or important or tough? When you did this you were using visual imagery and behavioral rehearsal. These processes helped you prepare to smoke. These same processes can help you prepare to never smoke again.

Grab a pencil. You will be writing a variety of personal scenarios, or specific coping plans, next. The writing is an important part of the overall process for retraining your thinking and action patterns. By writing things down you can visually imprint your solutions in your mind's eye. The written solutions will be very important to you later as you develop your final comprehensive list of nonsmoking self-management tools. You will begin this process with some specific nonsmoking plans: *early morning plan; driving plan; telephone plan;* and *tension-reduction plan.* This gives you a chance to write your own action plans based upon your former smoking habits and your typical daily needs. Let's get started.

Early Morning Plan

What will you do when you first wake up? Will you deep breathe, stretch, brush your teeth immediately? What will you do while you are waiting for the coffee to perk or the water to boil? Will you put the coffee or hot water pot on a timer so you won't have to wait? Instead of sitting at the table with the newspaper, will you sit in a chair instead where you will have to hold the paper with both hands? Think about your future mornings. Picture the scene in your mind's eye. What, specifically, are you doing? Think about it for a few minutes. Write your new nonsmoking morning plan on the lines below.

Your plan:

_____

_____

_____

_____

_____

Driving Plan:

Picture yourself sliding behind the wheel of your car. You turn the ignition switch and start the engine. Then you reach for the tapes and insert one into the tape player. Slowly you back out of the driveway and head up the street. What are you doing with your hands? Are you holding something? Are you talking on a cellular phone? Are you dictating into a microphone? Are you singing along with a music tape? Are you chewing or sucking on something? If so, what? What do you have in your ashtray? Do you allow other people to smoke in your car? If not, what do you say when they start to light up?

Your plan:

_____

_____

_____

_____

_____

Telephone Plan:

There you sit, trapped on the telephone. Restless. Impatient. A little tense. What are you doing with your hands? You open your desk drawer. What play objects come into view? Is there a hand grip for you to squeeze as you talk? Do you have gum, mints or toothpicks available? Are there flowers on your desk? Do you have a cup of tea or glass of water nearby? Are there some interesting pictures to look at or a telephone book to doodle in? Are you sitting back in your chair with your feet propped up? Are you hunched over your desk, pen poised over the paper in front of you?

Your plan:

_____

_____

_____

_____

Tension Reduction Plan:

Angry voices assault your ears. A family disagreement is in progress. Are you frowning? Do you rush in to referee? If so, what are you saying? Do you seek refuge as far away from the other people as possible? How are you feeling? Are you feeling muscle tightness anywhere? Are you breathing rapidly? What are you needing? What are you doing? Are you leaving the house? Are you taking a long shower to help you settle down? Are you putting on headphones to drown out the voices? Are you calling someone to get your mind off the argument? Close your eyes and picture yourself. Rehearse the scene as a nonsmoker.

Your plan:

_____

_____

_____

_____

More Scenarios—Your Plan Ahead Alternatives

Additional space is provided below for your particular special occasion plans, such as those for meetings or particular events, cocktail parties, business dinners, card games and so on. Give each one a title to help you identify it easily. Be creative. Be realistic.

Title: _____

_____

_____

_____

_____

Title: _____

_____

_____

_____

_____

Title: _____

_____

_____

_____

_____

Managing Up And Down Moods Without Smoking

Life seems to be full of ups and downs: good news and bad news, positive moods and negative moods, high energy and low energy.

Some days seem to have more ups than downs; other days are just the opposite. Your energies will vary too. Good news brings more energy, while bad news drains energy. Moods like anger and frustration seem to create energy, while loneliness and depression leave you tired. Smokers counter these ups and downs with cigarettes, using the nicotine for an upper or a downer as needed. Because mood management is such an important issue for almost everyone, let's turn now to the topic of managing your high- and low-energy moods without smoking.

High-Energy Moods

As suggested earlier, certain moods seem to generate energy: anxiety, irritation, anger, frustration, agitation. These moods escalate quickly and usually dissipate quickly. One high-energy mood spike can follow another in rapid succession, creating a lasting feeling of agitation and a sense of being "wired".

Think of your physical actions in response to these high-energy moods. Are your actions more abrupt, your words more sharp, your mind more scattered? What were your smoking responses like? Did you take short, rapid puffs? Did this increase your agitation? Were your hands fidgety? How did smoking settle you down? Did you need to move about? Did the search for a cigarette give you a much needed activity or outlet for release of energy? Did leaving the house to go to the store for a cigarette or to the vending machine at work provide a much needed release of pent-up tension? Did the need to buy cigarettes give you a safe way to physically leave an uncomfortable situation? What other actions, patterns or thoughts come to mind?

Think about the nervous agitation that accompanies the mental preparation for a performance, a contest, chairing a meeting, giving a speech. Many smokers puff rapidly on cigarettes when they are anxious or agitated in this way. The quick, small doses of nicotine act as a central nervous system stimulant which only increases the feeling of being "wired". Thoroughbred race horses, just prior to a race, display a similar nervousness, a similar agitation. Experienced jockeys walk their horses before the race to settle them down. In actuality, people need the same settling influence—they need motion.

Think about what you've been like when you were agitated, anxious or irritated. You aren't smoking anymore, so how will you manage your high-energy moods? What will you do when you are unable to sit still? Will you go to the kitchen for something to eat? Or will you go to the bathroom and brush your teeth with a strong toothpaste? Will you run an errand, run up and down a couple flights of stairs, close your door and do some stretching exercises, do some deep breathing exercises, get a glass of water or brew yourself a cup of tea and add a cinnamon stick to play with?

To repeat a few more suggestions made earlier, **keep things at your desk to play with:** pens and a telephone book for doodling, vise grips or a rubber ball to squeeze, coins or trinkets to manipulate. At home, keep simple mending or other mindless handwork items near the telephone, or even little table-top jigsaw puzzles that have fifty pieces or less. While this may sound silly and superficial at first, recognize that playing with cigarettes and lighters is just as superficial in the sense of having something to do with your hands, something to do to let you sit still.

Do something to directly slow yourself down. Guide yourself through some slow, measured deep breathing. The slow breaths will relax you. Talk aloud to yourself in calming terms. Lower, or deepen, your voice. This slows your rate of speech and this has a settling effect. People who are tense speak in a higher voice which allows more rapid speech. Rapid speech will further stimulate you and increase the tension. Lower your voice and s-l-o-w d-o-w-n.

Imagine yourself, now, in a tension-filled situation. Picture the details. As you bring the images into your mind, notice your own breathing rate, your body posture, your muscle tightness. **Imagine yourself doing something to dispel your tension,** to calm and

---

soothe your agitation. Close your eyes and observe the images carefully. What are you doing? What are you saying? Mentally talk to yourself in a calming voice, the same type of voice you use to calm and reassure an anxious child. Notice your breathing. Has it slowed a bit? If not, take a few slow, deep breaths. Sigh once or twice. Yawn. Stretch.

Continue to envision yourself bringing your tension down. When you are satisfied with what you see yourself doing to reduce your anxiety and tension, fix the image firmly in your mind. Then open your eyes and write down everything you did in that image on the lines below. **Write the information down before you forget it!**

Your High-Energy Mood Plan:

_____

_____

_____

_____

_____

You may be thinking that all of this sounds too involved, too unnecessary. Just remember… when you first quit smoking and you encounter stress and tension, these emotions will block your normal ability to think clearly. You will experience a type of momentary amnesia. You will still be thinking too much about smoking. That will further raise your anxiety and stress. **Smoking cravings will intensify unless you have prepared a solid list of specific things you can do to manage your tension, and then do something on that list.** Taking action will reduce feelings of helplessness and panic. Perhaps you won't feel helpless or panicked, but why wait to find that out? The best defense is a good offense. Plan ahead!

Low-Energy Moods

Shift gears a bit, now, and look at low-energy moods. They are not so abrupt or volatile as the high-energy moods. Low-energy moods tend to hang around longer. Low-energy moods include: depression, emptiness, loneliness, sadness, malaise. Fatigue is frequently a component of these moods. At these times, the energy required for anything but the most necessary tasks is less available. This, in turn, makes the accomplishment of other things more difficult.

What were your smoking patterns like during your low-energy moods? Did you sit back more, inhale more slowly and deeply? Did this further relax and slow you down? Did you escape from thinking by smoking? Did you avoid doing things you didn't want to do by smoking? Did you stare at the smoke? Do you caress the cigarette? Did you drag more deeply on the cigarette as you smoked? Were you able to escape interaction with others by smoking? During the day, were you able to rest for brief periods of time? Was smoking a necessary factor in giving yourself permission to rest or to take a break?

Many smokers in a low-energy state sit back, smoke their cigarettes slowly, taking long, deep drags. As you learned in earlier chapters, large doses of nicotine act initially as a stimulant but that is followed quickly by relaxation. Thus, the style of smoking just described serves to further relax or depress the central nervous system, thus compounding the low-energy cycle. The physical sensation of deep drags on the cigarette is soothing, though, and provides a feeling of physical comfort.

Think about what you can do to soothe or comfort yourself. Some people use gardening as a way to unwind; others use a walk, gentle to moderate exercise, playing with a pet or fiddling with a musical instrument. Some people cook, some paint, some do crafts, or woodworking, or car polishing, or house cleaning. Some people soak in hot tubs or bubble baths while others go to a movie (even a matinee). Some people talk on the telephone to people who make them feel good; others visit with friends or neighbors. Some people play with table or computer games, finding solace and comfort in solitaire, crossword puzzles, or computer chess or backgammon. Some people read, listen to records or tapes, or watch TV. Any of the last three tasks, if normally accompanied by smoking, should be done in a place where you never allowed yourself to smoke. If smoking has always been off-limits in your bedroom, read and watch TV on your bed. If you smoked everywhere but the bathtub, take your book to the tub to read.

Often, at times of emotional upset, the underlying issue is *fatigue*. Many people have difficulty recognizing fatigue; others notice it but are unwilling to let up on the pressure they exert upon themselves. You used to smoke to avoid doing things, to put off things by smoking in order to get a break. **You will still need the breaks, and a means for being periodically nonproductive.** Unless you are able to acknowledge and accept these needs, and to supply other means for being periodically nonproductive, you will be driven back to smoking. The emotional needs will be stronger than your mental resolve not to smoke.

In some instances, immediate rest or "time out" will not be possible, and rejuvenation of energy will be necessary. Get up and move about; deep breathe; drink some juice. The deep breathing will increase your oxygen level, thereby increasing your alertness. The moving about will increase heart rate and metabolic rate. The juice will bring up your blood sugar level. **Stimulation is what you'll need to get yourself going.**

Take a few minutes now to envision yourself during your low-energy moods. Picture what you are doing; think about what you are needing. Picture yourself doing something specific to manage your mood without smoking. When that picture is firmly in place, write down the specific actions you took to manage yourself on the following lines.

No Ifs, Ands, or Butts

Your Low-Energy Mood Plan:

_____

_____

_____

_____

Closing Thoughts

For a long time now, cigarettes have served as a coping tool to help you deal with your emotional self more effectively. The cigarettes, and the actions around getting and using the cigarettes gave you ways to express your emotions in a manner that outwardly looked controlled. You were able to endure tension-filled situations more easily because the cigarettes soothed, distracted, comforted or settled you. They gave you a way, perhaps, to mask the expression of your emotions. They certainly appeared to give you a better sense of control over yourself. Whatever the case, cigarettes are no longer a working part of your personal arsenal of coping skills.

If you feel a cigarette craving many months from now, it will not be the nicotine or even the cigarette itself you are craving. What you will be looking for is the *effect* of the smoking: the comfort, consolation, escape, relaxation, stimulation, comfort, companionship that were the result of your smoking. These effects can come from other sources. Find them. Use them. Make them as much and as consistent a part of your life as the cigarettes have been. Remember, **when you experience a cigarette craving it is the result, not the cigarette, you seek.** What is it that bothers you? What is it that you need?

Many of these ideas are not new to you. You've heard them before, and many of them were included earlier in this and other chapters. Many of the same ideas satisfy many different needs.

Before now you used primarily one tool, smoking, to meet most of your needs. If you find a few tools that have several applications, that will help you focus your energies on a few key tools, rather than spread yourself too thin by trying a vast array of them.

The very best way to help yourself is to write down a big list of tools to try and to make certain that whatever objects (cards, pens, books, toothpicks, crossword puzzles, etc.) you will need are readily available and visible. Once again, amnesia in the sense of being unable to remember what else you could do besides smoke, is very common in the early days of not smoking, particularly when you are overly tired or emotionally upset.

Until you experience need you will not be forced to find solutions. Hindsight is one of the best tools you have for analyzing what happened, what you felt, what could have been helpful. If you don't have ready ideas for what tools you can use, keep asking yourself, once the emotional upset has passed, *"What could I have tried?"* Write down your ideas, no matter how farfetched they may seem at the time. Add them to your Resource List. Keep the list handy for reference. Put it in your pocket or purse. Tape it to your closet door, the medicine cabinet mirror or the inside of a kitchen cupboard door. If you can't find the list, it won't be a helpful resource.

Make it as easy on yourself as possible to learn, to experiment and to practice. You don't need a cigarette to get you through emotional upset. You need a different tool. Keep experimenting until you find a few good, workable tools. Use them over and over again until they become habit. As for the cigarette craving, well, you can get yourself through ninety seconds of anything. Right?

Recommended Self-Study Exercises

Complete the scenarios and plans in this chapter.

Review the scenarios, highlighting the specific tools used. List the most frequently used tools on your Resource List (see page 325).

Maintaining Progress

III

The big moment finally arrived for **Jeremy** and his HAM radio kit: time to turn the switch to "ON". Jeremy's parents stood beside him as he turned the knob. Static. Jeremy fiddled with the other control knobs. Static. In a panic, Jeremy looked at his dad. "What's wrong?!" he demanded as tears filled his eyes.

Jeremy and his father, **Bob,** spent the next several hours trouble shooting possible problems. Jeremy was fidgety and impatient, finding the laborious process of retracing his assembly steps too frustrating to handle easily. Finally they put the tools down for the day, agreeing to work on it some more the next night.

Jeremy and his dad continued their investigation in one to two hour periods for three days before they located the problem. Each time something was tried that didn't correct the problem, Jeremy wanted to quit working on it. His dad would gently but firmly insist that they keep trying. "Remember when you fell off the horse last year?" Jeremy's father asked. "Remember how you never wanted to ride that horse ever again?" Jeremy nodded. "If you didn't get back up on that horse right away, do you think you would still love to ride horses as much as you do now?" Jeremy shook his head.

"Son," Jeremy's father said, "things don't always work out right the first, or second or even third time you do them. You have to keep on exploring, experimenting, refining your way of doing things until you do *get it right. Even then, sometimes something goes wrong. If you quit doing the thing right then and there you would never overcome the problem.*

"Besides, Jeremy," his father continued, "how do you think the great inventors handled their mistakes and set-backs? If Thomas Edison had given up after his first two or three attempts to create a light bulb, we might still be using candles."

"Oh, Dad!" Jeremy said in exasperation. "This isn't the same thing as doing a research experiment."

"Yes, Jeremy, it is," his father replied. "You are doing product research to understand why your product, your radio, isn't working. Then, after you find that out and get it working, you can discover new ways to use it, new ways to make it work best for you. You'll also learn ways to prevent the same problems from happening again. That's what the big companies do when they release a new product. They keep field testing and refining it. When things go wrong with the product they do more than fix it. They log the weaknesses and the solutions. Those repairs oftentimes lead to product revisions or enhancements—even to a new product."

The chapters in Section III will help you refine and strengthen your own product: your stop smoking action plan. You will undoubtedly encounter some snags and hurdles along the way. Don't let them get you down, or keep you down! Do your own product research to figure out how to work around the obstacles, ways to remove them altogether. The following chapters on Relapse Prevention and Recovery, Weight Control, Exercise, and Freedom From Smoking will assist you in reaching and maintaining your goal. Take time to study them carefully. Field test and refine them to suit your needs and strengthen your nonsmoking habits.

The final episode of Jeremy and his HAM radio is on page 301, in Section IV. Be sure to read it because it has an important message for you.

No Ifs, Ands, or Butts

Relapse Prevention And Recovery

9

The man who makes no mistakes does not usually make anything.

...Edward Phelps

Everyone likes to assume that once a job is completed or a change is made, the work is over. No problems. No effort. No relapse. Smokers who have quit smoking frequently feel that their work is finished after about three months of complete abstinence from cigarettes. If this is true, why do so many people return to smoking seven or more months later, or several years later? Certainly the problem is not nicotine addiction—that usually goes away within seven to ten days of complete abstinence from smoking.

Perhaps the answer lies more directly in peoples' response to emotional need, stress or pressure, to circumstance, or their need to play a variety of temptation games with cigarettes just to see how tough they really are. Sometimes the experimentation with just one cigarette is deliberate; sometimes it is accidental. Whatever the reason, the fear that one cigarette causes a complete reversion to smoking is something that all new nonsmokers must face directly.

Returning to an earlier notion that **all new learning, all new behavior patterns involve some mistakes,** some error in judgment

---

or technique, there is good reason to believe that similar mistakes or errors could happen to new nonsmokers. When mistakes do happen, fear and panic often result, maybe shame, anger or frustration as well. These feelings block the person's normal ability to think rationally, to create a solution to the problem of how to get away from smoking once again. Unfortunately, for many people the "one cigarette" becomes the first in a series of cigarettes which eventually leads the former smoker right back to his or her old smoking habits. The important message to keep in mind for yourself is: *this doesn't have to happen to you.*

One mistaken cigarette does not turn a former smoker into a return smoker if the former smoker has anticipated that mistakes can occur and has prepared, in advance, a carefully written plan for how to reestablish control immediately. **The issue is not failure; the issue is recovery from mistakes.** This is the focus of this chapter. Discussions about mistakes as learning tools, the setups to slip up, flexible control plans, stress and recovery plans will all serve to help you design your own best defense, an effective plan for relapse prevention and recovery. To help you prepare your thinking for the information in this chapter, take time to read the skater's story.

The Skater's Story

Martha and her children hurried to find seats along the side of the crowded ice skating arena. A famous figure skater was giving a skating clinic for the children who took lessons there. Only one minute remained until show time...

The overhead lights dimmed. Daylight filtered through the windows high above the ice. Voices were hushed. Everyone waited expectantly. The spot lights switched on as the music and the skater moved across the ice. The performance was flawless. The audience was enchanted.

The skater glided along one side of the arena, executed a perfect jump and proceeded up the middle. Not a sound was heard except for the music—and a collective gasp from the audience as she fell forward on the ice! The children's eyes were enormous. Their mouths were agape. Still, no sound. The skater picked herself up, listened for a moment to the music and then proceeded to finish her routine. The noise level increased rapidly as everyone compared notes about what they thought had happened. When the routine was finished, the skater moved to where the students were gathered. First she discussed what she had done to cause her fall. Then she reviewed some techniques for the students to use to avoid similar problems on the ice. What she told the audience next made a deep and lasting impression on everyone.

"It is very important," the skater told the children, "to push yourself beyond your limits when you practice skating. You will probably fall down many times when you practice. If I don't fall down at least once during every practice session, I don't feel I've worked hard enough. If I only do what feels safe so I won't fall, I won't ever learn to do something new."

The skater paused for a moment to let her words sink into the children's minds. She took a deep breath, then continued. "To become a skater, you have to take risks. What you risk is falling down and maybe even getting hurt. That's just the way it is with skating. If I stopped pushing myself after I learned how to do a single turn, just to keep from falling, I would never have learned to do a double. And I would never have learned to do jumps and spins.

"I want you to think very hard right now," the skater told the children. "I want you to pretend that you are competing in the biggest skating event of all, the Olympics. There you are, the spotlights following you all around the ice as you skate. You are doing well and trying hard to keep your mind on your skating. Then the most awful thing happens—you fall! All of the judges are watching you. All of the television cameras are bringing your picture into millions of homes all over the world. You want to crawl through a hole in the ice to hide, but you can't. You have to get up and continue skating—and keep smiling. You stumble and lose your balance for a moment but again, you must keep skating. You want to cry but you can't do that until you get off the ice at the end of your performance."

Everyone was silent. She continued. "The only way you learn how to keep skating with shaky legs, or when you're crying so hard you can't see the ice very well is to keep falling down when you practice. You have to learn how to get up from a fall, listen to the music so you can figure out *what to do, and then start skating again. The more you fall down, the more skilled you'll be at getting up. It's better to practice falling down and getting up in your training sessions than to wait until you're being judged in a competitive event."*

Martha thought long and hard about the skater's message as she drove home. She told her husband about it later that night. "It seems to me," he said, "that the most important message is about recovery from mistakes and regaining control. It reminds me of a phrase I've heard before in reference to sports: it's not losing the game that counts; it's how the game is played. Here, it's not falling down that counts as much as how you get up and keep going."

"Do you think that same message applies to everything we do?" Martha asked.

"I certainly do, and especially to you right now while you're trying so hard to conquer your nicotine problem. I'm proud of what you've done so far," he said as he got up from his chair and tweaked her nose in passing. "Just remember that without a few slip-ups there is no recovery training. And without recovery training there is less confidence and maybe even less skill at actually maintaining what you've achieved. Think about it."

How Mistakes Help You Learn

There is a powerful message in the skater's story. **Mistakes are a necessary part of learning. If you only do what feels safe you will never reach beyond what you already know how to do. If you never make mistakes you will never learn how to recover from them.** Learning to handle mistakes gracefully comes from repeated practice and that same practice is what builds your own courage, self-respect and pride.

Isn't it interesting how very basic a concept this is, and how well accepted it is when you are learning a new task or procedure? However, most people have a much harder time accepting the notion of mistakes when it comes to personal change. They seem to feel there should be no learning process, no training period. Many people believe that they should simply be able to make whatever changes they want to old, established habit patterns and never experience an error or a problem. This type of thinking reinforces a common practice of giving up after "messing up", rather than reestablishing control all over again.

The intent of this chapter is not to provide you with permission to go ahead and smoke. Neither is the intent of this chapter to suggest that you purposely set about to challenge your control needlessly in order to provide yourself with the opportunity to practice starting control all over again. **The purpose is to teach you how to recover control should you ever lose it, to help you avoid the real pitfall of one unplanned cigarette being the first step to becoming a smoker again.** The objectives of this chapter are to help you recognize the factors that can set you up for possible relapse, and to teach you methods for recovering control quickly and easily if you slip up.

Set Ups To Slip Up

Occasionally everyone trips, stumbles, or falls. Sometimes you can anticipate the circumstances that will put you off balance; other times you will just be caught off guard. In an effort to think ahead and avoid some future problems, there are a few common conditions to be aware of that can cause trouble in keeping yourself securely free from smoking:

Common Set Ups To Slip Up	
• Negative emotions	• "I don't care" attitude
• Stress or anger	• Social pressure
• Moods or mood changes	• Alcohol
• Interpersonal conflict	• Special occasions
• Temptation games	• "I deserve it" attitude
• Lifestyle imbalances	

Let's look at each of these troublemakers in more detail to help you protect yourself against them.

Negative Emotions

Negative emotions play a major role in setting the stage for potential relapse. Envision a gloomy, rainy day, the fifth such day in a row. You don't want to go anywhere, yet you're restless and bored. Your plans for the evening have been cancelled. The mail arrives and with it, a large charge account bill which you had been dreading. And there is a second notice from your dentist for the root canal you had two months ago. You don't even have the permanent cap on your tooth yet! Morosely, you head for the TV. Nothing of interest there. Next you try a book. No use. Back and forth you pace. Bored. Lonely. Worried about money. Anxiety builds. Restlessness increases. "I've got to get out of here!" you exclaim. You grab your keys and leave the house. Into the car. Nowhere in particular to go. Nothing in particular to do. More boredom. More loneliness. You drive aimlessly... This is not a happy picture. It is a dangerous one for the potential smoker. To avoid possible relapse in situations like this one, **keep a long list of alternative things to do, places to go, people to call.** Keep that list taped to the inside of a cupboard door where you can find it when needed.

Stress or Anger

High levels of stress or anger can interfere with your ability to carry out any task. Losing or changing jobs, moving, death, divorce, illness, confronting major tasks at work or school, rifts in important relationships all challenge the ability to abstain from smoking. Lighting up a cigarette will just add to the stress you already feel. **Use an alternative object or activity.**

Moods Or Mood Changes

The moods or mood changes that were once smoking triggers will still occur, at high intensity, and at unexpected times. Be careful to **give as much effort to having your cigarette alternatives with you** at all times and stashed in reserve in key places (near phones, at your desk, etc.) **as you used to expend in keeping cigarettes available and in easy reach.**

Interpersonal Conflict

Interpersonal conflict is highly uncomfortable for most people. Disagreements and emotionally charged confrontations raise many possible opportunities for relapse. The intensity of the discomfort triggers occasionally wild and erratic responses. People grab for what's easiest and what's most familiar. They don't think carefully. Easy availability of cigarettes can create an unplanned smoking binge. Don't let that happen to you. **Keep cigarettes far, far away. Keep alternatives very, very close.**

Temptation Games

Temptation games get many people into trouble. One game called "Russian Roulette" places the former smoker alongside a pack of cigarettes. The object is to stay within reach of the cigarettes until either the cigarette pack wins or the person moves out of the way. Another game, similar to the first, is called, "I Can Have Just One." This game is based on the idea that smoking one cigarette won't cause the former smoker to want, or to smoke, another cigarette. Both of these games are dangerous to one's own sense of integrity. The stakes are high. The outcome can be quite unpredictable when factors like fatigue, irritability, stress, sadness or longing are involved. **Better not to play these games at all, than to lose in the middle of your nonsmoking winning streak.**

Lifestyle Imbalances

Lifestyle imbalances play a strong role in occasional slip-ups. Too much work, too little sleep, too little exercise, too much food, too much stress all lead to too little control. You are very vulnerable then. Take time out. Take a nap. Take a "mental health" day away from work or projects. Go for a walk. Do something fun. **Lighting a cigarette will put you even more out of balance.**

"I Don't Care" Attitude

An "I don't care" attitude often arises when difficult situations in life frequently occur and recur. This leads to irritation, impatience, and frustration. That's when it becomes very easy to pick up a cigarette, just like you did in the old days, before you quit smoking. Beware of these times for they seem to sneak up and catch the unwary by surprise. Don't get caught off guard!

Social Pressure

Social pressure is a major influence upon many people's behavior. Your former smoking buddies may not include you in their exclusive gatherings, the ones you used to attend in your smoking days. They may not call to invite you to lunch or dinner. They may make sarcastic comments about your "reformation". They may hint that you'll never last as a nonsmoker. Your smoking buddies have something important to consider when you truly quit smoking: if you do it successfully, why can't they? Their pressure on you is aimed more at their comfort in continuing to smoke than at your discomfort for not smoking. Fortunately, there are many more nonsmokers than ever before. Even if it means trading friends for a while or for always, **seek the companionship of people who choose to live in ways that are compatible with you and your ways.**

Alcohol

Alcohol, even a little, relaxes and thus reduces overall control. Resistance to cigarettes is reduced also. Drinking and smoking are paired associations for many people. If drinking is a powerful smoking stimulus for you, **stay away from alcohol until you feel strong enough with your nonsmoking habits to be able to drink without smoking.** If you do resume drinking, drink less and change what you drink to something new or otherwise not associated with smoking. When you are in a drinking environment, take a nonsmoking friend with you to remind yourself that you, too, are a nonsmoker and intend to remain that way. The other person's presence will help to remind you of that intention.

Special Occasions

Special occasions can be a strong trigger, especially the first time you encounter them after quitting smoking. Holidays, family celebrations, visits from old friends are a few of the types of situations that occur less frequently, but used to be smoking occasions. Watch your reactions closely. **Plan coping strategies ahead of time.**

"I Deserve It" Attitude

The "I deserve it" attitude typically arises after you have been very good for a long period of time, or when you have worked extra hard and deserve a reward for all your effort. This is a true "wolf in sheep's clothing". It is a sabotage technique. Don't be fooled. You do deserve something special, something to celebrate with. A cigarette is not a celebration. **Find new outlets for joy and reward.**

What should you do about all of this? Subscribe to the motto, "the best defense is a good offense". **Plan ahead.** Determine your coping strategies, write them down, carry them with you and rehearse them in your head repeatedly. Be prepared!

Control Tactics

The results of your recent training gives you excitement and the resolve to stay away from cigarettes. This supplies the energy and momentum for you to keep working with your nonsmoking action plan. As with any moving object, though, momentum is affected by an opposing force called "drag". In the human experience, drag results from stress, fatigue, increased work load, social pressure, illness, and specific obstacles in the path of prolonged success. The intensity and speed of your nonsmoking progress is affected by how much drag you encounter, and the personal energy you have in reserve to overcome it.

Let's look at the process involved in driving a manual shift automobile as an example. As acceleration increases, you are forced to shift upward in gear until you have the correct gear for the speed and load on the engine. In this way, you are using momentum and the appropriate gear to overcome the drag caused by inertia, the upward incline of the road, the number of passengers in the car, the weight of the trailer you are pulling, and so on. At other times, your automobile coasts along easily. Once the cruising speed is obtained and if the roadway is flat, little extra drag is exerted on the engine. At still other times, you will down shift the gears to slow momentum, as you typically do when going downhill or approaching a sharp turn.

You have learned to respond to the sound and feel of your car's engine by shifting the gear up or down as needed. Shifting up in gears is relatively straightforward, with shift points occurring at anticipated intervals. Down shifting the gears takes more thought since you cannot always anticipate the precise speed at which you will navigate a turn, for example, or the specific gear you will need to pull a trailer uphill.

In the same way that you shift automobile gears according to momentum and drag, you will have to up shift and down shift the intensity of your nonsmoking efforts to match the amount of personal momentum and drag you encounter. The complexity and intensity of your daily activities, your personal needs and your energy levels will vary considerably. They may vary daily, hourly, even minute by minute in some circumstances. Like your automobile engine, you will not always be able to pull the same load, at the same speed. **This means that you cannot do all things the same way at all times.**

In recognition of your varying energies, available time and personal needs, the intensity of the effort made to manage yourself without cigarettes will have to vary also. You once turned to cigarettes to manage yourself through such situations and now you will be handling yourself without them. Learning to up shift and down shift to engage the appropriate tools and techniques to use for not smoking is a critical part of your overall success as a nonsmoker. The control tactics suggested in the remainder of this chapter address the concept of up and down shifting, and will instruct you how to let up at times without letting go. The same tactics will also enable you to recover control should you ever slip up momentarily.

As with driving an automobile, you first learn to drive under normal, unstressed conditions. You learn to handle the automobile without obstacles. You develop a set of typical driving procedures. With your nonsmoking action plan, you are learning to use a set of typical nonsmoking tools. As you proceed into increasingly more difficult circumstances, you will need to adapt these tools to fit within your daily energy levels and personal needs.

Until now you have been exploring and experimenting with your nonsmoking self-management tools. You have been using them and applying them to solve specific needs or problems. What is needed now is a **comprehensive action plan for long-range control.** This action plan needs to incorporate the best of your tools—the ones you have decided are workable and likeable, the ones you are willing to use for a long time. This action plan has to be *flexible* enough to bend with your daily stresses, and *clear* enough to help you reestablish control or balance whenever necessary. Your long-range control plan has three functions: a daily guide and reminder; a stress plan; and a control recovery plan.

Developing Your Long-Range Control Plan

In order to prepare your long-range control plan you will need all of your Cue Cards and your Resource List (starting on page 329). Spread them out in front of you and follow this procedure.

1. **Review the tools on your Cue Cards, removing any that you have not used, do not like or do not find effective.**

2. **Copy all of the usable tools from your Cue Cards onto the Resource List.**

3. **Review the Resource List looking for any tools you have listed more than once and combine them. Eliminate all tools from the list that are not achievable or liveable within your current lifestyle.**

4. **Assign numbers to all of the remaining tools on your Resource List,** using "1" for the very easiest tool for you to use, "2" for the second easiest tool on the list, "3" for the third easiest tool, and so on until every tool has an assigned number. Do this in pencil so that changes can be made easily if necessary.

5. **Discard all of your old Cue Cards** to avoid confusion. Your Resource List will contain all of the tools you want to use.

You will probably have more than seven tools on your Resource List. You may have many tools. To work with all of them at one time will leave you feeling overwhelmed and possibly even confused. It is far better to focus your attention on a few tools, using them frequently so that they will become habit. As your familiarity with the few tools increases, you will be able to turn your attention to additional tools, focusing on them until they too become habit.

As with any learning project, the tools you use first must be the simplest and most achievable ones. That is why you assigned numbers to the tools on your Resource List. You will be using a maximum of seven tools at one time from your Resource List, beginning with the "1" tool. The first seven tools can be copied onto a 3x5 index card, called a "Control Card" to distinguish it from your old Cue Cards. Like the Cue Cards with which you are familiar, Control Cards provide a quick and easy method for keeping yourself focused on the few tools you have selected for use at one time.

You will develop a series of Control Cards, each using a maximum of seven tools from your Resource List. **Taken altogether, these new Control Cards represent your graduated, sequential, long-range action plan for self-management without smoking.** Use the following procedure for preparing and revising your Control Cards.

6. **Prepare Control Card #1 using tools "1" through "7" from your Resource List.** Write Control Card #1 across the top of a 3x5 index card. Then write the number "1" tool on the bottom line of your Control Card, the number "2" tool on the line above, and so on, ending with the number "7" tool on the top line. In concept, this arrangement looks like rungs of a ladder, with the "1" tool being the lowest rung of the ladder, the "2" being the next highest rung and so on. Look at the following example.

Control Card #1	
7.	Take time for myself (book, movie, bath).
6.	Stay away from smoking people, situations.
5.	Exercise or walk to bring down stress.
4.	Talk with a support person daily (or hourly).
3.	Deep breathe through each craving.
2.	Leave the room if feeling panicky.
1.	Have nonsmoking aids (gum, mints, toothpicks, pens) in easy reach at desk, alongside the telephone.

7. **Concentrate only on the tools written on your Control Card.** The tools that aren't on this first Control Card remain on your Resource List for future reference.

8. **Look at your Control Card each day, using as many of the tools as you can.** Begin with the "1" tool at the bottom of the Card and work upward sequentially, using the "2" tool next, and so on. On some days you will use all or most of the tools on your Control Card. On other days you may have the interest or energy for only the "1" and "2" tools. Do what you can. Do not expect yourself to use every tool every day! This procedure is explained in detail in the section, Daily Guide and Reminder, on page 207.

9. **Update your Control Cards as needed.** Because the tools are numbered according to what is easiest, you will probably use the "1", "2" and possibly the "3" tools most often. In time these tools will feel familiar and "established." Then it will be time to prepare a second Control Card, moving the former "3" tool to the bottom line where it becomes the "1" tool on Control Card #2. Save Control Card #1 for use as a Control Recovery Card #1, explained later on page 209. To avoid losing the Control Card, tape it to the inside of your medicine cabinet door where you will be able to retrieve it quickly and easily.

You will prepare a succession of Control Cards, each numbered in sequential order (Control Card #1, #2, #3, etc.), until you have finally placed all of the tools on your Resource List onto a Control Card. By eliminating and adding two or three tools at a time on each new Control Card, you will eventually be able to work with each of the many tools on your Resource List. See the following example.

Control Card #2	
7.	No alcohol at night or at home.
6.	Start a hobby and do it while watching TV.
5.	Take time for myself (book, movie, bath).
4.	Stay away from smoking people, situations.
3.	Exercise or walk to bring down stress.
2.	Talk with a support person daily (or hourly).
1.	Deep breathe through each craving.

Control Card #3, continues this progression. As you become proficient with tools "1" and "2", prepare a new Control Card and add new tools from your Resource List.

Control Card #3	
7.	Begin daily exercise for 20 - 30 minutes.
6.	Learn meditation.
5.	No alcohol at night or at home.
4.	Start a hobby and do it while watching TV.
3.	Take time for myself (book, movie, bath).
2.	Stay away from smoking people, situations.
1.	Exercise or walk to bring down stress.

If this procedure seems complicated to you, take some time to go over each step carefully. In brief the procedure looks like this:

- **Cue Cards** as daily guides and reminders for exploration and practice of nonsmoking self-management tools.

- **Resource List** for consolidation and numbering of all desirable tools; and for continuing reference.

- **Control Cards,** developed in sequence, serve as daily guides and reminders of the specific tools you will use for your long-range, comprehensive nonsmoking action plan.

The **Cue Cards** represent a quick, portable, easy-to-use guide to help you remember which tools to use. They are a beginning step for exploring and experimenting with specific tools. You will evaluate the tools on these cards, eliminating or changing them as needed.

The **Resource List** represents an intermediate step, a method for consolidating and giving order to all of the tools on your various Cue Cards. The Resource List is also an on-going repository of new ideas or tools that come to mind as you solve specific problems or attempt to meet specific needs. The Resource List allows you to keep all your tools in one place. In this way, you won't lose track of your new ideas.

The **Control Cards** used for your comprehensive long-range action plan represent a systematic method for guiding you slowly through the daily practice necessary to build your tools into habit. Each Control Card gives you a flexible daily guide, allowing you to focus on a few tools at a time, and to work more or less intensely as your energy and available time permit.

Take time right now to do these steps.

1. Transfer the tools from your original Cue Cards onto your Resource List.

2. Destroy or store your original Cue Cards.

3. Assign numbers to the tools on the Resource List.

4. Prepare Control Card #1.

Using Your Control Cards

Control Cards are used in three ways: daily guide and reminder, stress plan, and control recovery plan. Let's look at each in more detail.

Daily Guide And Reminder

Under normal circumstances, each Control Card serves as a daily guide to help you remember, organize, plan, and use the control tools you selected. You will move up and down the lines of your Control Card, depending upon the energy and time you have for using the particular tools. This is the up shifting and down shifting concept in action.

The procedure is to begin at the bottom lines of the Control Card and concentrate on the simplest tools first. If your energy is high you may climb upward on the Control Card, adding tools "3", "4", "5"; maybe "6" and "7" on exceptionally high-energy days. On low-energy days you may use only tools "1" and "2". That is certainly acceptable. Don't force yourself to use too many tools on low-energy days. If you do, you can set yourself up for defiance, maybe even rebellion.

One key to effective use of your Control Card is to make certain that all necessary items like gum, mints, playthings for your desk and so on are available and in their expected places. Keep a shopping bag of extra supplies in your car. Then, if you run out of them at home or the office, you can draw from the reserve supply in the car.

You might find that the initial sequence of tools on your Control Card is out of order. For example, if it is easier for you to do the "3" item than it is to do the "2" item, reverse their position, placing each item where it most appropriately belongs.

You will use only one Control Card at a time. When one Control Card is exchanged for a new one, put the old one aside and use only the new one. Control Card #1 is special—be sure not to lose it. Tape it to the inside of your medicine cabinet door where you can find it easily for help in control recovery should you ever need it.

Make several copies of the Control Card you are working with so that you will always have one easily available. Keep one in your purse or wallet, your car, your desk drawer, taped to the bathroom mirror, even taped to the refrigerator. **The more times you see (read) the specific tools you want to use for maintaining yourself as a nonsmoker, the faster you will imprint them in your mind.** The better you imprint them in your mind, the easier it will be to remember them and use them consistently.

Stress Plan

Turn your attention to the vision of climbing a ladder. As with all ladders, you can occasionally lose your balance or footing. This frequently comes from overreaching, not paying attention, being distracted, moving too quickly, trying to climb too many rungs at one time, being too tired. Sudden, quick movements can also cause you to lose your balance, or even to fall.

Stress can cause you to lose your balance. It will be especially difficult to restrain yourself from smoking when your stress level is high. You may feel panicky about not smoking, and insecure about your ability to stay away from cigarettes. **As anxiety increases, clear thinking decreases.** You may begin predicting all the worst possible outcomes. You may become hard on yourself, demanding levels of performance you can't deliver. Negative self-talk may contribute to further loss of self-confidence. At times like this, you will probably be more attuned to your emotions than to rational thought.

What you will need most, at times like these, is to **regain a sense of balance or control.** You will need a simple guide to tell you what to do, a few well-defined but simple tasks that are so basic you will be able to do them without straining. This will help you focus your attention more effectively, and will help you clear some of the helpless or frustrated feelings out of the way. Action of any kind reduces anxiety. Taking a single step or two in the right direction can help you restore that sense of balance.

The Control Card you are currently working with can be used as a guide to help you restore and maintain your sense of balance without cigarettes, under stress. **Use your Control Card to tell you exactly what to do, at whatever level of difficulty you can handle comfortably.** If all you can manage is tool "1", concentrate all of your effort on that single tool. As your stress subsides, you will be able to climb slowly upward, managing each tool in succession until you reach your former level of performance. If your stress level varies substantially, adjust your daily nonsmoking plan to fit accordingly, moving up and down the list of tools on your Control Card as necessary. In this way, your Control Card functions as a *stress plan* to help you organize your thinking and adjust your efforts to reasonable and achievable levels.

Control Recovery Plan

Should you ever lose your balance and actually smoke a cigarette, the first step is to **destroy all cigarettes or remnants of cigarettes.** Remove all possible temptation. This will be difficult for you are likely to feel overwhelmed by failure and desire. There is no need for heroics or martyrdom. Get rid of the cigarettes first! Don't belabor your failure, and don't waste time thinking about it.

Next, grab Control Card #1—the one you taped to the inside of your medicine cabinet door. This becomes your **Control Recovery Card.** Write Control Recovery across the top of the card. Read the beginning step. No matter what it says, do it! Do it now! The objective is to manually force yourself to think in specific, stepwise fashion at a time when emotional reaction overtakes your normal ability to think rationally. This is analogous to mentally shifting yourself through your control gears: first gear, then second, third and so on until you are again at stable speed.

Ignore the lurking feelings of defeat. Ruthlessly put down the cravings. The single most important task for you at that time will be to stabilize yourself once again without cigarettes.

Slowly climb back up the levels of your Control Recovery Card, staying as long as you need to with each tool before climbing up to the next one. There is no hurry. Take it easy. Keep calm. Work with one tool at a time.

Your Control Recovery Card is all you need to get restarted as a nonsmoker. It contains the tools that helped you quit smoking initially. These same tools will help you quit smoking again if necessary. You won't need new tools to recover control—just the same tools you already know and are familiar with.

Avoid playing games with your mind. "Well," you tell yourself, "one or two cigarettes a day won't get me in trouble." Yes, they will. One or two cigarettes insidiously become three or four, then five or six, then a pack.

You may tell yourself, at such times, that you really do miss cigarettes and that you truly do want to smoke again. Don't be fooled into making that kind of decision in the heat of passion. Stabilize yourself without cigarettes first.

Some day, after you have reinstated yourself as a nonsmoker, if you really do want to return to smoking, you can make a carefully considered, conscious decision. In this way, you will not grab for cigarettes out of impulse, or weakness. You will not return to smoking just because you couldn't stay in control. Until that time of decision, if it ever comes, **you need to protect yourself as thoroughly as possible.** You owe yourself that much. You have worked hard to quit. You have gone through withdrawal. You have logged your behavior, thought about your patterns, developed alternative plans for living without cigarettes. Give yourself a chance to become strong as a nonsmoker.

Closing Thoughts

You have begun working with a complex set of changes designed to remove cigarettes from your life. It will be easy for you to assume that you should acquire skill and proficiency quickly. No doubt you will be immediately successful in many respects. But as you look at the sample situations given throughout the previous chapters, it is possible to imagine that you could slip up, that you could make a mistake. Emotionally, that mistake will feel like failure. Many people prefer to run away from failure, to quit doing the new things to avoid failing again.

Mistakes do not imply personal failure. They imply error in judgment, or error in execution, or error in selection. They imply failure of a tool or a technique, not failure of a person. Sometimes mistakes result from overload: too many things to do, too much stress, too little rest, too little time. People who are rigid in their approach to controlling outward behavior do not tend to let up when the going gets tough all around. Instead, they get out their "cat of nine tails" and attempt to flog themselves into continued performance of all tasks on all fronts—perfectly. No let up. No let down.

Look at what happens to your body when you push yourself too hard physically. Muscle cramps, pulled tendons, inflamed joints, chest pain and the like warn you to slow down. When you look at your psychological or emotional self, the warning signs may not be as clearly evident. The tendency is to ignore these warning signs as long as possible. Sleeplessness, mind wandering, excessive random movements, sharp verbal responses, irritability, impatience, reclusiveness and heightened cravings for cigarettes or food are only a few of the obvious signs of overload. **Ignoring the warning signs can lead to error, to discouragement, to disgust, to giving up the very things you want so much to achieve.**

Let up on yourself. Take some time away from projects and other demands to have a little fun. Use movies, books and magazines, spectator sports, activity, good friends, hot baths and the like to relax your mind and body. Use these as your anti-smoking projects in order to give yourself the needed permission to be nonproductive or self-indulgent. You once smoked to get time off, time out, self-pampering. You still have the same needs but now you don't have cigarettes. Nonsmokers have nonsmoking methods of providing relaxation and release for themselves. Find out what they do. You are a nonsmoker now. Their methods will be useful to you, too.

When cigarettes or their memory threaten your security, don't get scared, get mad! Anger generates energy. Use that energy to get the added momentum to push yourself uphill. Get your Control Recovery Card. Then bring out your best street language and aim it at the cigarettes. How dare they threaten your comfort and security! Haven't you already suffered enough discomfort? Get them out of your way! Out of your life! Out of your memory! If you stand firm, the power of the cigarettes will fade. Deep breathe. Distract yourself. Remind yourself, once more, that cigarette cravings pass away in thirty to ninety seconds. You've handled cravings many times before, successfully. You will handle this one too, successfully.

Some time ago, before you smoked your first cigarette, you were a nonsmoker. You saw yourself as a nonsmoker; you acted as a nonsmoker. Your very first cigarette probably didn't change that definition. In other words, one single cigarette did not make you into a smoker. You are a nonsmoker once again. Look at yourself as a nonsmoker; act as a nonsmoker. It took more than one cigarette to turn you into a smoker earlier in your life. It will take more than one cigarette to turn you back into a smoker—if you let that happen. You have the tools to prevent your return to smoking. Use them.

Recommended Self-Study Exercises

Prepare Control Cards (see item 6 on the list on page 203.)

Resource List, beginning on page 325.

Keep you Control Recovery Card handy as described on page 209.

Weight Control 10

Quitting smoking does not have to mean gaining weight.

Many smokers consider weight gain to be their major worry after quitting smoking. Many smokers choose not to quit smoking because of anticipated weight gain. Will you be one of those who gains weight after quitting smoking? You don't have to be. This chapter and the next, "Exercise", will give you a set of usable tools for helping you control your weight effectively. No specific diet plan is given in this chapter. If you prefer to have specific dietary guidelines for reducing calorie intake, consult a dietitian or your physician for assistance. The emphasis of this chapter is on your eating habits.

This chapter focuses on tools for controlling weight by limiting or reducing calorie intake. It is similar in design to Chapter 7, "Self-Management Tools for Nonsmokers." A wide variety of suggestions is given. Some of them will appeal to you; others will not. Some of them will be effective; others will not. As with your nonsmoking tools, the weight control tools you select need to fit your needs, personality and lifestyle. They need to be tools that you are willing to use over a long period of time. If a suggested food doesn't appeal to you, don't eat it. If a suggested eating control tool doesn't appeal to you, don't use it. The objective is to identify a few concrete, usable tools to help you build a long-term, practical, achievable, flexible eating control plan. Sound familiar? Before getting into the specifics of what to do, look first at the factors which influence weight gain.

Physical Factors

Nicotine does inhibit hunger contractions in the stomach for as long as one hour. And nicotine does cause a slight increase in blood sugar level and a deadening of the taste buds. According to UCLA researchers, food remains in the stomach of smokers for a longer period of time than for nonsmokers, which causes some sensation of fullness and some perceived decrease of appetite.

Elimination of nicotine reverses these responses. New nonsmokers may notice more frequent hunger pangs due to lower blood sugar levels. And when the stomach empties more quickly, hunger contractions may be stimulated more frequently. Reawakened taste buds enhance the enjoyment of food and thereby increase the desire to eat.

These are a few of the physical factors that pave the way for possible weight gain as a result of stopping smoking. **Increasing exercise and decreasing food intake can offset these factors.**

Psychological Factors

Like smoking, eating is a well-practiced, over-learned set of behaviors which occur with considerable frequency. Eating, unlike smoking, is acceptable under a wide variety of settings and circumstances. These settings and circumstances become signals to eat, often triggering an eating response whether or not the person is noticeably hungry beforehand. Without cigarettes, particular foods may be frequently used to achieve stimulation, relaxation, pampering, comfort, time out, thinking, socialization and isolation. Because smoking and eating are such common, easy-to-use tools for meeting these needs, it seems natural that more emphasis would be placed on the one tool (eating) in the absence of the other tool (smoking). Thus, **transference occurs easily from dependency upon smoking to greater dependency upon eating.**

For many years cigarettes have provided a way for people to manage their tension and discomfort, which quite possibly resulted in smaller food intake. Cigarettes are an "end of the meal" cue for many people, meaning that a cigarette smoked at the conclusion of the entree signalled an end to further eating. Rather than eating second or third helpings of food or even dessert, smokers often light up a cigarette instead. This practice not only reduces the urge to eat more, it keeps the smoker's hands occupied. In this way fidgety people can resort to something other than food to keep themselves busy.

Moderate to heavy tension levels cause a general restlessness and inability to sit still for many people. Without cigarettes, former smokers may notice stronger tendencies to clench their jaws and grind their teeth. They may also notice they have excessively restless hands. Foods that require grinding or crunching are particularly useful for reducing jaw tension. Foods that require cutting, shelling and peeling offer more hand activity and for people with restless hands, these foods provide a welcome distraction from the old habit of holding a cigarette.

Eating provides a most intimate and sensual type of touch. There is very definite physical pleasure in sucking, chewing and swallowing. It may be hard for you to imagine feeling sensual when eating lettuce and carrot sticks, but think about how you feel when you are eating ice cream, chocolate, cheese or warm bread!

Eating is intertwined in the recreation, relaxation and social activities of most people. You may be all too well aware of this, and perhaps you used cigarettes to combat eating urges in such circumstances. For this reason, it is important to have an array of eating control tools for social situations to enable yourself to withstand food temptations successfully.

There are numerous positive rewards for eating and, as with smoking, these rewards are felt immediately. The negative consequences of eating too much or eating the wrong foods are delayed, and perhaps not even noticeable until the weight gain is substantial. You may discover that your friends or family members, in their efforts to support your not smoking, will become food pushers, offering up meals or tempting goodies to cheer you and reward you for not smoking. You may feel good about this at first, or until your clothes become too tight. You may be more lenient with yourself around food, using it to meet needs formerly associated with smoking.

Weight change needs to be approached gradually, especially during the early weeks without cigarettes. **It is unwise to attempt significant weight loss at the same time you are quitting smoking.** Too much pressure is created from trying to make too many changes all at one time. The result? Sabotage. Rebellion. Return to old habits—all of them!

Decrease Your Calorie Intake

Reducing your daily calorie intake can be accomplished with one or more of these general approaches:

- **Switching to lower calorie foods.**
- **Reducing portion size.**
- **Reducing the frequency of eating.**

Simply stated, switching to lower calorie foods primarily means cutting down on obvious fats like butter, margarine, mayonnaise, and salad dressings, and cutting down on foods with high levels of hidden fat like peanut butter, nuts, hash brown potatoes, cheese, chocolate chip cookies. Reducing portion size is fairly straightforward: the less you eat, the less you gain. Cutting down on eating frequency generally refers to "extra" eating, or snacking. Two approaches to snack control are to find similar but lower calorie foods to substitute for the snacks currently being eaten, or to find other activities to accomplish the same result (i.e., relaxation break, pampering, etc.). A wide variety of tools and methods for meeting these objectives are given throughout this chapter.

Getting Started

The action plan used in this chapter is the same as in previous chapters. Here is a brief review.

1. **Read through all of the suggested tools in each category. Place a check mark (✔) alongside each of the tools that seem most interesting and important to you.**

2. **Prepare a Cue Card for each category you want to work with.** Use a 3x5 index card. Write the name of the category across the top (i.e., Remove Temptation, Dining Out, etc.), and list the tools for each category that you wish to experiment with. List no more than seven tools per card.

Remove Temptation	
6.	Eat only at the kitchen or dining room table.
5.	Send extra "company" food home with the company.
4.	Order food in single-serving portions only.
3.	Store all left-overs in the freezer.
2.	Keep acceptable low-calorie foods available.
1.	Eat tempting foods away from home only.

You may want to list the tools in order of their apparent difficulty, using "1" for the very easiest tool for you to use, "2" for the second easiest tool, "3" for the third easiest tool and so on. Place the "1" tool on the bottom line, the "2" on the next line above, and so on.

Dining Out: Restaurants	
7.	Destroy excess food on plate immediately.
6.	Order smaller portions of high-calorie foods.
5.	All sauces and dressings "on the side".
4.	Order toast, sandwiches, etc. dry.
3.	Alcoholic beverages with the meal only.
2.	Wear fitted clothing.
1.	Eat a 4:00 P.M. snack to control hunger.

3. **Select one of the following categories of tools to work with initially:** Removing Temptation, Mealtime Control, Reducing Fats, Improving Shopping and Food Storage Practices, Dining Out, and Snack Control. Add additional categories of tools one at a time, as you feel ready. There is no hurry!

4. **Evaluate the tools you are using to find those that are effective, that meet your needs and fit into your lifestyle. Determine those you are willing to use for an extended period of time. Eliminate or modify all tools that are not usable, likeable or effective.**

As you did with your nonsmoking tools, read through the eating control tools in each category, think about them, experiment with no more than seven at a time, and practice with the ones you find useful. Don't attempt to bite off more than you can comfortably chew at one time!

Remove Temptation

Many people respond to obvious suggestions to eat. The easy visibility of specific foods, their smell or even the ease with which they can be reached affect what and how often a person eats. The idea is not to keep yourself from eating pleasant foods. If these foods are too easily seen or too easily obtained, you will find yourself eating too much of them too often. If you eat them away from home you are more likely to think first and not just eat them automatically, and you can control how much of them you eat by buying them in smaller quantities. The following tools are designed to help you reduce automatic, high calorie snacking at home with foods that tempt you "because they are there!"

❏ **Remove especially tempting foods from your house, car, and office.** Eat those foods away from home, in single serving portions. This is particularly important for snack foods and other foods often considered to be "forbidden."

❏ **Keep left-overs and other more interesting foods in opaque containers or in brown paper bags.** What you can't see won't tempt you.

❏ **Keep all food in storage containers in the kitchen.** No bowls of candy by the TV or boxes of crackers in the bedroom.

❏ **Make it easier to eat lower calorie foods and much more difficult to get to the higher calorie foods.** Store more appealing high-calorie foods in hard-to-reach places, in the backs of cupboards or in the back of the highest shelves, or place them in hard-to-open containers. Then place lower calorie foods you would rather eat in easy-to-reach, visible places.

❏ **Eat only at the kitchen or dining room table.** No eating in front of TV, in a favorite chair or on your bed. This is especially important for snacks and will help you reduce the amount of snacking. Use a calorie-free beverage while watching TV, reading, playing cards or doing other social activities.

❑ **Stay out of the kitchen unless you are specifically preparing or eating food.**

Mealtime Control

Mealtime eating is an important part of overall balance with respect to energy and nutrients, to relaxation and enjoyment. The objective is to control food intake in ways that are achievable, practical and even potentially enjoyable.

❑ **Eat a small amount of fruit, vegetable, whole-grain bread or breadsticks, juice, soup, rice cakes or other low-calorie crackers in the late afternoon** to raise energy and blood sugar levels, and to prevent uncontrolled eating at dinner.

❑ **Wear clothes with definite waistbands for every meal.** Loosely fitting clothing encourages excessive eating. When you are at home, wear jeans to the table. In this way, all extra food servings will be noticed by the fit of your waistband.

❑ **Eliminate alcoholic beverages prior to the start of the meal** because they stimulate appetite and lower control. Sip one drink during or after the meal if alcohol is desired.

❑ **Eat slowly, taking smaller bites and chewing thoroughly.**

❑ **Eat bulky, filling foods** like baked potatoes, acorn squash, corn on the cob, pasta, and sturdy rolls or bagels. Some of these foods provide substantial chewing. Mouth activity is an important factor for smokers and eaters alike. Also, the bulkiness of these foods satisfies the need for stomach fullness. This often feels comforting or soothing to people when they are agitated or otherwise upset. Be sure to exchange the high-calorie toppings like butter and sour cream for the lower calorie alternatives listed in the next category, Reduce Fats.

- ❏ **Keep serving bowls off of the table whenever possible** to prevent yourself from taking unwanted extra helpings.

- ❏ **At home, use smaller plates, bowls, glasses and even spoons** to reduce the size of the portions, and of the bites. This practice helps in reducing food volume.

- ❏ **If too much food arrives on your plate at home or in a restaurant, pour generous amounts of salt, pepper or hot sauce over foods you want to leave uneaten.** If you do this at the very beginning of the meal it will help you resist eating everything on the plate. This is a useful strategy when you cannot control what, or how much food is served to you.

- ❏ **Remove your plate as soon as you've finished eating** to prevent yourself from reaching for more food. Put a beverage cup in front of you and use that as an "end of the meal" cue.

- ❏ **Get up from the table as soon as possible after you've finished eating.** Ask others to talk with you in the family or living room, or anywhere else not normally associated with eating or smoking. Take a calorie-free beverage with you if desired. Chew on a clove, sugarfree mint, gum or toothpick if you still want something in your mouth.

- ❏ **Brush your teeth immediately following meals or snacks, or even when experiencing an urge to eat (or smoke).** The strong, refreshing taste of the toothpaste provides some stimulation for the tongue and at the same time, counteracts the desire to eat.

- ❏ **Keep yourself away from tempting foods whenever possible.**

Reduce Fats

Fats are the most concentrated source of energy in the human diet. Fats are nine calories per gram, compared to pure protein and pure carbohydrate which are each four calories per gram. Most protein foods contain some amount of fat, and many carbohydrate snacks and convenience foods have added fat. **The overall strategy is reduce or eliminate the fat from every food you eat.** Here's how you can accomplish this:

Purchase food items with the lowest possible fat level.

❑ **Drink 2%, 1% or skim milk instead of whole milk.**

❑ **Eat lower fat cheese instead of regular cheese of the same type.** Use the low-fat varieties of cream cheese and swiss, cheddar and jack cheeses. Use ricotta cheese on bread or toast, and part-skim mozzarella for snacking. Read the package labels carefully to make certain the grams of fat in the new item are truly less than the grams of fat listed for the old item.

❑ **Use graham cracker pie crust instead of regular pie crust.**

❑ **Eat nonfat frozen yogurt instead of ice cream.**

Remove all visible fat from protein foods before and after cooking.

❑ **Remove all visible fat and skin from animal products prior to cooking.**

❑ When using ground beef in soups, casseroles, etc., **brown the meat in a skillet, then rinse thoroughly in a strainer with hot water to remove most of the excess fat.**

❑ When preparing tuna fish, **rinse the tuna thoroughly in hot water first to remove excess oil.**

Substitute low-fat snack items for high-fat snack items.

❑ Eat pretzels or plain, unbuttered popcorn instead of chips.

❑ Use Raisin Squares, Oat Squares, or other sweetened, low-fat snack-style cereals instead of cookies.

❑ Substitute Chocolate Nips (hard candy), orange slices, licorice, or even Tootsie Pops for chocolate or candy bars.

❑ Eat Melba Toast, Ak Mak, Bran-A-Crisp, Lavosh, rice cakes, or bite-size shredded wheat biscuits instead of regular crackers.

❑ Use oven-dried garbanzo beans (chick peas) instead of roasted nuts.

Reduce over-all fat content in dressings and toppings, sauces and condiments.

❑ Add apple butter or natural fruit jam to toast, bagels or muffins instead of butter or margarine.

❑ Use syrup, jelly, apple butter or apple sauce only (no margarine or butter) on pancakes and waffles.

❑ Use cottage cheese, yogurt, mustard, salsa or stewed tomatoes on baked potatoes instead of butter, margarine or sour cream.

❑ Add fruit juice instead of butter or margarine to moisten sweet potatoes, yams or squash.

❑ Use salad dressings sparingly. Have the dressing brought in a separate dish. Dip the fork tines in the dressing, then spear the vegetables.

❑ Add mustard, catsup, barbecue sauce, horseradish, relish or chutney to sandwiches instead of butter, margarine or mayonnaise.

Improve Food Purchase, Preparation, And Storage Practices

Shopping, food preparation, and clean-up offer many opportunities for impulsive eating as well as eating unconsciously. Successful management of food intake during these times can result in many fewer calories eaten each day. **Remember these two main strategies: reduce your contact with food, and where involvement with food is necessary, limit it as often as possible to times when your control is likely to be higher.**

Shopping

❏ **Do not shop when hungry or very tired.**

❏ **Shop from a specific list.**

❏ **Shop quickly.**

❏ **Don't buy your favorite flavors of high-calorie foods.**

❏ **Buy only small packages of hard-to-resist foods.**

Preparation

❏ **Prepare food at times when your control is highest.**

❏ **Prepare lunches and snacks at the same time another meal is being cooked.**

❏ **Use a quarter teaspoon for tasting.**

❏ **If you prepare more than one meal at a time, cook each portion in a separate container and freeze the extra portions immediately.**

❏ **Use smaller containers for mixing, baking and cooking to reduce portion sizes.**

Clean Up and Leftovers

❑ Package and label usable leftovers for a specific meal or snack.

❑ Freeze containers of leftovers for soups or stews.

❑ Make your own TV dinners out of leftovers.

❑ If there is no good use for a leftover food, add it to a compost pile or throw it out.

Dining Out

Restaurant eating and dinner parties typically result in excess calorie intake. Part of the problem stems from the feeling of specialness that accompanies eating away from home. Many people look to meals out as a way to pamper and reward themselves. Other people look upon those meals as freedom from the effort of cooking and clean-up. And some people eat out for convenience. You've paid once, in money, for the service, the ambience, the convenience. Why pay a second time, in frustration or bad feelings, because you ate everything available?

While reading through this section, keep the following motto in mind: **eat the best and skip the rest.** Eating out should not be a battle to make yourself eat plain salad, dry baked potatoes and uninteresting fish if you find these items to be unpleasant. The objective of this section is to teach you tools for controlling the amount and calorie levels of the foods you do like; to teach you *how* to have the foods you like.

Restaurant Dining

❑ Eat a low-calorie 4:00 P.M. snack or eat a small amount of some low-calorie food just prior to leaving your home or

office to go to the restaurant. You will have greater control at the table if you aren't ravenous.

❑ **Wear fitted clothing.** This will boost your resolve to eat less food.

❑ **Drink only nonalcoholic beverages before the meal is served.** If you choose, have your wine or beer with your meal.

❑ **Order foods with high "play" value** like steamed clams, crab or lobster left in the shell, artichokes, cioppino, relish trays or fruit platters; eat Asian foods with chopsticks. The busier you keep your hands during a lengthy meal, the easier it will be to avoid cigarettes and extra food.

❑ **Reduce the portion size of the meals you order in restaurants.** Order appetizer portions of higher calorie entrees, side dishes or half orders; order a la carte; share orders with someone; or even take half of the order home for another meal.

❑ **In a restaurant, when too much food arrives on your plate, immediately remove a portion of it by placing it on a small plate and either offer it to others at the table, or send it back to the kitchen with your server. Or, use salt, sugar, hot sauce or some other substance to destroy the extra food so that you won't be tempted to eat it later in the meal.**

❑ **Order salad dressings and sauces "on the side".** Dip the tines of your fork in the dressing or sauce first and then add the food item. This allows you to get enough taste of the dressing or sauce with each bite without adding excess calories.

❑ **Order your sandwiches dry and request mustard or catsup to use in place of butter, margarine or mayonnaise.**

❑ **Use syrup, jelly, apple butter or apple sauce only (no margarine or butter) on pancakes and waffles.**

❏ Order one serving of a favorite high-fat food (i.e., fries, ribs, bacon, etc.) in a restaurant to be shared with everyone at the table.

❏ When ordering Asian foods, order double the quantity of rice and half the quantity of entree.

❏ If you want something sweet to end the meal, try one of these ideas: order two or three chocolate mints to eat with your coffee or tea; order one dessert to share with another person or with everyone at the table; order a half portion of the dessert for yourself.

❏ Resist the impulse to order too much food initially. Order modestly at the beginning of the meal and if you are still hungry at the meal's end, then order an additional item. People who order too much also tend to eat too much.

Buffets and Cafeterias

❏ Use the techniques listed earlier for **eating something beforehand, wearing fitted clothing** and **drinking nonalcoholic beverages before the meal is served.**

❏ Eat a plate of salad first.

❏ Use a serving spoon for servings; use a teaspoon for tastes. If you want to sample some items that look appealing and you use a serving spoon to put some on your plate, you are likely to get a larger serving. Then, if your tendency is to eat everything on your plate, you will eat a larger serving.

❏ Use a salad plate instead of a dinner plate or cover half of your dinner size plate with green salad. This will help you control the amount of food that gets onto your plate.

❏ After eating, clear away your dishes before having coffee or tea.

Dining in Other People's Homes

❏ Use the techniques listed earlier for **eating something beforehand, wearing fitted clothing, drinking only nonalcoholic beverages before the meal is served.**

❏ **In other people's homes, take servings of only two or three items the first time the serving plates are passed around.** Then take servings of the rest of the items the second time the serving plates are passed. This practice allows you to feel like you've had second servings but in reality, you've only had one helping of each food.

❏ **When coaxed to have more food, say that you'll have more later on.** This disarms the hostess and reduces the immediate pressure to take more food.

Snack Control

Random or continuous snacking is less often a response to hunger than to boredom or restlessness, or the need for temporary distraction, diversion, comfort, reward, pleasure, time off from "projects" and the like. In this respect, snacking serves much the same function as smoking once did. Sometimes there are specific food cravings to deal with, like those for sweets, ice cream, cheese and chips. **Strategies for controlling snacking fall into two categories: alternative foods and alternative activities.** In both instances the objective is to use substitution of different foods and different activities to meet obvious preferences and needs.

Betheny smoked her last cigarette four weeks ago. She had many battles with herself over the temptation to smoke, but she steadfastly refused to give in to her cravings. Betheny always prided herself on her remarkable self-control and her grim determination not to give in to what she called her "soft side". Bob had been her sole source of support and advice. She laughingly told him that the money she saved from buying cigarettes only covered half of her telephone bills.

Betheny dialed Bob's number in a panic. She had just weighed herself and she had gained another pound. "I just can't afford to get fat!" she wailed to Bob during her telephone call.

"What's your biggest problem with food?" he asked.

"Snacking, I think," she answered. "It seems like I'm always in the kitchen, looking for something. I want to eat while I read and while I watch the late news on TV."

"That's understandable," Bob told her. "You smoked a lot at night. You used cigarettes for relaxation, comfort, tension release, and breaks from your usual routine. Eating satisfies many of the same emotional needs. Eating is also good 'occupational therapy', something to keep your hands busy and leave your mind free to wander. In the sense that eating also involves your hands and mouth, exchanging smoking for eating, and eating for smoking appears to be a particularly workable trade-off."

"Do you mean that I've just traded one bad habit for another?" Betheny asked.

"In some ways, yes," Bob replied. "You smoked for many years, and you have firmly established the function of cigarettes in managing your moods and emotions. While nicotine has a definite pharmacological impact on your nervous system and upon your moods as well, various foods also affect your moods. How many times have you turned to sugar or caffeine for stimulation? To gooey or creamy foods for comfort or relaxation? To chewy or crunchy foods for tension release? How many trips have you made to the kitchen for something to do, or wandered about the house in search of food out of anxiety or restlessness rather than hunger? Eaters search for food in much the same way as smokers search for cigarettes. The movement provides tension release; the activity supplies the break from routine."

"I guess that all makes sense," Betheny said thoughtfully. "What can I do about it? I absolutely do not want to gain more weight!"

"There are two main strategies you can use for snack control," Bob told her. "The first is to **exchange lower calorie foods of the same characteristics for the higher calorie foods you are now eating.**"

"It sounds like you're suggesting that I trade the chips in for something less fattening like carrots," Betheny said.

Bob laughed. *"Not exactly. Chips are dry, salty, crunchy. Carrots are wet, bland, crunchy. That's not a good exchange. Pretzels would work better. So would seasoned bite size shredded wheat biscuits, or some seasoned low-calorie crackers."*

"Have you got a good substitute for chocolate?" Betheny asked wickedly.

"Sure," Bob answered. *"Tootsie Pops. They're only 55 calories each and they last for a while. I know the texture's not the same, but I think they'll work pretty well for you."*

"I don't know about the Tootsie Pops," Betheny laughed, *"but I understand what you're trying to tell me. What's the second strategy?"*

"One you've heard about before when you were studying the tools to quit smoking. **Find other leisure and time-filling activities that meet your emotional or psychological needs.** *You need to take time off to relax, Betheny. You used to smoke. Now you eat. You still need to relax. You still need to fill your time with little undemanding things to do. You need to do a better job of finding things to keep you amused at night."*

Alternative Foods

The purpose of using alternative foods is to preserve the enjoyment and sensation of specific foods while, at the same time, lowering the fat and calorie content. Start thinking about your favorite foods. Grab a pencil and look at the Alternative Foods List, page 239.

1. **Write your favorite snack foods on the list,** in the left-hand column.

2. Think about the characteristics of the snack foods you put on the list. **Alongside each food item listed, write the following information in the appropriate column:**

    a. The predominant **taste** of each food. Is the food salty, spicy, bland, sweet, tart, tangy? If these words don't apply, use any words which describe the taste to you.

b. The predominant **texture** of each food: crunchy, chewy, gooey, thick, sticky, juicy, etc..

c. The **temperature** at which each food is eaten: hot, warm, cold, frozen, room temperature.

Look at all of the characteristics for each food. If ice cream is one of the items on your food list, the characteristics are sweet, frozen, creamy. Many people find ice cream to be an especially comforting or soothing food, one they use when upset or in need of a reward. What alternatives come to mind for ice cream? Carrots, celery and apples don't meet the need for sweet, creamy, frozen foods. These are wet crunchy foods and will only be satisfying when wet crunchy foods are craved. Frozen yogurt, frozen fruit bars, creamsicles, sorbet, low-calorie fruit and yogurt bars are a few examples of lower calorie sweet, creamy, frozen foods which make acceptable substitutes for higher calorie ice cream. Each of these foods is comforting and soothing in the same manner as ice cream.

One of Betheny's problem foods is chips, a salty, dry, crunchy, room temperature food. Perhaps that's a problem for you as well. The fattening component of chips is the fat content. If you can find a lower fat, similar type of food to munch, the potential amount of weight gain from eating "salty, dry crunchies" would be reduced. Alternative foods that come quickly to mind include: pretzels, pop corn, salted bread sticks, seasoned Chex cereals (dry), seasoned bite-size shredded wheat biscuits, and thin, wafer-style low-fat crackers like Ak Mak or Lavosh.

Sometimes sweet-spicy, warm, "bready" foods are desired, especially for their comforting value. Foods like cinnamon rolls, sweet breads, bread puddings or apple dumplings are not easily replaced by dry crunchy foods. Baked apples, baked yams moistened with orange juice, or hot cereal served warm with raisins, a bit of sweetened yogurt or spicy apple butter can make desirable alternatives.

Use a calorie guide to help you determine whether or not the alternative foods you are selecting are truly lower in calories than the foods you are replacing.

3. **List your "alternative food" ideas in the last column for each food item on your list.**

4. **Buy them and place them in visible, easy to reach places** in your cupboards, refrigerator or freezer.

5. **Remove the higher calorie foods that are troublesome for you.** This leaves only the alternative foods available for immediate use.

6. **Experiment with the alternative foods you selected.** Keep the ones you like readily available for times when you need an edible alternative to cigarettes.

7. **Tape the Alternative Food List to a visible place in your kitchen** to serve as a daily reminder.

8. **Use the Alternative Food List to develop a shopping list** for purchase of the alternative items.

Substitutes for cheese and chocolate are not easy to find. For this reason it is useful to keep both food types out of the house and eat measured amounts of them away from home only. Sometimes less palatable versions of a food are helpful in reducing the desire for large amounts of them. Low-salt, low-fat cheese; pepper cheeses; extremely rich cheeses that make you feel "sicker sooner" are useful in reducing the amount of cheese eaten at one time. When good quality cheese is important, go to a cheese store and buy a measured amount and then eat it very slowly, savoring each small bite. As for chocolate, many people have success with these suggestions: hard chocolate-flavored candies like Chocolate Nips, very rich chocolate which becomes nauseating if too much is eaten, or very long-lasting forms of chocolate like the hard chocolate "pops" made by many local candy companies. Easy to eat, mildly sweet chocolate candy like M&Ms and chocolate bars are difficult to control because they tantalize, rather than satiate, the palate.

A good rule to live by is to **keep all tempting food out of the house.** Make it easier for yourself to eat lower calorie, acceptable foods and correspondingly more difficult to obtain higher calorie, hard to control foods. Remember, you can't eat what isn't there!

Alternative Activities

Bob and *Betheny* continued their conversation about alternative activities.

"Once you begin to recognize the moods, feelings or emotional needs which set you up to want something to eat," Bob said, *"you will see that certain of them are 'triggers' that create psychological hunger. This type of hunger can be handled successfully in nonedible ways once the dynamics are clearly understood."*

"I know I get keyed up during the day and I need to unwind or spin down my tensions at night," Betheny admitted. *"This makes me restless and fidgety. I just mindlessly prowl around the house."*

"Smokers typically occupy themselves with cigarettes, something you have chosen not to do as a result of quitting smoking," Bob said. *"What you will do instead largely depends upon what you psychologically or emotionally need, what appeals to you, and what tools or materials are readily and easily available to use."*

"I know we talked about things to do at night when I first stopped smoking," Betheny said. *"I just never found anything that interested me. Maybe doing some exercise at night will help."*

"That will help a lot," Bob agreed. *"But you can't exercise all night and all weekend long. You have to come up with more ideas, or you'll just go back to eating."*

"I'll take out the list I made when I quit smoking and look for ideas. I guess I can look for something different to do, something I've never done before. Maybe I can start a collection of some sort, like stamps or coins. I think something more creative would interest me more. My secretary makes beautiful beaded jewelry. Maybe I can learn how to make something like that."

*"Good idea, Betheny. **Try as many ideas as you can without censoring them first.** You won't always know for sure that something will or won't work for you until you try it. Keep an open, curious attitude. **Discover new activities.** Build an extensive list of workable ideas. Put your ideas on a list. Also write the supplies you will need to do them on the same list. Then tape the list to the inside of a kitchen cupboard door, where you will always have it available as a resource."*

"Knowing me," Betheny said, "I should probably tape the list to the refrigerator door. That way I won't be able to avoid reading it."

Like Betheny, **you will need to explore new ideas and new ways of amusing yourself without eating or smoking.** Use the Alternative Activities List on page 240 to keep track of your ideas. If you are having difficulty finding interesting things to do:

- **Ask other people what activities they use for leisure or relaxation.**

- **Browse in craft and hobby shops, looking for ideas.**

- **Visit stores that specialize in games and puzzles.**

- **Explore and experiment with new ideas.**

- **When you find something that works for you, write it on your Alternative Activities List, along with the needed supplies.**

- **Purchase the supplies and store them in easy to reach places.**

- **Keep your Alternative Activities List taped to a visible place so that you can refer to it often.**

The objective is to find a few items that provide distraction or diversion, or items that offer a genuine source of interest and involvement. Either way, an array of items readily available for amusing and entertaining yourself can help to divert you from excessive snacking. As with smoking and eating, you will use whatever is within easy reach. Therefore, keep these nonedible, nonsmokeable items placed where you can most easily see and obtain them.

Your Action Plan

Quitting smoking does not have to mean gaining weight. **Review your patterns and needs** for cigarettes to help you anticipate where you might turn to food as a cigarette substitute. Take time to **study this chapter.** Think about what you have read. **Explore new ideas. Experiment** with the ones you have selected. **Use your Cue Cards and the Alternative Foods and Activities Lists** to help you organize and limit your efforts to whatever level you can manage comfortably. As with your nonsmoking tools, it is far better to concentrate on using a few eating control tools consistently.

The development of a **comprehensive action plan for eating control** follows the same guidelines used to develop your comprehensive action plan for not smoking. You may want to review the detailed instructions given for this procedure in Chapter 9, page 202.

- **Work on one category of tools at a time and no more than seven tools per category.** Use eating Cue Cards for daily guidance.

- **Evaluate, modify, combine and eliminate tools** as you discover what works effectively and comfortably for you.

- **Condense all of the workable eating control tools onto a Resource List,** page 241.

- **Numerically rate all of the tools on the Resource List according to what is easiest for you to do:** "1" for the easiest tool, "2" for the second easiest tool, "3" for the third easiest tool and so on until every tool has a number.

- **Destroy your original eating Cue Cards and prepare a Control Card (page 242) using tools "1" through "7".** Place the "1" tool on the bottom line, the "2" tool on the next line above and so on.

- **Use the Control Card for eating control in the same way you've been using your nonsmoking Control Card, as a daily guide and reminder, and also for control recovery.** Review Chapter 9, page 191 for guidance in the use of Control Cards.

- **Replace your first Control Card for eating control with a new one when tools "1" and "2" become habit.** Prepare the new Control Card with the former "3" tool on the "1" line of your new card. Move all remaining tools to your new card and add the next two tools from your Resource List to the "6" and "7" lines of the new card. Continue in this fashion, preparing new Control Cards until you have used all of the tools on your Resource List.

- **If desired, prepare a separate Control Card for listing your alternative foods and another one for listing your alternative activities.**

- **Prepare individual Control Cards for guidance in handling eating control situations of special or anticipated difficulty:** Thanksgiving, Christmas, dinner parties, vacations, and so on. Take the Control Card with you and refer to it often. For example:

Control Card: Thanksgiving	
7.	Seal left-overs and freeze for later.
6.	Share a piece of pie with someone.
5.	Take one serving of three other favorite foods next.
4.	Take one serving of three of my favorite foods first.
3.	Provide a tray of cut vegetables for snacking.
2.	Wear fitted pants.
1.	Eat a bagel at 4:30 P.M. to reduce appetite.

The Control Cards, Alternative Foods and Activities Lists, and Resource List are designed to help you think constructively at times when your thoughts are more attuned to excessive eating, or even to smoking. Use them regularly to keep yourself "on track."

Closing Thoughts

Controlling your weight effectively will take some concentrated effort. There are some steps you can take to make the process easier to live with.

Keep-high calorie, tempting foods out of your way for a while. The sugarfree gum and mints, cloves, seeds, toothpicks and swizzle sticks you use as options to put in your mouth in place of cigarettes will work equally well to replace food when physical hunger is not the issue.

Keep your activity level up. If you gain a few pounds, don't panic. You would have to gain a great deal of weight to create as much damage to your heart and body as you did when you smoked even one pack of cigarettes per day.

Don't go overboard and put yourself on a severe diet. A small weight gain of four or five pounds can be easily remedied.

Get away from food. Keep yourself busy. Seek the company of people who will help you maintain control. Go to a movie. Take a hot bath. Go for a walk.

Above all, remember that all of the stress you feel from not smoking and not eating will let up with time. Just hang on tightly to your goals and tackle it all, one urge at a time.

Recommended Self-Study Exercises

The Alternative Foods and Activities Lists and the Resource List for use with this chapter are all included at the chapter's end. Use 3x5 index cards for your Control Cards for eating control. The page numbers listed below are for the instructions for use of each item.

Alternative Foods List, page 230.

Alternative Activities List, page 233.

Resource List, page 235.

Control Cards, page 235.

References

Information for this chapter was adapted from the following sources:

1. Ferguson, T. *The Smokers Book of Health.* New York: G.P. Putnam's Sons, 1987.
2. Waltz, J. *Food Habit Management.* Tucson, AZ: Northwest Learning Associates, Inc., 1986.
3. Witters, W. and Jones-Witters, P. *Drugs and Society.* Monterey, CA: Wadsworth Health Sciences, 1983.

Alternative Foods List

Food Item	Taste	Temperature	Texture	Alternative Food

Alternative Activities List	
Activity	**Necessary Supplies**

No Ifs, Ands, or Butts

Resource List

Control Card:

7.	
6.	
5.	
4.	
3.	
2.	
1.	

Control Card:

7.	
6.	
5.	
4.	
3.	
2.	
1.	

No Ifs, Ands, or Butts

Exercise

11

Strong reasons make strong actions.

... William Shakespeare

Cigarettes once satisfied a variety of your personal needs—a topic addressed often in earlier chapters. Among those needs were stress reduction, appetite suppression, increased metabolic rate (which burns more calories), and mood elevation. These are important benefits from smoking. The good news is **you can get these same benefits in a more healthful way through exercise.**

Perhaps you already exercise regularly and are wondering, "Will I have to do more?" Maybe you have never considered yourself to be an "athlete" and the idea of consistent, regular exercise is unappealing. Whatever your personal perspective, don't skip this chapter. Please read it with an open mind, looking for ways to introduce, increase or improve the effectiveness of some type of exercise in your life so that you can recover those nice benefits lost through withdrawal from nicotine.

If you are concerned about potential weight gain as a result of quitting smoking, consider this. When an over-one-pack-per-day smoker quits, there can be a decrease in heart rate of as much as ten to twenty-five beats per minute, and a decrease of ten percent in basal metabolic rate. This decrease means that the body requires fewer calories to maintain itself, so it converts the excess food into fat.

Your objective will be to somehow increase the number of calories burned to compensate for the decrease in metabolic rate. The strategy for increasing calorie burn is to increase overall activity at a level high enough to facilitate weight loss. This ultimately means aerobic activity, intense enough to make you "work", long enough to be effective (thirty to forty minutes), and frequent enough to make a difference (four to six times per week).

Benefits Of Aerobic Exercise

Aerobic exercise has many benefits for former smokers. Let's look at a few of the most obvious ones:

Benefits Of Aerobic Exercise	
• Raises metabolic rate	• Reduces stress
• Decreases percent body fat	• Improves quality of sleep
• Maintains or increases lean body mass	• May help lower risk for osteoporosis
• Increases body's ability to use fat for fuel	• Creates higher levels of energy
• Increases collateral circulation	• Improves feeling of emotional well-being
• May help lower blood pressure	• Increases self-confidence, self-esteem and self-image
• Strengthens heart muscle	

That's considerable benefit from a thirty- to forty-minute expenditure of time and effort! The resistance many people feel to the concept of regular exercise, if they are not exercising regularly already, is based in the challenges of finding the time to do it and managing boredom. Personal preferences for solitary or communal exercise, competitive or noncompetitive activity, indoor or outdoor exercise and the like all play a critically important role in the adoption of an effective, likeable, manageable and consistent exercise routine.

Keep in mind that **exercise is approximately twenty percent "bodywork" and eighty percent "headwork"**. What this means is that the hardest part of exercise, for many people, is getting themselves in the proper frame of mind to do it. The hardest step you'll take in exercising may be the very first step out of the house! Mental headwork—a positive attitude—is the key to getting going. Once in motion, the benefits of the exercise will demonstrate for themselves.

The purpose of this chapter is to raise your awareness of the benefits of exercise, to help you develop positive attitudes about exercising, and to give you some guidelines to get you started. This chapter will not provide you with the complete guidelines for a comprehensive exercise or fitness program. There are many resources in your own community to guide you in developing an appropriate exercise program that meets your needs and physical condition. If you are already exercising regularly, you may prefer to skim through this chapter briefly, looking for some ideas for enhancing what you are already doing. If you have not been exercising regularly, or even at all, this chapter will give you some information to think about and some suggestions for how to get started.

This chapter begins with a section about increasing exercise that is designed for currently inactive people, followed by sections devoted to type, intensity, frequency and duration of exercise, and a concluding section for developing your own exercise plan. As you have done with other chapters in this book:

1. Read through this chapter once for information.

2. Think carefully about what you have read.

3. Draw up an initial plan for exploration and experimentation. Try a few different types of exercise to see what you like best. Experiment with different settings for exercise (i.e., alone or with others, at home or at an exercise facility, etc.). Try different times of day, and different days of the week to find out what suits you best.

4. As you find ideas that appeal to you, place check marks (✔) alongside them in the book or make note of them in the book margins.

5. Prepare a Control Card for exercise as explained later in this chapter on page 258.

Experiment with a variety of activities; explore the resources in your own community and even in your own home. Think of ways to make exercise more fun. A seldom-used exercycle can be more appealing, for example, if you listen to novels on tape while pedalling, or pre-record some TV shows for viewing while exercising. Once you have investigated the available options and have determined what you want to commit yourself to doing, follow the guidelines discussed in the final section of this chapter.

An important word of caution: **before beginning or increasing any type of exercise program, check with your physician first.** This is especially important before beginning rigorous, sustained exercise, such as jogging, aerobic dance, volleyball or tennis. A thorough physical examination which includes a review of your personal and family history for the presence of heart disease, and tests of blood glucose, serum cholesterol (including "good" and "bad" cholesterols) and triglycerides should be scheduled. An exercise stress test is recommended for all adults, especially for those over forty years of age. These tests will help to identify the presence of coronary risk factors which may influence the type and intensity of your exercise. The objective is for you to exercise safely and effectively.

Following your physical examination, consider enlisting the guidance of a professional exercise specialist. He or she will be able to help you increase your exercise safely and will have many ideas for ways to have fun and maintain your motivation to exercise regularly.

Begin By Moving More

Consider what your movement patterns have been for the past several months or years. If you have moved principally from the house to the car to the office to the restaurant to the bedroom, you will need to begin with gradual increase of movement. If you have been more active, but only for brief periods of one or two weeks at a time, you will also need to begin incorporating exercise more gradually.

If you have never exercised on a regular basis, or haven't exercised regularly in a long time, approach the idea of exercising more cautiously. Your first objective is to increase your movement patterns. Here are some suggestions to help you do this.

❑ **Rather than sitting down immediately after a meal, do something more active** like playing with your children, taking the dog for a walk, or working on a hobby or craft project.

❑ **Increase your opportunities to bend down** by dropping things or storing frequently used kitchen or workshop items in the cupboards below the counter. Be careful to do this by bending your knees and keeping your back erect, rather than bending from your waist which puts extra strain on your back.

❑ **Make two trips out of one** when carrying the laundry or groceries by carrying fewer items at a time.

❑ **Use the telephone and the bathroom farthest away** to increase your movement patterns inside your home or work setting.

❏ **Get rid of the remote control channel selector on your television set** so that every time you wish to change the channel, you'll have to get up and do it yourself.

❏ **Find a parking spot as far away from the door as possible** when going to the store, to increase your opportunity to walk.

❏ **Get off the bus three or four blocks before your usual stop** so that you can walk the few extra blocks to your destination.

❏ **Walk to the mail box** rather than drive.

❏ **Use the stairs instead of elevators and escalators.** If you are currently not using the stairs at all, begin by climbing only the first flight of stairs and then use the elevator or escalator for the remaining flights. After a few days, gradually increase the number of flights climbed until you no longer need to use the escalator or elevator.

❏ **Take a walk break instead of a coffee break at work.** Add a fifteen-minute walk at noon and another ten-minute walk later in the afternoon.

❏ **Use household chores as an opportunity for developing flexibility and even a little strength or endurance.** Wash and wax your car yourself instead of using a commercial car wash. Mowing the lawn, raking, digging, sweeping, hauling dirt and clippings all expend calories, and contribute to better physical condition. Housework will pass more quickly if you put on some peppy music and work vigorously. Bend, reach and stretch as much as possible.

The objective behind these suggestions is for you to move your body more often, over increased distance and for longer periods of time. This will help you prepare your mind and your body for more intense exercise later on.

No Ifs, Ands, or Butts

When you feel ready to begin a more formal pattern of regular exercise, **start out slowly.** Begin with a five- or ten-minute walk, for example, and slowly increase the time by adding five minutes each week until you reach an initial level of twenty to thirty minutes. Multiple exercise periods (two or three per day) of short duration (five to fifteen minutes each) are recommended for beginning exercise, before building up to longer time periods.

As your physical capacity improves, you may want to increase your exercise period to thirty to forty minutes. Later on you can increase the time further if you choose to, but in the beginning stages of getting used to exercising, moderate exercise periods will feel more comfortable.

Actually, limiting exercise periods to thirty minutes may be more practical in terms of fitting exercise into a crowded schedule. If you don't resent a half-hour of exercise, you will probably be willing to do it more frequently. If you are fighting with yourself because you've insisted that you do sixty minutes of exercise or more, you are less likely to exercise very often, and frequency is important.

Explore different activities. *Investigate* a variety of exercise facilities or programs. *Experiment. Evaluate. Do what feels good.* Look for companionship or incentive. If you enjoy the activity, you will be more likely to do it. If you don't enjoy the activity, you will probably abandon all exercise before you have had a chance to discover the benefits.

Once you've had your physical exam and improved your physical condition and stamina, you may decide to vary the type of exercise you do or increase the intensity and frequency of your workouts.

What Type Of Exercise Suits You?

A simple and effective remedy to offset a lower metabolic rate is to increase exercise levels, using aerobic exercise (walking, biking, swimming, rowing, stair climbing, jogging, aerobic dance or cross-country skiing). Daily workouts which include thirty or more minutes of sustained aerobic exercise can effectively counteract the body's lower fuel needs as a result of nicotine withdrawal. In a manner of speaking, the effect of sustained aerobic exercise on metabolic rate is analogous to turning up the thermostat in your house—more fuel is burned.

If solitary exercise appeals to you, walking, biking, jogging, rowing, swimming and cross-country skiing may offer the dual benefits of effective exercise and time alone with yourself. On the other hand, if you need the presence of other people for incentive, stimulation or companionship, look for aerobic classes, a personal trainer, walking or running partners, or biking or skiing companions. If you require the thrill or incentive of competition to keep you moving, look for community running and biking events, walkathons, competitive swim events and crew events for rowing. If your only option is to exercise at home, perhaps an aerobic exercise tape will provide some motivation, guidance and companionship. In the winter months consider week-end sports like cross-country or downhill skiing, and ice skating.

Many people prefer competitive sports. Tennis, racquetball, handball, squash, volleyball, basketball, soccer and softball are a few high-energy sports that offer the combined benefits of calorie burn, a good sweat, tension release and a lot of fun. If this appeals to you, look for partners, a league or even an instructional program to get yourself going.

Many activities will give you a good workout; others will offer challenge, involvement and a much needed release of tension. Consider bowling, sailing, canoeing or kayaking, fishing, horseback riding, hiking, and camping. While some of these activities burn more calories than others, they all offer mental relaxation and some physical exertion. They will help you forget about problems, excess food and cigarettes.

This is not an all-inclusive list of exercise and activity options, but it will get your thinking started. Write down ideas of your own. You may prefer to work with only one exercise option as, for example, walking. Or, you may prefer to vary your routine, walking two or three days, for example, and swimming one day; playing tennis one day and walking three days; aerobic dance classes two days and stationary biking three days; volleyball one night, horseback riding one day, and walking or biking two days.

Whether you use predominately one type of activity or mix and match them, the important factor to keep in mind is this: **your exercise plan must be reasonably enjoyable for you to do it, it must fit into your schedule for it to happen consistently, and it must be within your current physical capacity.**

Select one or more exercise options from the chart on the next page by placing a check mark alongside the one(s) that most appeal to you. Space is provided for you to write in exercise options that don't appear on the list.

Explore the options for doing the exercises you marked. Can you find a facility that offers the space and equipment you require that is within reasonable distance from your home or office? Does that facility have professional, qualified staff for consultation and guidance? Is that facility open during times when you will be able to use it? Does that facility have the necessary amenities like showers, hair dryers, secure lockers? Do you feel comfortable with the people who use that facility?

If you are looking for social, competitive sports activities, do you have available partners from among your current friends? If so, are they willing to play at agreed upon times so that you can plan ahead? If not, perhaps enroll in a club that offers access to people who play that sport (i.e., golf, racquet sports), or enroll yourself in a series of private or group lessons to get started, and to meet others who like the same sport. If league sports like volleyball, basketball or softball are your preference, call community recreation centers, community

What Type Of Exercise Suits You?		
Aerobic	**Competitive**	**Recreational**
__ Walking	__ Tennis	__ Bowling
__ Biking	__ Racquetball	__ Golf
__ Running	__ Squash	__ Horseback Riding
__ Stairs	__ Handball	__ Canoeing
__ Swimming	__ Paddleball	__ Kayaking
__ Rowing	__ Volleyball	__ Downhill Skiing
__ X-Country Skiing	__ Basketball	__ Skating
__ Hiking	__ Soccer	__ Camping
__ Aerobic Dance	__ Softball	__ Sailing
__ Trampoline	__ Hockey	__ Vigorous Dancing
_____	_____	_____
_____	_____	_____
_____	_____	_____

college evening programs or even children's leagues for information and possible contacts.

How Much Exercise?

No matter what sport you select, **be careful to build up your intensity gradually.** If you have been sedentary, your endurance, strength and flexibility will all have to be improved. To jump into intense exercise without gradual conditioning puts you at risk for a number of things: muscle soreness, joint soreness or swelling, ex-

No Ifs, Ands, or Butts

haustion, even risk for heart attack. And it puts your positive attitude toward exercise at risk too.

The focus of this section is on sustained **aerobic exercise** (those listed in the left hand column of the previous list). All of the other exercise options have a stop/start aspect to them, and the intensity of your exertion will vary throughout the exercise. Aerobic exercises like running and biking, for example, require a more constant and prolonged level of exertion. It is important to measure the level of exertion (intensity) to ensure that you are working strenuously enough to be effective but not too strenuously to cause potential harm. If you are uncertain what "strenuously enough" and "potential harm" mean, in the practical sense, consult an exercise specialist for guidance.

Keep in mind that there is little advantage to overtaxing yourself, for that will only result in shorter exercise periods. **There is more benefit to be gained from working at a moderate intensity for a longer time than from working at a higher intensity for too short a time.**

Five of the very best exercises for weight loss are long-distance walking, biking or running, hiking and cross-country skiing. Think about activities like these for week-ends. Whether you are considering rowing, paddling, swimming, skating, riding, dancing, tennis, etc., use your week-ends for longer workouts.

When doing aerobic exercise, **you should be working strenuously enough to be breathing deeply, but not so strenuously that you are unable to talk while exercising.** This is a somewhat subjective measure of intensity. A more accurate measure is to calculate your "training heart rate range" and adjust the intensity of your exercise to maintain that range. The next section will show you how to calculate your training heart rate range.

Calculating Your Training Heart Rate Range

Your training heart rate range should be between sixty percent and eighty-five percent of your capacity. To calculate this, you will first need to become familiar with taking your pulse accurately. Place the first two fingers of your hand along the inside of your opposite wrist, pressing just firmly enough to feel your pulse. Or, you may prefer to gently press the same two fingers along the side of your neck just beneath the back of your jaw. Take a moment now to find your pulse following the diagram below.

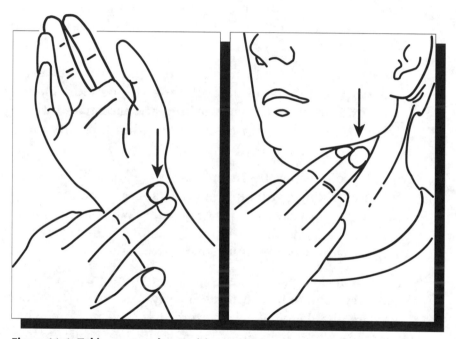

Figure 11-1, Taking your pulse. Feel for your pulse at your wrist or on your throat as shown.

If you have never taken your pulse, stop in at your doctor's office or an exercise facility and ask someone to show you how to do it.

Next, you will need to know your training heart rate range, the number of heartbeats per minute during exercise for safety and effectiveness. The formula for calculating your training heart rate range is shown below.

Calculating Your Training Heart Rate Range

For Men:

205 - ½ your age x .60 = _____ heartbeats per minute at 60% capacity
205 - ½ your age x .85 = _____ heartbeats per minute at 85% capacity

For Women:

220 - your age x .60   = _____ heartbeats per minute at 60% capacity
220 - your age x .85   = _____ heartbeats per minute at 85% capacity

Example for a 40 year old man:

205 - 20 = 185 x .60   = 111 heartbeats per minute
                        = 18-19 beats per 10 seconds.
205 - 20 = 185 x .85   = 157 heartbeats per minute
                        = 26 beats per 10 seconds.

Example for a 40 year old woman:

220 - 40 = 180 x .60   = 108 heartbeats per minute
                        = 18 beats per 10 seconds.
220 - 40 = 180 x .85   = 153 heartbeats per minute
                        = 25-26 beats per 10 seconds.

Calculate your own training heart rate range:

____ - ____ = _____ x .60 = ____ heartbeats per minute at 60% capacity
____ - ____ = _____ x .85 = ____ heartbeats per minute at 85% capacity

---

After you have warmed up and begun your workout, stop periodically to take your pulse. **Count the number of heartbeats for**

ten seconds and multiply that number by six. This will give you the number of heartbeats per minute. This number needs to be within your training heart rate range. Do this periodically during your workouts for the first several days. Note what it feels like to be close to seventy percent capacity. Confirm this each time you check your pulse. Before long, you will be able to determine your safe, effective exercise level without frequent pulse checks.

CAUTION: If you are taking medication which controls your heart rate, or have emphysema or any other respiratory illness which impairs your breathing, please consult a physician and an exercise specialist for guidance. You will not be able to use this system for monitoring the intensity level of your exercise. An alternative system of monitoring will need to be developed for you.

A Target Heart Rate Chart is included on page 265 for greater ease and convenience in keeping track of your heart rate during exercise. This chart is the one used at Canyon Ranch Health and Fitness Resort. To use it, find your age (left-hand column) and then look at the numbers for your sex in the 60%, 70% and 85% columns. These numbers are the **heartbeats for ten seconds** of time. Copy these numbers and carry them with you when exercising. Stop periodically during your workout to take your pulse for ten seconds. The number of heartbeats you count during that ten seconds should be no lower than the number in the 60% column or higher than the number in the 85% column.

Remember, **to realize the full cardiovascular and weight loss benefits from sustained aerobic exercise, you must be working between 60% and 85% of your maximum heart rate (your training heart rate range).** Less than 60% is too little and more than 85% percent is too much.

Begin your aerobic workouts with three to five minutes of warm up. Moderate paced movement should precede vigorous exercise in order to gradually increase blood flow and warm the temperature of the muscles. The heart and lungs will be stimulated gradually and progressively. The muscles and tendons will be slowly stretched, preventing muscle soreness and unnecessary injuries.

Finish your aerobic workouts with ten to fifteen minutes of cool down. Gradually reduce the speed of your activity, allowing yourself to slowly decrease your heart and breathing rates. Do this for five minutes or so, and then do approximately five to ten minutes of stretching. Careful and extended stretching of muscles will help to prevent tightness and soreness, and will help you maintain good flexibility.

How Often To Exercise

To be maximally effective for weight loss, you should build up to a level of four to six exercise periods per week. For maintenance of body weight, plan to have no less than three exercise periods per week. This may seem like a great deal of exercise to you, especially if you have been sedentary.

It is helpful to begin with more interesting, fun-oriented activities first. Beach walking, biking with a friend, playing tennis or golf are just a few ways to get yourself up and moving. When you are enjoying yourself, the added exercise doesn't feel like work. Perhaps one or two of these activities on the week-end, and two brisk walks during the week would be a good starting point for you. Or, perhaps two aerobic classes per week and two morning walks with a dog or a friend will feel good.

If you are more physically fit, you might walk briskly on two days and swim or aerobic dance on three days. Or, you might bike on two days, play tennis on two days and hike on one day. You might use an aerobic exercise class on two days, a trainer on one day, and jog on two days. Varying the type and intensity of the exercise options you use will provide more interest, and will help you avoid the pitfall of looking at exercise as just one more burden in your life.

Creating Your Own Exercise Plan

You might not be physically ready for a high-powered workout. If not, set up a plan for *gradual* increase of activity. This plan can be written to look just like the Control Card you used earlier in developing your nonsmoking and weight control action plans. Look at the example below.

Control Card: Exercise	
7.	30 minute walk, bike or tennis game
6.	25 minute walk, bike or aerobic tape
5.	20 minute walk, yard work or bike ride
4.	Use stairs at work
3.	10-15 minute walk
2.	5-10 minute stretching
1.	Walk to mailbox; use farthest bathroom / telephone

This example demonstrates a progression of exercise based on *amount of energy and time available*. On a high-energy day, you might be able to do a workout lasting twenty minutes or more. On a low-energy day, a stress day, a hurried day, or a not feeling well day, level "1" or "2" might be all you are capable of doing. While level "1" or "2" does not amount to a full scale aerobic workout, each of them allows you to do something that feels a little disciplined, something that will feel good to do physically. This will help to increase your sense of control. As with your nonsmoking and weight control plans, you will have to be flexible in your exercise plans or you will not maintain them comfortably.

Perhaps you are already physically active and capable of more extended or intense workouts. Perhaps you are easily bored with exercise and need to plan a more varied routine. Using the Control Card concept once again, establish a plan allowing for variety of activity as well as varying levels of intensity. **No matter how physically fit you are, you will have more energy on some days than others; you will feel more like exercising on some days than others; you will need different kinds of exercise on some days than others.** Vary your activity, and the time and intensity of your workout accordingly.

The example below illustrates a variety of weekday exercise options to the left of the +, and weekend activity options to the right of it. No specified number of days is given in this example. You set the number of days as best fits your schedule.

Control Card: Exercise	
7.	45 min. jog / bike / swim / trampoline + hike / ski
6.	40 min. jog / bike / trampoline + tennis singles
5.	35 min. jog / bike / swim / racquetball + volleyball / dancing
4.	30–35 min. jog / bike / tennis singles + sail / golf
3.	25–30 min. walk / swim / bike / or tennis doubles
2.	20–25 min. walk / swim / or stationary bike
1.	10–15 min. walk / aerobic tape / or dancing

What will your progressive exercise plan look like? Think carefully about what you like to do. Think about where you will go or the equipment you will need in order to do the type of exercise you like. Grab a pencil and map out your own exercise plan on the following page. Remember to place the easiest activity on the bottom line. Experiment for a while, making modifications to your plan based upon what feels good to you and what works best within your daily routine.

Control Card: Your Exercise Plan	
7.	
6.	
5.	
4.	
3.	
2.	
1.	

An Exercise In Realism

Bob called **Betheny** late one night to find out how she was progressing with her weight reduction plan. "I'm so glad you called!" Betheny exclaimed. "I'm not losing weight very fast and it's making me nervous."

"What about exercise?" Bob inquired. "I thought you were going to sign up at an exercise club."

"I did," Betheny told him. "It's a very nice club, and the people who use it seem pleasant. The problem is that I never get there. My schedule has been so hectic lately. I know that sounds like an excuse, but it's the truth."

"Then you'll have to find another way to exercise," Bob said. "You need regular exercise to handle your tension as much as you need it for weight loss."

"What do you suggest I do?" Betheny demanded testily. "I already have more to do than I have hours to do it in."

"Not so long ago you had time to eat, didn't you?" Bob asked.

"That's not fair!" Betheny responded angrily. "I ate while I did other things."

"You also ate to get time off from being busy, and to help you manage your stress. That's also why you smoked. You aren't doing either of them, now, and you still need tension release, and time away from using your head to do the work you drag home from the studio."

"Yes," Betheny admitted in a quiet voice. "I do need something. But exercise has never been one of my hobbies."

"That's alright, Betheny. I'm not going to suggest anything too in-volved, especially right away. I know you have a videotape machine hooked up to your TV. I want you to rent a few stretching and aerobic tapes for review. Also, I want you to review your music tapes for ones that make you feel good emotionally. Ones that get your legs moving.

"Then I want you to honestly see if the video tapes offer something positive to you for at home exercise, and if the audio tapes would be helpful to listen to while you walk or use a stationary bike."

Betheny agreed to Bob's request. She found some good tapes at the library, and also at the video rental service near her home. While at the library, Betheny found some novels on audio tape. She always loved to have someone read to her so she took three of them home for trial. She called Bob to tell him about it.

"That's great, Betheny. Now, how do you plan to use them? I know you well enough to be certain that you won't go jogging in Central Park in the dark."

"You're right about that!" Betheny said. "I've been looking into renting some exercise equipment to use at home. That will help during the week. I can use the exercise club on the week-end. Someone at work told me about the racquet club she belongs to. Maybe I'll play tennis if I can find a partner."

"You've got the picture," Bob told her. "It will be especially important for you to keep busy on the week-ends. Don't you have some friends who have horses?"

"Yes, I do," Betheny answered. "And I have some friends who like to hike. I work with a couple of people who sail on the week-ends. I guess I can find lots of ways to keep busy and burn some calories too."

"The biggest and most important part of exercise," Bob said, *"is getting yourself out to do it. Make it fun. Find others to do it with you. Try new things. Take lessons to improve your skill at something that interests you. Ice skate and ski in the winter. Hike, ride and sail in the other months. And when you won't leave your apartment, put on those tapes you found and exercise at home."*

Bob's message to Betheny was clear. She won't do things she doesn't like to do, and she won't use facilities that she can't find time to get to. You won't either. Realism, when it comes to exercise, is very important.

Be realistic in your approach to exercise. If you are willing to be outside only when it is sunny and the temperature is mild, use indoor exercise options on inclement days: stationary bicycle, treadmill, rowing machine, cross-country ski machine, aerobic exercise tape, indoor track, indoor pool, gym or exercise facility.

Be realistic about the time you select for exercise. If the only time of day that you have control of your schedule is in the morning, do your exercise early. Getting up will probably be the hardest part of the whole routine, but once you are used to rising early, the early morning exercise will get your day off to a good start. Alternatively, late afternoon exercise, on the way home from work or school, may be very beneficial for reducing stress and re-energizing yourself. Take your gym bag with you so that you can use your momentum to get yourself to the exercise facility.

Many people find that they have an energy let-down once they arrive home, and are less able to drag themselves out of the house again, especially during the winter months. If this applies to you, do your exercise before arriving home. Noon times can be effective exercise times as long as you can reliably get yourself out of your work environment, have sufficient time for exercise and for the required shower and grooming activities, and have an exercise outlet that is reasonably close to your office.

Be realistic about how often you are willing to exercise. While five to six exercise periods per week are best for weight loss, you are still farther ahead to commit yourself to three or four exercise periods if you know that is the most you are willing to do. If two exercise periods seem like a lot to you, start with that, and maybe add a fun activity for the weekend. In time, you may find that you want to exercise more often.

Be realistic about what kind of exercise suits you best. While aerobic exercise is most beneficial for weight loss, any kind of exercise that gets you moving or out of the house is important. Do what feels good. If you enjoy the activity, you will be more willing to exercise more often.

Be realistic about how far out of your way you are willing to go to exercise. If you are unwilling, or unable, to join an exercise club thirty or more minutes' drive from your home or office, no matter how wonderful a club it is or how much you like it when you are there, you are not likely to get there very often. You will do whatever is easiest and if that means having exercise videotapes or a stationary bike at home, plan accordingly.

Closing Thoughts

Exercise plays an important role in reducing stress and tension, two factors that create excessive eating and cigarette cravings. Develop a more active lifestyle by adding recreational sports (tennis, golf, bowling, sailing, scuba diving, horseback riding, badminton, volleyball, softball, skiing, hiking) to fill time in meaningful ways, provide outlets for social activities, help in mood management and keep you away from both cigarettes and food.

There are additional benefits to exercise. Remember the increased endorphin levels you used to get when you smoked? Sustained exercise will cause your brain to increase its production of endorphins, causing you to feel more euphoric and more relaxed, more optimistic and exhilarated.

Exercise makes you feel good physically and psychologically. It increases your self-confidence and gives you a greater sense of personal control in your life. It reduces appetite and takes your mind off of smoking. Again, that's a lot of benefit from one thirty-minute addition to your daily routine!

Recommended Self-Study Exercises

Calculate your training heart rate range, page 254.

Find your 10-second target heart rates on the chart on page 265.

Prepare Exercise Control Cards for daily use, page 258.

Target Heart Rate Chart

To use the chart below, find your age in the left-hand column. Then look across the line, finding the number of beats per ten seconds of time in the 60%, 70%, and 85% columns for your sex. Copy those three numbers on an index card or piece of paper to carry with you when you exercise. As you do your exercise, stop periodically to take your pulse for ten seconds. The number of heartbeats you count in that ten seconds should be no lower than the number in the 60% column or higher than the number in the 85% column.

TARGET HEART RATES (for 10 seconds)						
	60%		70%		85%	
Age	Men	Women	Men	Women	Men	Women
16–19	20	20	23	24	28	29
20–22	19	20	23	23	38	29
23–25	19	19	23	23	28	28
26–28	19	19	22	22	27	27
29–31	19	19	22	22	26	27
32–34	18	19	21	21	26	26
35–37	18	18	21	21	26	26
38–40	18	18	21	21	26	26
41–43	18	18	21	21	26	26
44–46	18	17	21	20	25	25
47–49	18	17	21	20	25	24
50–52	18	17	20	20	25	24
53–55	17	17	20	19	25	23
56–58	17	16	20	19	25	23
59–60	17	16	20	19	24	23
61–65	17	15	20	18	24	22
66–70	17	15	19	18	24	22
71–75	16	14	19	16	23	20

References

The most important resources in the development of this chapter are the three technical advisors listed below whose professional expertise and commitment help people like yourself establish or improve the quality of exercise in their lives. Additional references and suggested books for you to use if you want to explore specific aspects of exercise further are also included.

Technical Advisors:

Eric Chesky, Exercise Physiologist, Canyon Ranch Resort, Tucson, Arizona.

Gary Holzsager, Exercise Physiologist, Canyon Ranch Resort, Tucson, Arizona.

Karma Kientzler, Executive Fitness Director, Canyon Ranch Resort, Tucson, Arizona.

Additional References:

Ferguson, T. *The Smoker's Book of Health.* New York: G. P. Putnam's Sons, 1987.

Skog, D. "Developing Your Personal Exercise Program,", Waltz, J. *Food Habit Management.* Tucson, AZ: Northwest Learning Associates, Inc., 1987.

Witters, W. and Jones-Witters, P. *Drugs and Society.* Monterey, CA: Wadsworth Health Sciences, 1983.

Additional Reading:

Anderson, R. and J. *Stretching.* Fullerton, CA: Andersons, 1975.

Cooper, K. *The Aerobics Program for Total Well-Being.* New York: M. Evans & Co., 1982.

Cooper, M. and K. *Aerobics for Women.* New York: M. Evans Publishing Co., 1972.

Freedom
From Smoking

12

Tough times never last but tough people do!

... Robert Schuller

The tough times involved in quitting smoking are most noticeable during the first few weeks, and then begin fading in strength, frequency and length of time. The periods of time between struggles increase; the intensity and length of the struggles decrease. Occasionally, though, certain circumstances may combine in a particular way to cause you to think about smoking, or to long for a cigarette. These are temporary desires and they will fade quickly when you understand how to handle yourself during these times. As you gain mastery over your temporary desires to smoke, you will achieve a feeling of freedom from cigarettes' influence in your life. This will be the beginning of your psychological independence from smoking.

There are four phases to the process of firmly establishing your psychological independence from smoking: the decision to quit; withdrawal from nicotine; habit retraining (including relapse recovery); and long-term maintenance. You have completed the first three phases and thus, your formal training program. You have studied your smoking patterns, and the underlying emotional, psychological and physiological needs for smoking. You have battled through withdrawal from nicotine. You have learned the strategies, tools and techniques for establishing nonsmoking habits and patterns. You have studied, experimented, applied and modified what you have learned to fit your needs and your lifestyle. You have prepared for relapse recovery, and for managing yourself under stress without cigarettes. You have worked hard. You have achieved a great deal. You should feel justifiably proud of yourself!

The long-term maintenance phase of your stop smoking training has no time constraints; it has no formal closure. You have entered "the long haul", as some people term it. There is less excitement to this phase. There is less urgency, less turmoil and less attention from others. There are fewer personal battles over the desire to smoke. Living without smoking becomes routine.

While the objective of all your recent hard work was to establish your new nonsmoking habits and patterns as simple routine, **there is a potential danger in thinking that your work is finished the moment you have completed your formal training.** Consider that new habits are similar to seedlings, the tender new plants that will one day become the sturdy bearers of seeds, fruit or flowers. These new seedlings must be protected when first planted outside. They must be sheltered from harsh, destructive elements: too much wind, rain, dryness and cold. They must be given food. Eventually they will be strong enough to exist without much assistance.

So it is with your tender new nonsmoking habits. They must be protected at first. They must be sheltered from neglect because of too little time, attention, planning and thought. They must be nurtured and cultivated regularly. **If you, like many new nonsmokers, allow your new habits to fend for themselves too soon, they can fade away altogether, causing you to revert back to smoking.** The objective of this final chapter is to help you succeed as a long-term, permanent nonsmoker. You will learn tools for maintaining your new nonsmoking patterns, achieving emotional separation from cigarettes, resisting the temptation to return to smoking, and getting yourself successfully through the occasional tough times.

Some of the information in this chapter will not be new to you. **The very tools that helped you quit smoking are the very same tools that will help you remain free of smoking.** The tools used in this chapter are organized to help you maintain your progress, to reinforce what you have already accomplished. There is nothing magical here, just good common sense.

Maintaining Your New Habits

Think again about your personal smoking history. Remember how you carried your cigarettes everywhere? You always had a supply. You were willing to inconvenience yourself to buy them, even late at night. You were willing to swallow your pride and ask others for cigarettes, or borrow money to buy them yourself. You were willing to leave the company of others to obtain them, or to get away from others so that you could smoke. You were willing to stand up in the face of opposition to maintain your smoking habits. That's a substantial investment in smoking!

You will need to make an equally substantial investment in *not* smoking. Look what you've done so far:

- ✔ Tracked and analyzed your smoking patterns.
- ✔ Developed a Resource List of usable tools.
- ✔ Prepared Control Cards for daily use.
- ✔ Purchased cigarette replacements like gum and mints.
- ✔ Prepared a Control Recovery Card.

You will need to keep your Control Cards and cigarette replacements with you and use them as regularly as you once used cigarettes. You will sometimes need to borrow money to purchase a pack of gum or mints. You will occasionally need to leave a room to get away from the urge to smoke. And you will sometimes have to oppose others when you refuse to smoke. You've done all this before so that you could smoke and you can certainly do it all again—without smoking!

Strengthen And Maintain Your Nonsmoking Habits

❑ **Use your Control Recovery Card (Control Card #1) as a daily guide during particularly shaky times.** Follow the steps as written. Don't argue about it—just do it. Review the instructions for control recovery on page 209.

❑ **If cigarette cravings are becoming a problem, identify the triggers or underlying needs that are causing them.** You may not have identified all the possible smoking triggers or needs in earlier self-study exercises. Write any new information you think of on the Smoking Log, page 308.

Set a plan for dealing with the smoking triggers or needs you identified. Consult the lists of nonsmoking tools in Chapters 5 and 7 and set an action plan. Write that plan on a Control Card for easy reference.

Keep your plan simple. Select no more than seven tools that are within your ability to perform. It is far more effective to focus on a few tools and use them well than it is to try everything at one time and wind up feeling overwhelmed, frustrated and discouraged. This is when many people give up their action plan as well as their good intentions. Don't let yourself get caught in that trap! Use your Control Cards to guide you.

❑ **Keep a big supply of cigarette replacements stored in reserve,** whether or not you think you will need them. Gum, mints, tooth picks, cinnamon sticks, low-calorie foods or beverages are all helpful. Keep them stashed in pockets, purses, drawers, desks, even in the ash tray of your car. You cannot anticipate when a sudden spike of tension, frustration, anger, fatigue, worry, relief or other mood may send you into a temporary desire to smoke.

This desire will fade quickly, especially if you can do something to calm or distract yourself, change your thoughts or delay your getting up to search for a cigarette.

Buy your nonsmoking tools in bulk!! Remember that one pack of cigarettes means twenty cigarettes. One pack of gum, by contrast, means five pieces. If you formerly smoked thirty cigarettes each day, you will need to have at least thirty pieces of gum, or six packs, available every day. If gum is your chosen replacement for cigarettes and the gum isn't available when you need it, you will miss cigarettes even more. You don't need that kind of stress, especially now. Teach yourself to buy your nonsmoking tools the same way you once bought cigarettes: in bulk. And store them the same way: lots of little stashes, everywhere. Keep a reserve supply in your car, easily available when your home or office supply runs out.

When necessary, borrow gum or mints from others, or borrow the money to buy them from vending machines. If you were once willing to borrow cigarettes from others, don't let false pride get in your way now. Borrow what you need, then replace what you borrowed the next time you go shopping. These other items are just as important as the cigarettes they are replacing!

❑ **Keep cigarettes out of your sight and far, far away from your reach.** This is especially important if you have close friends or family members who still smoke. You will need to be careful of the cigarettes left behind by others. Don't save them; destroy them. Subscribe to the motto: make it easier to do what you want to do, and harder to do what you don't want to do! If cigarettes aren't around or in easy reach, and other tools are, you will turn to whatever is most quickly and readily available. Don't underestimate the power of ease and convenience. These same factors helped you establish your smoking habits; use them now to help you maintain your nonsmoking habits.

❑ **Resist the influence of others who challenge your ability to stay away from cigarettes,** or who tempt you to return to smoking. Surround yourself with nonsmokers and strengthen your commitment to remain smoke free.

❑ **Use your Control Card as your stress plan or recovery plan** at times when you feel overwhelmed, or when you have a temporary slip up. These are the very reasons you originally prepared Cue Cards. Use them as intended. Review Chapter 9, page 191.

❑ **Use this book for continued reading, training and reinforcement.** Leave it in your bathroom or on the kitchen table as the only reading material available for the next few months. Read it over a second time for reinforcement. Browse through it frequently. Use it for quick reference, and as a guide for specific problem solving. Use it to stimulate your motivation and commitment. Read it for information, as a guide and also for encouragement. As your skill and familiarity with these tools and techniques increase, you will need higher level reinforcement. The information in this book will provide that for you, especially the later chapters.

❑ **Practice, practice, practice.** This is what will make you a skilled and confident nonsmoker. The more you use your nonsmoking strategies and tools, the more proficient you become in applying them. The more often you use them, the more familiar and comfortable they will feel to you. The more comfortable you feel when using them, the more confident and secure you will feel with yourself as a nonsmoker. This concept is very basic, and very important.

A Practice Exercise For You

For your own amusement you might want to see for yourself how important and effective repetition, or practice truly is. To help you do this, look at the sample Circle Exercise on the next page. Use a timer from one of your table games or set the oven timer for one minute. Start the timer and in that one minute put your finger on as many circles as you can, beginning in sequence with numbers 1, 2,

3, and so on. When the timer signals the end of the minute, look at the number of the last circle you touched. Write that number on a piece of paper.

Reset the timer and repeat the same exercise seven or eight times. At the end of the seventh time, look at the number of the last circle touched. Is it a higher number than when you first did the exercise? Do the exercise once more. Was the last number higher this time? Most people find that the more often they do something, the better and faster they become in doing it. If your final number became higher with practice, that will show you in a small, concrete way how important practice is for improvement and greater comfort in doing the task. Try it for yourself.

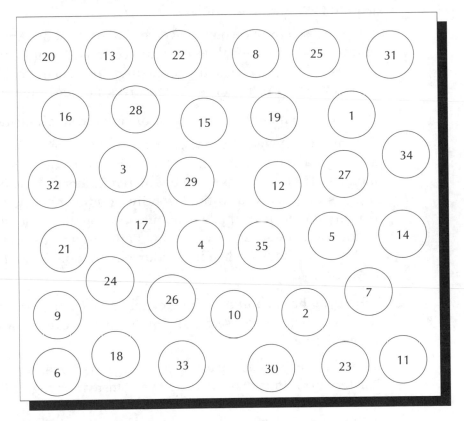

Figure 12-1, Circle exercise.

Resisting The Temptation To Smoke

Many things can ignite a little mental flirtation about having "just one puff" or "just one cigarette". Fatigue, moods, stress, social pressure, overconfidence and periodic resistance to change are a few of the most common reasons for needing to test yourself, or to relax your rigid control "just a little". These topics were discussed in earlier chapters. Chapter 9, Relapse Prevention and Recovery, can help you recover if self-control does weaken momentarily. Below are listed the few **very effective tools** to keep foremost in your mind, to help you through most of the difficult times:

❑ **Remain cautious of the moods, situations and people that once caused you to want to smoke.**

Keep yourself from becoming overconfident too soon. Any situation, mood or personal need that once caused you to smoke always has the *potential* to trigger an urge for a cigarette. This is especially true during times of high stress, fatigue or illness.

❑ **Remove all remnants or mementos of your old smoking habits:**

This means ALL cigarette cases, tobacco pouches, pipes, lighters, ash trays and any other items that can affect you at a weak moment. The objective is to remove all reminders of smoking, all triggers to cause you to think fondly of smoking. The fewer reasons you have for thinking about smoking, the easier it will be for you to establish new thinking patterns, new associations and new methods for handling yourself emotionally and psychologically.

❑ **When you have an urge to smoke, get away from the cause of the urge, distract yourself and slowly deep breathe until the urge subsides.**

Should you experience an unexpected urge to smoke, don't view it in terms of, "I'm not ready to quit yet." Instead, recognize it for what it is—a leftover from an old, no longer used habit. Take action immediately!

❑ **Let other people know you have quit smoking.**

Don't hide it or make it seem unimportant. Most new nonsmokers have difficulty in letting anyone know what they are doing. This is protection against the embarrassment of potential failure. This can get in the way of your ultimate success. The more open and direct you are about what you are doing, no matter how shaky you feel about it, the likelier you will be to stay in control when the going gets rough. Don't give yourself an easy way out of control.

❑ **Develop a nonsmoking reputation.**

Do it in affirming words as well as actions. *"Yes, I used to smoke after a meal, but not anymore." "I always had to have a cigarette with my coffee. Now I drink tea with lemon instead, and cigarettes just don't fit with tea."* This practice serves to alert you as well as others to your newly developing habits.

❑ **Be firm and definite in your refusals when other people offer cigarettes to you.**

Sometimes it is difficult to bring to mind the actual words to use in refusing a cigarette or in saying a nonsmoking affirmation. Write some simple ones on a Control Card labelled: Refusals/Affirmations. Refer to it frequently, especially in difficult social situations.

"Definitely not! I am no longer smoking." "No, I wouldn't like a cigarette, thank you, but do you have a piece of gum?" Disarm more insistent people with comments like, *"You have always been so supportive of me. I know you wouldn't purposefully cause tension for me by giving me a cigarette right now."* Remember that each "no" is a deeper bond to not smoking. It is also stronger evidence of your personal "goodbye" to smoking.

❑ **Do as much socializing and as many activities as possible in a nonsmoking place, or with nonsmoking people.**

Sit in the smoke-free section of your local library to study or write reports, or just to get your desk work done. This will take you away from the normal distractions and the familiar triggers which cause you to think about smoking.

❑ **Stay in frequent contact with people who naturally give you acceptance and support for not smoking.**

Being in their company will help you to want to stay smoke free. One certain way to sabotage your progress is to spend too much time with your old smoking buddies, especially the ones who are upset by your success. After all, if you are successful at quitting smoking, what excuses do they have to say they can't quit? You were once one of them, and you quit.

❑ **Reward yourself when you need something special, or when you need a break from work or your daily routine.**

Reward yourself with little things: a paperback book, a rental movie, a restaurant meal, tickets to a play or sports event, a leisurely bath or any other indulgence that feels good and doesn't remind you of smoking. Don't wait until you feel you deserve it and don't wait for other people to suggest it. When you need a little extra bit of fun or pleasure, go get it. Cigarettes once did that for you, many times each day. A little time off for relaxation or a little extra money spent for enjoyment will be helpful to you now. You once spent a considerable amount of money for cigarettes. Use some of the money you are saving from not buying cigarettes to buy yourself other indulgences.

❑ **Keep your Control Cards readily available at all times.**

Read them daily. Use them for control recovery by following them methodically until you once again feel stable. Resist the thought that you shouldn't need to use your Control Cards, that you should be able to control yourself without any help at all. This type of thinking will only sabotage your long-term control.

Don't waste time on pride. Just find the Control Cards and use them! Better yet, keep a set of them in your pocket or purse at all times!

Periodic resistance to change is normal and natural. It will be more obvious when you are tired, agitated or feeling burdened by the pressures of life. New ways of doing things feel awkward and strange for a while. This creates additional tension. Recognize the resistance for what it is: your response to extra pressure. Let up on yourself. Give yourself a break. Go for a walk, take a bath, go to bed early, get together with a friend, go to a movie. As you become more comfortable with not smoking, the resistance will diminish.

Achieving Emotional Separation From Cigarettes

Tim and *Martha* sat down together for their last session of the hospital's Quit Smoking Program. *Sue Burns* and her assistant, *Steve,* were warm in their acknowledgement of each person's dedication and hard work toward quitting smoking successfully.

Sue looked directly at Martha and said, "You deserve a special round of applause from the group. You have not only stayed in the program, but you have done all of the assignments and worked very hard to break your smoking habits." The group members applauded loudly. "Now, when you are ready," Sue continued, "you can gently wean yourself away from the nicotine gum. Dr. Anderson will help you with that, and Steve and I can be resources for you if you need us."

Tim nudged Martha. "Good job! One step down and one to go. I know you'll be able to do it!"

Martha grinned, then turned her attention back to Sue.

"Right now all of you are feeling positive and enthusiastic. That's wonderful. It's probably hard for you to imagine that you won't always feel this way, but emotions are not always steady. Emotions can be a powerful tool to boost yourself up, and also to tear yourself down. You

have had a great deal of emotional involvement with smoking and that is what I want to talk to you about today.

"There is a particularly hazardous kind of emotional involvement on the pathway to your success in remaining long-term nonsmokers," Sue warned. "It has to do with your own emotional responses to leaving cigarettes.

"When smokers quit and then return to smoking three months, five years or even ten years later, the issue is not nicotine addiction. Nicotine and the other chemicals cleared out of their bodies long ago. Yet some former smokers still talk at length about how they occasionally miss smoking; about how they haven't completely lost their desire for a cigarette. In some respects, this longing for contact with the cigarette resembles the emotional longing we experience for an intimate friend who, through relocation or death, is no longer around. We miss the good times, the times of relaxation together, the times of closeness and sharing. You have shared similar moments with cigarettes so it is understandable that you will miss them in similar ways, especially at times of deep emotional need. Cigarettes used to be there when you needed them and now you are learning to manage without them."

*"Perhaps **companionship** and **intimacy** are the two most common words which sum up the loss most smokers talk about when first quitting smoking. Collectively, cigarettes have been the closest and most intimate of companions for you. They were always present. They demanded no conversation and little physical effort. They were soothing. They were with you at all times. They were easy to relate to. The negative effects were not readily apparent, especially when viewed through the hazy good feelings that came with the emotional satisfaction of smoking. As we've said before, smoking is very seductive. Perhaps it is this seductiveness that allowed you to ignore the obvious relationship between cigarettes and poor health, between cigarettes and high risk for fatal illness. How could something that feels so good be so bad?"*

"I've asked myself that same question many times," said a man seated at the back of the room.

"How did you answer it?" Steve asked.

"I didn't have an answer," the man replied. "It was just my way of talking myself into continuing to smoke."

"That's what many people do," Sue commented. "It may be difficult for you to keep from being tempted by the seductiveness of the cigarettes. You may hear yourself saying that 'one puff won't matter'; that 'one cigarette won't hurt'. You may even hear yourself saying that if you could have 'just one cigarette to calm your nerves', or 'keep you company' just this one time, then you would be willing to stay away from them from then on."

"That really hits home!" Tim exclaimed. "I can hear myself saying those same words."

The mood of the group noticeably changed. Uncertainty, even fear, showed itself in people's expressions. Sue was quick to reassure the group. "My reason for bringing this up today is to **prepare you ahead of time** to defend yourselves against this faulty reasoning, this seduction to smoke. If you know what to expect and how to deal with it in advance, you won't be trapped by it later on.

"Think about the visual imagery strategy we discussed earlier. It will be especially important for you to increase your awareness of the negative feelings that come with smoking: the burning in your throat, the cough, the congestion, the clogged sinuses, the tightening in your chest, the elevated heart rate, the cold hands and feet, the irritation in your eyes from the smoke. Absolutely turn yourself away from the emotional picture of the 'innocent, abandoned friend', the cigarette. Turn your attention, instead, to the physical struggle of your heart to pump blood through smaller passageways; of your lungs, unable to rid themselves of mucous and other foreign particles because the cilia are paralyzed; of your throat and nasal passages which are constantly irritated by the smoke."

"Pay attention to how you have been feeling without the cigarettes. Take pleasure in long, deep breaths without coughing, in exercising without being short of breath. Notice all the wonderful scents around you once your nasal passages have returned to normal. There are wonderful fragrances everywhere: dew on the grass in the early morning, delicate flowers in the spring, herbs growing wild along the roadway. You will appreciate the subtle scents of shampoo and body lotion, even the familiar smell inside your house once the cigarette odor has been thoroughly cleaned away."

"In a way," Sue continued, "removing the smell of old cigarette smoke from your clothes, house, office and car interior is similar to removing heavily flavored salad dressings from salads. Bleu cheese dressing, for example, completely covers the delicate tastes of the vegetables in the salad, and you are left only with the taste of the dressing. With cigarettes, you are left with the smell of the smoke and not the more varied and interesting scents of the world around you."

Sue paused in her dialogue to let her words imprint deeply in her students' minds. She glanced at Steve who was carefully scanning the faces in front of him for clues about the people's reactions to Sue's words. He remembered how he felt the first time he heard Sue give this same lecture. Feelings of anxiety and worry got in the way of understanding what Sue was actually saying. Later on, when he was feeling more secure with himself as a nonsmoker, Steve was able to recall Sue's comments and think about them more rationally.

"After I first heard Sue give this same lecture," Steve told the group, "I went immediately to a restaurant and ordered bleu cheese salad dressing just to see if she was right. For the first time, I noticed that I didn't taste the vegetables, only the dressing. I've never ordered bleu cheese dressing again," he laughed. "It was a good way to help me see that cigarette smoke worked the same way in the rest of my life. Everything smelled like smoke to me once I noticed it. I hadn't paid any attention to smell before, so I never realized I couldn't smell things like other people did. At first, that didn't seem important to me. Now, however, I do appreciate my improved sense of smell. This is just one of many good things that come into your life when cigarettes aren't around anymore."

"Let's talk about **companionship** for a few minutes," Sue suggested. "Companionship may be an important part of your emotional attachment to cigarettes. This does not necessarily mean that you have a strong need for human company. Actually, the cigarettes provided release from human contact, in many instances. You will perhaps miss the cigarette the most when you crave solitude, for it was in the lack of human company that the cigarettes' companionship was likely to be most deeply felt. If this has been important to you, you will need to find a new companion, a new object to keep you company."

"I know just what you mean," Tim said. "I liked to watch the smoke. It almost seemed that something live was in the room with me. Maybe that sounds silly."

"Not at all," said Sue. "A lot of people feel that way." Several people in the room nodded in agreement. "Try using candlelight. The warm glow of a candle on your desk or in the room where you are sitting gives the emotional feeling of warmth, and a sense of something 'live' in the room with you."

"The **physical touch** involved in smoking was important to me," Steve told the group. "I am a very physical person. I like to be hugged and touched by people close to me, except when I am cranky. When I smoked, I felt physically comforted and soothed by the feel of the cigarette in my hand and in my mouth. I liked the deep inhalation. When I first quit smoking I noticed that I missed that sense of touch from cigarettes. "I started to eat when I wanted to smoke, looking for some kind of comfort. I went after my favorite comfort foods, too: candy, ice cream and pastry."

"And that's when I had a long talk with him," Sue cut in. "Sex, eating and smoking provide some of the most sensual and intimate touch we allow for ourselves. Many smokers are particularly touch sensitive, deriving security, reassurance and comfort from touch. When we are most emotionally upset, the needs for reassurance and comfort are especially strong. Yet these are often times when the touch of another person is not welcomed. What is needed is some solitary time for self-healing. Food and cigarettes are popular in the self-healing process because they feel physically nurturing. They are also readily available in a way that bubble baths and a fire in the fireplace are not.

"If touch is important to you, it will be absolutely necessary that you find ways other than smoking and eating to bring healing touch into your life," Sue said. "You women might enjoy giving yourselves a facial, manicure or pedicure, or just soaking your feet or your whole body in warm water. Back rubs are wonderful when you can talk someone into giving them to you! If you don't have a buddy around to give you a back rub, treat yourself to a regular massage."

"Even men enjoy that!" Steve grinned.

Sue smiled. "Stretching, deep breathing, even running your hands through your own hair, clasping your hands behind your back as you walk, putting your own hand on your own shoulder are all ways you can provide that sense of physical comfort without smoking. These are all good ways to provide reassurance and acceptance from yourself to yourself, and we all need that when we are emotionally upset or feeling insecure."

Martha raised her hand. "I have a Persian cat at home who loves to curl up in my lap whenever I sit down. Except for having a lapful of long cat hair whenever she gets up, I do enjoy playing with her tail and feeling her fur in my hand as I pet her."

"That's a terrific suggestion," Sue responded. "Many people enjoy petting or hugging an animal, playing with it and even training it. If any of you do have pets, use them to gain that sense of companionship and touch."

"All I have is a big teddy bear," Steve said. "Will that work?"

Everyone laughed, but Sue was more serious. "Teddy bears are wonderfully cuddly. You can hold them and pet them, and they never complain or have to be fed.

*"Maybe this all sounds too involved or too burdensome to think about right now," Sue continued. "Just pay attention to your feelings, especially during times when you are overly tired, stressed or emotionally upset. **Provide comfort for yourself in any way that seems realistic and useful.** If you begin to think about smoking more than usual, review the ideas written on your Resource List or the ones provided in your book. Look for some new tools to use. Talk to others who quit smoking and ask them for ideas. The most important thing you can do for yourself is to actively explore new ways to handle your emotional self. You dare not sit back, helplessly, and wait for something or someone to magically take the struggle away for you! That is a sure road back to smoking. **If you need something, figure out what it is and figure out how you can get it.** Then get up and get it. **Anything, that is, except cigarettes!"***

Getting Through The Tough Times

There are some very important elements to keeping yourself going with any task or goal. Three of the most important are *encouragement*, *belief* and *patience*. Encouragement provides that extra "push" to try a little harder, keep going a little longer. Belief refers to faith in yourself and in your ability to succeed at the goals you have set for yourself. Patience is the element most often found in short supply. Most people are anxious to reach their goals, impatient to get started and demanding of continuous progress. The harder and faster you push yourself to succeed, the greater the chance for error, frustration and relapse. Let's look more closely at each of these three elements.

Encouragement

Visual imagery is a powerful tool for developing, changing or maintaining a particular point of view. Use a little visual imagery, now, to help yourself understand the importance of encouragement.

Picture a large oval running track, the kind of track seen at most local high schools. Then picture a high school track meet involving several different schools. As the racers line up for the first event, four adults move to the inside of the track, one adult at each end of the oval and one adult midway down each side of the straight sections. The adults are wearing the colors of the home team. The gun is fired and the first race begins. As the home team sprinter reaches the closest adult, the adult leans forward, hands cupped around his mouth, and shouts something to the racer. The racer speeds up, then starts to slow down a bit just before reaching the second adult. That adult leans forward and shouts something, and again the sprinter speeds up. As the racer passes the third and fourth adult, the same procedure takes place.

You have probably heard good coaching language before. You have probably heard encouraging phrases like: You're looking great!; Pump your arms, stretch your legs, keep your speed up!; You're doing it, you're almost there!; Keep going! You're powerful!!. If you were a home team sprinter, would encouragement like that keep you moving at top speed?

Wouldn't it be wonderful to have your own personal coach who would encourage you to reach a little higher, try a little harder, hold on a little longer whenever you felt discouraged or disheartened? Wouldn't it be wonderful to have an inner coach who carefully guided you through the specific control strategies whenever you felt a strong urge to smoke? Sometimes people are lucky enough to find personal coaches who will encourage, motivate and guide them through specific trials or tasks in life. Not all people are so fortunate. Most people have to be their own coaches, to learn about **the power of positive coaching** for themselves.

Think about your own inner coaching language, the way you talk to yourself. Is it supportive? Or does it bring out the worst in you? Do you flog yourself into action? If you do, your very own language may be getting in the way of your ability to feel good about what you are doing and the success you are achieving. Are you continually reminding yourself about what you haven't yet achieved, rather than what you already have achieved? Do you discount your successes by reminding yourself that you haven't succeeded often enough or frequently enough to really matter? Do you discount other people's positive comments by stating that you still have a long way to go or much more to achieve?

Some people find that it is easier to be critical than supportive. **Critical self talk will wear you down emotionally and psychologically.** Mentally beating yourself over mistakes doesn't help you feel good about yourself nor about not smoking. Getting through the tough times requires positive support, especially from yourself. Below are some tools which you can use daily to keep your own support system strong.

No Ifs, Ands, or Butts

❏ **Positive self talk.**

Speak in terms of improvement. Here are some examples: I can! I am doing it! I am succeeding! I am a little stronger each day! I am proud of myself for what I have accomplished so far!

❏ **Talk to others about your progress rather than your struggles.**

Let them know how hard you're working. Tell them about how many cravings you have withstood. In the beginning you will have fewer days of nonsmoking, but a vastly higher number of cravings. So, discuss the cravings first. It is impressive when, in the early days of quitting, you are able to say, *"Yes, it's true that I've been a nonsmoker for one week, but that week represents more than 659 cravings I have successfully overcome!!"* Later on, you will have a greater number of days without smoking to talk about.

A big mistake many people make when quitting smoking is to assume that they are boring others by discussing their successes. They completely forget or just don't realize how much time they used to spend complaining about their bad habits, their lack of success in changing them and how disgusted they were with themselves. Continual positive talk is far easier for other people to listen to than all the negative things you used to say!

❏ **Talk to your nonsmoking support person every week.**

Explain what you are doing, how you are doing it and what your progress has been. This reinforces your awareness and attention to detail. When other people know more precisely what you are doing, the easier it will be for them to support you and your efforts. Besides, this is a pleasant way to get a little extra positive attention for yourself.

❏ **If assistance is needed from someone, make a very specific request.**

Generalized requests leave people confused and uncertain about what to do. A request like, *"I need you to watch over me at the party tonight,"* is not nearly as specific or as helpful as a definite request. Here is an example of a more specific request for help. *"If I feel my control is shaky, will you go outside with me for a few minutes so I can get some fresh air? Let me tell you about what I am doing to keep myself from smoking. And will you tell me I am doing a good job at not smoking when you know how tempting it is for me to just give in and have a cigarette?"*

While these words may not fit you or your manner of speech, remember that this style of request forces you to *think in detail* about what kind of support is helpful, and it lets someone who cares about you learn how to be more appropriately helpful. Choose your own words but remember *to be specific and direct* about what you want. Such requests reduce confusion, frustration, misunderstandings and hurt feelings.

Belief

Faith and belief in your own ability and in your own success as a nonsmoker are fundamentally important to helping yourself get through the challenges to your control and your resolve to remain smoke free. Yes, there will be tough days and tough times. You've worked your way through them many times before in your life, and you can do it again, even without cigarettes!

If you genuinely believe that you will be successful, you will be. If you doubt your own ability, you will have to work much harder at keeping your self talk positive. Do your very best to keep yourself from saying something like, *"Well, I've gone two months without smoking, but that's not nearly long enough."* Words like that only undermine your conviction that you will achieve your long-term goal. Better to say, *"Yes, I've gone two months without smoking and I'm still going strong."*

If other people doubt your ability to remain a nonsmoker, that's their problem. Your goal should not be to convince others of your commitment or your ability to succeed. Your goal is to remain a nonsmoker. Ignore the challenging or negative comments from others. The longer you go without smoking, the more convincing you will become automatically. In time, there will be no more doubt about your staying a nonsmoker because you will have been a nonsmoker for a long time. Your belief in yourself is most important. The belief of other people is helpful but not nearly as critical to your ultimate success as your own belief.

Focus your attention upon each little success, each little personal victory over cigarettes. There will be many negative things to dwell on if you allow that to happen: the feelings of awkwardness with your new habits, the periodic sense of emptiness without cigarettes, the effort of finding nonsmoking alternatives for managing your daily moods and energy levels. These are all temporary issues. They will become a little less burdensome and a little less important each day. Each day you will become a little stronger, a little more sure of yourself, a little more secure in your own ability to live well without cigarettes. Put that into your conscious mind every day.

Counter every negative thought with a positive one; every doubt with a statement of conviction in your ultimate long-term success. Remind yourself that you are establishing a track record without cigarettes, one day at a time, each and every day. *"I have quit smoking,"* you remind yourself. *"I have not smoked for _____ days. I am not smoking today. I will not smoke tomorrow. I am finished, once and for all, with cigarettes!"*

Should you stumble and have a cigarette by accident, think about the skater's story on page 192. In the words of Martha's husband, *"It's not falling down that counts as much as how you get up and keep going."* Your mistake gives you the perfect opportunity to use your control recovery plan and to practice your recovery skills. One cigarette did not make you a smoker initially. One cigarette alone will not make you a return smoker. *"Yes, I messed up,"* you can tell yourself. *"I need to be better prepared for difficult situations. I have my Control Recovery Card and I am using it. I am a little nervous because of my slip-up but I will recover quickly. I am feeling better already."* Perhaps these are not the words you would use with yourself, but whatever words you do use, keep the meaning behind them supportive. Don't let your own negative words undermine your own belief in yourself. Use the power of positive coaching to keep your internal language positive and supportive.

Patience

Exercising patience may be the hardest aspect of quitting smoking. Most people want complete success—yesterday! It took you many years to build your current smoking habits; it will take a while to retrain yourself and establish new, nonsmoking habits.

Think about the difference in the psychology and training of a sprint runner versus a marathon runner. Think about your nonsmoking goal. Are you in this for the long haul? Are you running a sprint or a marathon? You cannot do both at the same time. As with running, you will have to sacrifice speed to gain distance, or sacrifice distance to gain speed. If distance (sustained nonsmoking) is your goal, then let up a little on speed (how hard you push yourself). **Aim for consistency and stability with a few tasks at a time.**

Many marathoners set their goals, during the race, in increments: one water station to the next; one mile to the next; one hour to the next; and so on. Set your goals in increments too: one hour to the next; one day to the next; one month to the next. In this way you will be less likely to feel overwhelmed. Thinking about not smoking for the rest of your life may seem like too much too deal with, like too big a commitment to make all at once. Though, in fact, you are making a lifetime commitment, keep your daily objectives more short-term. As with any runner, you will reach the finish line, one step at a time.

If you are used to seeing results quickly in the work or projects you typically do, concentrate on your smaller, more immediate victories over smoking. Notice that you did handle a craving without smoking; that you chaired two meetings without smoking one cigarette; that you get up from the table after meals rather than linger with a cigarette; that you went through one more day without a single cigarette; and so on. Pay attention to the little things. They will occupy your thoughts and keep you feeling good about what you are doing. In time, you will have established yourself as a nonsmoker of many months and eventually a nonsmoker of many years. In the words of an ancient Chinese proverb, *"Patience is power; with time and patience the mulberry leaf becomes silk."*

Closing Thoughts

You will undoubtedly feel cautious of your success in the beginning. Most new nonsmokers fear loss of control for quite some time. You will gather greater strength in your commitment and your conviction to be smoke free with each successive month without smoking. Your psychological independence from smoking will come when you know, with certainty, that you no longer need or want to smoke; when you know that cigarettes have lost their control over you; when you realize that you can indeed live contentedly without smoking; when you see that you can handle yourself successfully without smoking; when you become aware there are more important or more interesting things to think about than cigarettes; when you know there is nothing to go back to anymore. Will the day really come when you will know all of these things? If you are willing to stick to your stop smoking goals, no matter what, if you are willing to be diligent in your use of nonsmoking tools and strategies, and if you are willing to be patient long enough for your nonsmoking habits to become firmly established, the answer is, "yes".

Follow the guidelines you have set for yourself. Reread this book to keep your attention focused upon managing yourself without smoking. Do whatever is necessary to strengthen your habits and your commitment to never smoke again. Gather support however and whenever you can. Don't be afraid to get up and leave a room if that helps you refrain from taking a cigarette. Look to former smokers and nonsmokers for encouragement and support. Most of all, be supportive of yourself. Gentleness and patience with yourself will enable you to get through the tough times. Remember this message from Robert Schuller, minister, author and promoter of positive thinking and living—*"Tough times never last but tough people do!"*

Recommended Self-Study Exercise

Each of the chapters in this book is complex, with many ideas to think over and many suggestions to explore. **If you have gone through the book fairly quickly, return more leisurely to each chapter and study it thoroughly.** Take a week, even two or three per chapter if you really want to firmly fix the concepts and the tools securely in your thoughts and actions. Review the self-study exercises, or work on them now if you have not had enough time to finish them. Stopping smoking is a major project worth every bit of time and attention you can give it. That time and attention will pay off later in the ease and stability of living without cigarettes.

If you have studied the chapters carefully already, then settle down with the Smoking Profile Questionnaire, your Resource List and your Control Cards. Study them. Post them in obvious places. Follow the specific tasks as directed. **Read. Think. Explore. Experiment. Modify. Practice.** If you make a mistake, use your recovery plan. Stabilize yourself. Then just keep on doing what you've been doing: reading, thinking, writing, experimenting, practicing. As the Roman poet Ovid said, *"Practices become habits."*

Epilogue

13

Habit is a cable; we weave a thread of it every day, and at last we cannot break it.

... Horace Mann

Each time you use your nonsmoking tools and techniques, they become a little stronger. Each time you say "no" to the urge to smoke you become a little more confident of yourself as a nonsmoker. Each time you pick yourself up from a setback or a slip up you become more resilient and secure in your ability to recover from error. Each day you live and act as a nonsmoker, your nonsmoking habits become stronger, more comfortable and easier to live with. Just as the individual threads of a cable become strong and unbreakable when woven together, the individual threads of your nonsmoking habits gather strength as they are interwoven in your daily thoughts and actions.

Each of the six main characters who appeared throughout the pages of this book strived to apply the knowledge and skills necessary to achieve their goals. Some were more successful than others; some certainly struggled harder than others. Each of them learned something unique and important along the road to quitting smoking. Each of them has a final message to share with you.

Bob, *always one to keep in touch with old friends, decided to call everyone who sat at his table for the last class reunion six months ago. He had been in close contact with Betheny, had bumped into Tim on the street one day, and had gotten a couple of telephone messages from Randy who was looking for materials for his Smoke Out Campaign. Bob knew they had all been trying to quit smoking, each in his or her own fashion and he was curious to know how successful each of them had been.*

Betheny was first on his list. "How are you doing?" he asked her.

"Actually, I'm doing very well," she answered. "And I've got some good news. You know I've been running regularly with two women from the studio. Well, they ran in the New York Marathon last year and they want me to train for it with them. It's six months away from now so I'll have time to build up my stamina. What do you think?"

"I think it's a long way away from where you used to be," Bob answered. "Not so long ago I couldn't imagine your doing anything physical!"

Betheny laughed. "I couldn't either. These two women pushed, coaxed and humored me along until I finally understood what they meant about the 'runner's high'. I guess you could say that I'm as much into running as I was once into smoking. The only difference is, I look much better now. And I feel so much better, too. I can breathe deeply and easily. I have so much energy. The three of us meet at Central Park every morning, or we run on treadmills at the exercise club at night. We take trips out of town every couple of weeks so we can run hills, explore shops and generally unwind."

"You sound like an ad for running," Bob exclaimed.

"It is a bit much, I agree," Betheny said. "But I'm so excited by it right now. I'm also excited that I haven't wanted even one cigarette for the last month. I thought that would never happen for me. You told me to have faith, but it was very hard to believe in myself for a long time. I think I finally trust myself. The running gives me daily incentive to never, ever smoke again. What do you think of the New York Marathon idea?"

"I think it's fantastic!" Bob replied. "I'll even fly in for the event so I can be at the finish line to take a picture of you."

Bob was pleased as he thought about Betheny later. She had been his special project for the first three months following the reunion, and though he hadn't talked with her in the past month and a half, he felt a special closeness to her. He was excited about her new goal. She hadn't mentioned her weight, once a serious concern, but he figured it was no longer a problem now that she was running daily.

At the end of their conversation, Bob had asked Betheny what she thought was the most important thing she learned in the process of quitting smoking. Not surprisingly, she felt that **having a new and consuming interest was terribly important to pushing thoughts of cigarettes out of her mind.** Betheny's passion for running replaced her preoccupation with smoking. She began to view cigarettes as a hindrance to her goals as a runner. Betheny was slowly changing her self-image from "smoker" to "runner".

Bob felt secure about Betheny's ability to remain a nonsmoker. He did not have the same feelings when he called Louise the next day.

Louise was still deep in therapy and struggling hard to build a sense of security within herself. She had stopped and started smoking several times, but she joined a Smokers' Anonymous group three weeks ago and was gamely trying to quit one more time.

"I know it's got to work out for me sometime," she told Bob. "I've tackled so many other, bigger things in my life that I have to believe that I can quit smoking too."

"I'm sure you can," Bob agreed, "when the timing's right. Perhaps your other struggles have delayed quitting smoking for a while, but you'll be successful once you no longer need to depend upon cigarettes emotionally or psychologically."

"You're right about that," Louise admitted. "I think the most important part of quitting smoking, besides personal commitment, is to **have a strong support system.** I have that now in my new group."

Bob agreed with Louise about the importance of social support, especially for people who derive strength from the approval, attention and acceptance of others. He knew that wouldn't be important to Betheny who prided herself on independence, but he knew that Louise was deeply lonely and needed the strength of other people to bolster her own self esteem.

Bob took a two-day break from the telephone and then called **Randy.** "How did those posters I sent work out for your Smoke Out Campaign?" Bob asked.

"They were great!" Randy answered. "Thirty kids gave up smoking during the campaign, and twenty-one of them are still not smoking."

"That's wonderful," Bob said warmly. "That must give you a great deal of personal satisfaction. What about you? Have you stayed free of cigarettes?"

"Yes, I have, though barely so at times," Randy answered. "There is tremendous pressure in being a model for other people to follow. Besides the kids, there was a parents' club of people who were trying to quit smoking too. I found myself talking so much about cigarettes that I couldn't get my mind clear of thinking about smoking. I slipped up a few times, but I felt so much pressure to 'stay quit' that I somehow got myself back on track each time. I still think about smoking, though. The cravings aren't too tough anymore, but the desire is still there."

"Don't get too discouraged about that," Bob advised. "The desire will fade with time, especially as you become more secure with yourself as a nonsmoker."

"I know, in my mind, that you're right," Randy said, "but I'm not sure that I feel it yet in my heart."

"You will, eventually," Bob reassured him. "What do you think was most important in helping the kids and their parents quit smoking?"

"Information about what happened to them when they smoked seemed pretty important," Randy answered. "Not statistics about heart disease and stuff like that, but information about what cigarettes did to them chemically. I think most people, myself included, have never really thought much about how nicotine and carbon monoxide actually affect the body.

"The most important thing that helped everyone," Randy continued, "was **having a specific list of tools to use to quit smoking.** I really believe that it's not enough to just want to quit smoking. You have to know how to do it and what else to do instead."

"That's so true," Bob agreed. "What tools seemed to last the longest?"

"Deep breathing during a craving," Randy answered easily. "And distracting themselves when they thought about cigarettes. Having some nonsmoking friends seemed to be pretty important too."

This is all very interesting, Bob thought to himself. He reflected back to the time when he quit smoking to see if he could remember what was most important to him at that time. Tools and social support were important, he remembered, but he had something else to keep him going: anger. Bob hated to be told what to do by anyone, despite his warm and seemingly compliant exterior. He had hated being controlled by cigarettes. He remembered telling Betheny about using anger as a weapon in her fight to become independent from nicotine. She never mentioned much about using anger as a tool and Bob suspected that the more positive aspect of finding a replacement interest was much more useful to her. As Bob thought more about anger toward cigarettes, he remembered Martha who always seemed like such an angry person to him. He called her next.

"I'm so surprised to hear from you," **Martha** said when she heard Bob's voice. "What's the occasion?"

Bob laughed. "There's no occasion specifically, but I've been in touch with almost everyone at our table for the class reunion, and I want to talk to you too."

"That's nice," Martha replied. They chatted pleasantly about what everyone was doing. Finally the conversation turned to Martha and how she had fared since her hospitalization.

"I stopped smoking cigarettes three months ago," Martha told him, "but I've only been off of nicotine for a month. I used nicotine gum first, then a medicine called Clonidine which helped decrease the nicotine cravings. That helped me the most. Dr. Anderson was wonderful!"

"Would you suggest that other people use the same tools you used to quit smoking?" Bob asked her.

"I had a very tough time quitting smoking," Martha said somberly. "I had plenty of good reasons for quitting: bronchitis and emphysema... serious enough that I probably wouldn't have lived to see my children graduate from high school if I continued to smoke. It was still hard for me to give it up. Tim and I took a class together at the hospital to help us quit. Tim did it without too much trouble, but I struggled so hard. I think that **for anyone who has real difficulty quitting or staying away from cigarettes for more than a couple of days at a time, either nicotine gum or Clonidine could be critically important to helping that person be successful.**

"Did you use the information you learned in the class?" Bob asked.

"Yes, I did. The suggestions were helpful, and I still use many of them. My struggle was less about smoking and more about nicotine. I didn't miss smoking nearly as much as I missed nicotine. That's why Dr. Anderson finally gave me the Clonidine. It is a prescription medicine used to control high blood pressure. Dr. Anderson told me that it has been used for Methadone detoxification and recently, it has been used very successfully for nicotine withdrawal. You can't get it without a doctor's prescription."

"I hadn't heard about Clonidine," Bob told Martha. "I'm glad to know about it, and also to know that you're at last on the road to becoming truly free of nicotine. Congratulations!"

Bob thought about Martha for a long time, and marveled once more at the complexities of the human mind. Of all the people at their table, Martha had the most to lose by smoking, yet she had the most difficult time quitting. Leaving cigarettes is not an easy task for anyone, he thought, but some people seem to have a much tougher time of it than others.

Bob made his final information update call, this one to **Tim.** His wife answered the phone and they talked for a few minutes before she summoned Tim from the garage. "How are you?" Bob asked.

"I'm fine, thank you," Tim answered.

Bob shared all the information he had heard from the others with Tim. "I can't believe Betheny is actually going to train for the New York Marathon! She never seemed the type to go out for anything athletic."

"I was a little surprised myself," Bob agreed.

No Ifs, Ands, or Butts

"Martha and I took the stop smoking class together so we've seen a lot of each other," Tim explained. "Other than that day when I saw you in town, I haven't seen or talked to anyone else from the group. I'm glad to hear all the news from you."

"Martha finally seems to be on her way to success," Bob said. "Have you had much trouble giving up smoking?"

"Not much," Tim answered. "I have a new marriage and my wife doesn't tolerate cigarette smoke. That was my incentive to quit. With a new person in my life, a new house and new routines, I didn't miss smoking all that much until I got into the office. I had some help there, too. About two months after I quit, my boss decided to make the whole office nonsmoking. All the carpets and curtains were cleaned. No one could smoke inside. No more smoking during meetings. His timing was perfect for me."

When asked what factors were most important to him when quitting smoking, Tim said, "I think that **changing the environment somehow is important, and also changing routines.** When you sit in the same old places, expecting cigarettes to be there, why wouldn't you miss them? When you smell old smoke in chair and curtain fabric, it just reminds you of smoking. When you do the same things in the same sequence and smoking used to be part of that sequence, of course you would think of cigarettes."

"Not everyone can refurbish a house, or change living or working conditions," Bob remarked. "What would you advise people to do when they can't change those conditions?"

"Anyone can change a routine in some way," Tim answered. "The progression of things you do when you first arrive home or enter the office, the sequence of activities when you first get up in the morning, all the little rituals of life can be changed enough so that smoking will not be obviously missing."

"You're right about that," agreed Bob.

"Cleaning carpets and curtains, painting a few walls, detailing a car and sending clothes to the laundry or cleaner is a nuisance but it does make a big difference to overall comfort without cigarettes. I've been luckier than many people because some of my environmental conditions *changed naturally, but if they hadn't, I would have created some changes anyway. I really think that **one of the important keys to success without cigarettes is to change your triggers.** If you are naturally triggered to think of things other than cigarettes, to do things other than smoke, much of the automatic response part of smoking habits goes away over time.*

*Bob and Tim talked on for another fifteen minutes. After he concluded the conversation, Bob thought about what he had heard from each person. Everyone had a different slant on what was helpful for quitting smoking. The responses were as varied as the personalities of the people who spoke them. "Isn't that what it's all about anyway?" he said aloud. **Each person has to find the correct approach to fit his or her own personality, living and working situation, lifestyle, emotional or psychological needs, even the social circumstances that influence his or her behavior.** It's a wonder, sometimes, that people can be so successful at something that is so complicated. I guess that's what makes for challenge, he mused.*

Bob remembered an old Hebrew proverb: "Change takes but an instant. It's the resistance to change that takes the time to overcome." How true that is, he thought. Martha, Louise and maybe Randy seemed to show more resistance to quitting than the others. I used to think that was just lack of commitment. Not anymore. Not after I quit. I used to tell myself that each "No!" to cigarettes meant severing one more link in the chain of my bondage to cigarettes. The mental image of that chain made me so mad that I'd swear at the image of cigarettes in my mind.

I talked out loud to myself in those days, Bob remembered. People used to ask me who I was swearing at. Bob chuckled to himself. I wanted freedom from smoking. I was willing to fight anyone and anything to get it. So I fought resistance, and sabotage and seductive smoking memories. I stayed away from smokers. I forced down every craving. Right now none of that seems so hard to do, but it was difficult at the time I had to do it. Like surgery, the pain went away after a while. Not the memory, perhaps, but the pain. That's true for most things in life.

*Bob's attention turned to his son, **Jeremy.** He thought about the HAM radio project they had worked so hard on together and realized how similar the lessons in life truly are. There didn't seem to be much difference in the way he, as an adult, approached smoking from the way he, as a youngster, built and learned to use a HAM radio. There has to be a basic* *plan of operation for both, he mused. There has to be an overall plan, or strategy, to follow. There also has to be a set of tools and some clear directions for their use. You have to experiment with the tools so you understand how they work and then figure how to use them to get the project done.*

Then there's the trouble shooting, Bob thought, the many hours of trying to figure out why something doesn't work, and a great deal of 'head scratching' until the correct solution is found. He remembered how discouraged and frustrated Jeremy became when something didn't work properly, or when the solution wasn't easily found. I was pretty frustrated myself at times, he reflected.

No learning is complete without the daily practice, Bob thought. He smiled as he remembered the countless hours he and Jeremy spent together, sending and receiving Morse code until Bob began to hear everyday conversation in terms of code. He laughed. He thought about quitting smoking once again. "I think my quitting smoking was the best preparation in the world for helping Jeremy!" he said aloud.

Bob stopped his reverie and went to look for his wife and son. He had thought about cigarettes and smoking much too much for one day. Going to a movie sounded like a good idea right then.

This is a good time for you to take a break from thinking about cigarettes and smoking. Maybe a movie sounds good to you, too. Whatever you decide to do at this moment, make it fun or rewarding or relaxing and, of course, smoke free. Like the people in this book, you are well along on the road to your freedom from cigarettes and from smoking. May you travel in good health and good spirits!

No Ifs, Ands, or Butts

Self-Study Exercises IV

Jeremy's HAM *radio was fixed at last. His eyes shined with pride as he looked at it. "You've done a wonderful job, Son," Jeremy's father told him. "Now you will have to practice using Morse code so you can really use the radio. I have this old book that gives you the code. I also have this little machine I made for myself a long time ago when I needed to practice sending Morse code. It has a light, a buzzer and a key pad so you can see and hear exactly what you are doing."*

Jeremy was excited! He put the practice machine on the dining room table next to the radio. He opened the book and began experimenting with the machine. His father smiled as he watched, lost in memories of his own.

By the end of the week, Jeremy's code sending skills had improved dramatically. He practiced every day. Immediately after supper every night, Jeremy's father sat across the table, blindfolded, and interpreted the messages Jeremy sent with the practice machine. Jeremy thought that was great fun. So did his dad.

Before long Jeremy was ready for the next project: learning to receive code. It was like learning a foreign language. He had to quickly translate the code in his head. Jeremy's father sent some messages to his son on the practice machine, but Jeremy was obviously much more proficient at sending messages than receiving them.

"Here, Jeremy," his father said. "I have some tapes for you to use to help you recognize the code by ear, and some coded messages for you to translate."

"Thanks, Dad," Jeremy said quietly. "I don't know if I'll be able to do it."

"Use the printed guide in the book, and just listen to the tapes without trying to understand everything. Play with them. Put the tapes on while you're doing other things so that you get used to listening to the code without the oscillator to help you. In a few days we'll listen to the tapes together and see how well we do at translating them. Alright?" Jeremy nodded.

The following week-end was a busy one for father and son as they practiced sending and receiving code, and translating the tapes. Jeremy's mother was impressed. She commented about how much each of them had improved. Jeremy's father laughed. "I haven't used Morse code in years. It won't be long before Jeremy will be faster than I am at sending and receiving messages."

Two weeks later Jeremy's father raised the issue of an amateur radio license. He bought some books for Jeremy to study in order to prepare for the test. He explained that there would be a skills proficiency test for sending and receiving Morse code, and a written test covering Federal rules and regulations, electronics theory, how antennas and transmitters work, and other similar topics.

Jeremy looked worried. His father understood. This was a great deal of technical information to learn. "I'll tell you what we'll do," his father said. "We'll set up a study guide and some practice exercises. We'll even have some practice tests. We'll do a little every week until you feel ready to take the test. I'll even give you a big practice test on everything before you take the real one. How does that sound?"

"It sounds hard," Jeremy said.

"It is," his father agreed, "But I know you can do it. You will have to study and use the practice exercises. Write down your questions and mark the things you don't understand. We'll go over them together later."

Jeremy studied diligently for the next three months. He and his father discussed, reviewed, practiced, and tested themselves on their knowledge. They continued to send and receive code regularly. They took field trips to radio stations, and to electronics stores that carried antennas and transmitters. They even joined a HAM radio club for teen-agers and their parents. Jeremy tested his knowledge and skills in many different ways. At last he felt ready to take the test.

Like Jeremy, **you have your own test to take, your own skills and proficiency to develop.** This section of self-help exercises is intended to assist you in gaining the self knowledge and understanding necessary to enable you to quit smoking completely. It contains a specialized collection of questionnaires, self-observation worksheets, assessment forms, planning guides and pages for your specific action plans.

Some people, when faced with quitting smoking, prefer to find some established guidelines for how to proceed and follow them accordingly. Other people are full of questions. How? Why? When? What will this mean for me? Some people enjoy studying their own behavior by tracking their daily patterns on paper. Others like to write down specific action plans. Whatever your personal style, you will find something of interest and importance in this section.

Consider this an enhancement section. The exercises are recommended to guide you in developing the specific insights and skills necessary to stop smoking most successfully. If you are using this book in a group or individual counseling program to help you stop smoking, some of these exercises may be assigned to you. If you are reading and following this book on your own, follow the recommendations given at the end of specific chapters.

Tracking Your Smoking Patterns

The farther back you can look, the farther forward you are likely to see.

... Winston Churchill

The more you understand about yourself and your smoking habits, the better prepared you are to quit smoking successfully. Hindsight learning is something most people understand. By reviewing the past, you can pick up valuable information for dealing with the future. By reviewing past and present performance, you are better able to anticipate your future needs, and the potential pitfalls in the path toward success.

Watch yourself in action for a while. Study your smoking habits and patterns: their origins, their role and function in your life, their benefits for you on a daily basis. Why do you smoke, and when; how often do you smoke and how many cigarettes do you consume; what triggers you to light up and what are the benefits of smoking at these times?

You may already have formed a set of impressions about *when*, *where* and *why* you smoke. For this reason you may not think that tracking your current smoking patterns is necessary. You certainly can quit smoking based upon those impressions. Keep in mind, though, that impressions are formed based in part on observable data and part on our interpretation of that data. If your thinking has changed in the past few weeks or months, it will be most helpful to review your current patterns once again to confirm that your impressions are current and accurate. To do this, two or three days of tracking will be sufficient. If you are not reasonably certain of the factors that underlie your smoking habits and patterns, take more time for observation. **Much the same way that observation is a critical first step to a chemical or biological experiment, observation is just as critical for experiments or changes in human behavior.**

Take one week to study your smoking patterns before entering into nicotine withdrawal. If you are waiting for the first day of a scheduled stop smoking program, or waiting until courage and conviction overtake you before actually withdrawing from cigarettes, use this time to your own best advantage. Smoke as usual during this week, but use each time you smoke as an opportunity to gather some important information about your current smoking habits and patterns.

Smoking Log Sheets

Eight Smoking Log sheets are included with this exercise. Remove them from the book or photocopy them so they can be carried with you and your cigarettes. Use one each day for up to eight days. The more days you are willing to track your patterns, the better for helping you see a broader range of self information. High-stress days may result in different smoking responses. Weekday patterns may be different than those for Saturday, or for Sunday. Travel days, conference days, special event days, low-energy days and the like may each make a definite difference in your physical and psychological needs for smoking.

How The Smoking Log Works

The reason for using a Smoking Log is to gain answers to some obvious questions about *when* and *why* you smoke, *how* strong your desire for each cigarette is, and *what* the importance of each cigarette is for you at the time you smoke it. This may sound more complicated than it actually is. Look at the example below.

SMOKING LOG			
DAY:		**DATE:**	
WHEN	**WHY**	**NEED (L, M, H)**	**COMMENTS**
6:15 am	groggy	H	enjoy with coffee
8:10 am	bored	M	driving
8:40 am	habit	M	sitting at desk
9:15 am	restless	L	attending meeting

The **WHEN** column is for the time of day or evening each cigarette is smoked.

The **WHY** column is for recording the reason(s) why you lit each cigarette. Reasons may include: anxiety, stress, tension, boredom, loneliness, depression, sadness, enjoyment, fatigue, habit, reward, stimulation, taste, to name a few. Other reasons may include an object or person that triggered a desire to smoke, the need to settle or soothe yourself, defiance or rebellion. You will undoubtedly have many reasons of your own.

The **NEED** column has a low, medium, high gradient: L = a mild want; M = a moderate desire; H = a strong, urgent craving. Write in the number that fits the level of need behind each cigarette you light, even if you don't smoke all of it.

The **COMMENTS** column is available for any tidbits of information you want to keep track of. Examples can include: "first cigarette of the day", "smoked only half of it", "borrowed it from secretary", and so on. You may want to use this column for noting the benefits of smoking each cigarette: relaxation, pleasure, something to do, and so on. Individual comments may not seem very significant at the time you write them but when looked at overall, they can shed light on important facets of your smoking behavior.

Using The Smoking Log

Enter the day and the date at the top of one log sheet. Then fold it up and slip it inside the cellophane wrapper of your cigarette pack along with a small pencil. You may prefer to put the pencil inside the pack alongside the cigarettes. Each time you reach for a cigarette, remove the log sheet and enter the information while you are enjoying your first few drags. Think about the information being asked of you. Use your smoking time to reflect about the role and importance of smoking each time you light up.

Ideally, you will write some information about each cigarette you smoke. Practically, you probably won't track every single cigarette you touch. Do the best you can to record as much as you can. Keep in mind that **some information is better than none; that a partial day of recording smoking patterns is better than no recording at all.** This information is for you: your awareness, your understanding and your ability to make effective change. The more you know about yourself, your smoking needs, and the habits and patterns you currently have, the easier it will be for you to take appropriate, practical, livable steps to separate yourself successfully from cigarettes.

Remove the log sheets from the book or take your book to a photocopy machine. Then grab a pencil and the first log sheet and place them in your cigarette pack. You're all set to begin your week of observation.

SMOKING LOG #1			
DAY:			**DATE:**
WHEN	**WHY**	**NEED (L, M, H)**	**COMMENTS**

SMOKING LOG #2			
DAY:			**DATE:**
WHEN	**WHY**	**NEED (L, M, H)**	**COMMENTS**

SMOKING LOG #1

DAY:			DATE:
WHEN	**WHY**	**NEED** **(L, M, H)**	**COMMENTS**

SMOKING LOG #2

DAY:			DATE:
WHEN	**WHY**	**NEED** **(L, M, H)**	**COMMENTS**

No Ifs, Ands, or Butts

SMOKING LOG #3

DAY:			DATE:
WHEN	**WHY**	**NEED** **(L, M, H)**	**COMMENTS**

SMOKING LOG #4

DAY:			DATE:
WHEN	**WHY**	**NEED** **(L, M, H)**	**COMMENTS**

SMOKING LOG #3

DAY:			DATE:
WHEN	**WHY**	**NEED (L, M, H)**	**COMMENTS**

SMOKING LOG #4

DAY:			DATE:
WHEN	**WHY**	**NEED (L, M, H)**	**COMMENTS**

No Ifs, Ands, or Butts

SMOKING LOG #5

DAY:			DATE:
WHEN	WHY	NEED (L, M, H)	COMMENTS

SMOKING LOG #6

DAY:			DATE:
WHEN	WHY	NEED (L, M, H)	COMMENTS

SMOKING LOG #5

DAY:			DATE:
WHEN	WHY	NEED (L, M, H)	COMMENTS

SMOKING LOG #6

DAY:			DATE:
WHEN	WHY	NEED (L, M, H)	COMMENTS

SMOKING LOG #7

DAY:			DATE:
WHEN	**WHY**	**NEED** **(L, M, H)**	**COMMENTS**

SMOKING LOG #8

DAY:			DATE:
WHEN	**WHY**	**NEED** **(L, M, H)**	**COMMENTS**

SMOKING LOG #7			
DAY:			DATE:
WHEN	WHY	NEED (L, M, H)	COMMENTS

SMOKING LOG #8			
DAY:			DATE:
WHEN	WHY	NEED (L, M, H)	COMMENTS

Your Smoking Profile

Forewarned, forearmed; to be prepared is half the victory.

... Cervantes

While the above sentiment applies well to armed battle, it is equally important for personal battles like quitting smoking. The more you understand about what triggers your desire to smoke, the benefits you enjoy as a result of smoking, and the social and environmental factors connected to your smoking, the better prepared you will be to do something constructive about it. Analyzing and synthesizing the information will enable you to focus your attention upon a smaller, more manageable number of factors that have special meaning for you. This will help you avoid the pitfalls of being overwhelmed with too much information, and the scattered thinking that arises when you try to tackle everything at one time.

Take a few minutes right now to think about how you have handled other major changes in your life. Were you consistent in your efforts to make those changes? Who supported your achievements and who hindered your progress? How did you deal with those people? Did you deliberately sabotage or interfere with your own progress in some way? If so, recognition of your potential to get in the way of your own achievement and your methods for doing it will be critically important to your ability to reach your stated goals.

The Smoking Profile Questionnaire

Whether you choose to log your current smoking patterns first or base your answers upon your impressions, **the Smoking Profile Questionnaire is an essential preparation tool for quitting smoking successfully.** The questions in the Smoking Profile Questionnaire have three purposes:

1. To help you analyze and group the information you have about your smoking patterns;

2. To help you look ahead toward the potential needs and problems you expect to encounter when you quit smoking;

3. To help you identify the potential resources at your disposal for making it easier and more comfortable to quit smoking.

Complete the questionnaire before you begin withdrawal. If you have already gone through withdrawal, complete the questionnaire before studying the self-management tools in Chapter 7. The information in Chapter 7 is correlated closely to questions 4 and 5 of the Smoking Profile Questionnaire.

Using The Smoking Profile Questionnaire

If you have tracked your smoking patterns by completing the Smoking Log, spread all the partially or fully completed Logs out in front of you and use them to help you answer the questions on the Smoking Profile Questionnaire. If you prefer not to use the log sheets first, then base your answers to the questions upon your impressions. Place a check mark (✔) alongside each item in each question that best describes your smoking patterns most of the time. Add information of your own where indicated.

Questions 4 and 5 require the use of a numbering system to designate the most correct response for each item within each category of questions. These categories are based upon the most common reasons people smoke: habit, physical pleasure, psychological support, stimulation, and relaxation and tension release. You will also be asked to total the number of points within each category to help you determine which reasons are most important to you. Follow the directions as indicated on the questionnaire.

Take the time needed to complete the Smoking Profile Questionnaire. Think about your answers. Let your mind work out potential solutions to the problems and needs you've identified. This little bit of advanced planning will go a long, long way toward helping you prepare yourself adequately for withdrawal—and to face the process with greater confidence!

Smoking Profile Questionnaire

Smoking Patterns

1. **I smoke an average of** _____ **cigarettes per day.**

2. **I smoke most often in the:**

   __ Mornings

   __ Afternoons

   __ Evenings

   __ Late evenings

   __ Other _____

3. **My need to smoke is strongest: (mark every item that applies to you)**

__ before breakfast	__ after meals	__ at my desk
__ while watching TV	__ while reading	__ while driving
__ talking on phone	__ with coffee	__ with alcohol
__ before bed	__ when angry or upset	__ when lonely
__ when bored/restless	__ when tired	__ other _____
__ other _____	__ other _____	__ other _____

   Note: When answering questions 4 and 5, use the following numbering system to designate the most correct response for each item:

   5   Always

   4   Frequently

   3   Occasionally

   2   Seldom

   1   Never

A space is provided for writing down the total points for each category of responses.

4. When smoking I often:

a. __ smoke the entire cigarette

a. __ light up automatically when doing specific things

a. __ light a new cigarette while the old one is still burning

a. __ smoke without awareness of doing it

_____ total points for "a", **smoking habit**

b. __ inhale deeply

b. __ play with the cigarette pack

b. __ hold or caress the cigarette

b. __ enjoy the feel of the cigarette in my mouth

_____ total points for "b", **physical pleasure**

5. Smoking helps me to:

c. __ have time for myself

c. __ not feel lonely

c. __ reward myself

c. __ feel comforted

_____ total points for "c", **psychological support**

d. __ think better

d. __ have more energy

d. __ keep myself going

d. __ change the taste in my mouth

_____ total points for "d", **stimulation**

e.   __ unwind or relax

e.   __ settle myself when nervous

e.   __ have something to do with my hands

e.   __ feel in control of myself

_____ total points for "e", **relaxation and tension release**

Potential Needs And Problems

6.   **The times of day I think will be the hardest for me not to smoke are:** _____

_____
_____
_____
_____
_____

7.   **The situations I think will be the hardest for me not to smoke in are:** _____

_____
_____
_____
_____
_____

8.   **The people I think will be the hardest for me to be around without smoking are:** _____

_____
_____
_____
_____
_____

9. The activities I think will be the hardest for me to do without smoking are: _____

_____

_____

_____

_____

_____

10. The strongest emotional needs I think I will have when I'm quitting smoking are: _____

_____

_____

_____

_____

_____

11. I worry that I will do these things to sabotage my success in quitting smoking: _____

_____

_____

_____

_____

_____

Potential Resources

12. The people I can look to for help and support while I'm quitting smoking are:_____

_____

_____

_____

_____

_____

13. The places I can go where it will be easiest for me not to smoke are:_____

_____

_____

_____

_____

14. The activities I think will calm and settle me while I'm quitting smoking are:_____

_____

_____

_____

_____

15. I will do these things to help myself when I notice that I'm sabotaging my potential success:_____

_____

_____

_____

_____

16. Some positive messages I can write down and read or say to myself for encouragement and self-support while I'm quitting smoking are:_____

_____

_____

_____

_____

Resource List

What happens to the sudden flash of inspiration, the marvelous idea, the long-awaited solution to a thorny problem when you don't write it down? Do you forget it? Is it like the dream that you remember upon awakening, but cannot recall later in the morning? Many people carry paper and pencils with them for jotting down messages to themselves, notes about important ideas or plans, solutions to problems. They make lists of things to remember or things to do. **The advantage of list making is that what is written is remembered; what is seen is most often done. And when all of the ideas are contained on one list, it becomes much easier to set up a workable, comprehensive plan of action.**

In Chapters 5 through 8 you will learn about many tools for helping you achieve freedom from smoking. Within each chapter you will be using Cue Cards for listing and tracking the tools you wish to experiment with. As you move from one chapter to the next you will be adding more and more Cue Cards. The list of potentially usable tools will grow accordingly. You will eventually feel the need for consolidating everything onto one list.

The Resource List provides a simple method for helping you merge all of the usable tools from individual chapters onto one or two sheets of paper. The Resource List also serves as a guide to help you determine the order and sequence of the specific tools you will use to develop your final comprehensive action plan for eliminating and replacing your old smoking habits.

Selecting The Tools

As you read through the chapters of your book you will find many tools that have appeal or value to you. Mark them or note them in the margins of the book. As instructed in item 6 on page 128, copy these tools onto 3x5 index cards, called Cue Cards, for daily use. Cue Cards provide an easy method for limiting the number of tools you can work with at one time. They are ideal for guiding you through the initial exploration stage.

As you work with the tools on your Cue Cards, you will see that you do not like some of them, that some of them don't work well for you and that others don't fit your needs or lifestyle. *Eliminate them.* You will see that you never get around to using some of the tools. Eliminate them also. Some tools may need modification to make them work more effectively for you. *Change them* as needed. And some tools either apply to more than one need or they function in the same way as other tools. *Combine them.* This will reduce the number of viable tools for use in your final action plan.

Once you have finished exploring, experimenting, modifying, combining, adding and eliminating specific tools from your Cue Cards, you are ready to consolidate the remaining tools.

In brief the procedure is this:

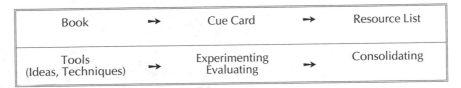

Book	→	Cue Card	→	Resource List
Tools (Ideas, Techniques)	→	Experimenting Evaluating	→	Consolidating

Preparing The Resource List

You will notice two columns on the Resource List: a narrow column to the left and a wide column to the right. Use the wide column for recording the tools. Keep adding tools to the list as you progress through the book. When interesting ideas or useful solutions occur to you, add them to the List. The Resource List becomes the repository for all of your viable tools.

Review your Resource List every few weeks in order to eliminate, modify, combine or exchange tools as needed. Updating and revising the List is important so that you don't create such a large resource of tools that it becomes overwhelming, impractical or simply unusable. Use a pencil for writing on your Resource List so that you can change or eliminate tools more easily.

Arrange Your Tools By Ease Of Use

Once you have finished making revisions to your Resource List, assign a number to each remaining tool. The numbers can be placed in the narrow column on the left side of the page.

Numbers are assigned in the following manner. First, **evaluate each of the tools according to what is EASIEST for you to do.** Not what is most important. Not what is most logical. You are looking for what is the very easiest of all the tools for you to use. That tool becomes #1, and a "1" is placed in the narrow column alongside it.

Next, look for the second easiest tool and place a "2" in the narrow column alongside it. Place a "3" alongside the third easiest tool and so on until every tool on the list is assigned a number. Look at the example below.

	Resource List
7	Watch TV on bed where I normally don't smoke.
1	Remove all cigarettes, lighters, ash trays!
6	Spend time with nonsmoking buddies.
5	Use cordless phone so I can move around.
8	Nonalcoholic drinks only.
3	Keep gum, mints, cinnamon sticks handy.
4	When tempted to smoke, distract myself.
2	Deep breathe during cigarette cravings.

Most people tend to rate things according to importance. Often the seemingly most important tools are also the most difficult to use. If you rate the tools on this list according to importance, and the most important tools are also the hardest to use, what do you think will happen to your motivation and progress when you begin with the "1" tool on that list?

Instructional manuals of all kinds begin with the simplest, easiest items first and progress gradually in difficulty and complexity. There is a reason for this. Success is what keeps most people excited and motivated to keep on learning or practicing. This will be true for you as well, and especially true when it applies to changing very established habits like smoking.

Using The Resource List

The Resource List is a *master list of tools* from which your Control Cards will be developed. Control Cards are discussed on page 203. For right now, content yourself with adding tools to your Resource List. The tools will come from primarily four sources: the chapters in the book, your Cue Cards, your own ideas and techniques you've heard or read about elsewhere. As you collect the tools, evaluate them to determine whether or not they are helpful, likeable and practical.

As you experiment with the tools on your Resource List you may find some tools are out of sequence, that the "4" item is actually easier to do than the "3" item, for example. Change the numbers accordingly. Your best clue that a particular tool is too difficult is your own performance. If you are not getting around to using a particular tool very often, or you are avoiding it by doing other things instead, or you feel some resistance or resentment toward using the tool, change the tool!

The Resource List will be most useful in helping you prepare your long-range comprehensive action plan to keep yourself smoke free. Directions for using the List in this way are in Chapter 9, page 202. Three blank Resource List forms are included at the end of this section. You are welcome to make extra copies if you wish.

Resource List

No Ifs, Ands, or Butts

Resource List

Resource List

Withdrawal Diet Plans

by Linda Connell Hadfield, M.S., R.D.

To many smokers, it's more than just a bad habit—nicotine is a physical addiction. Research tells us that the body's attempt to maintain a certain serum nicotine level can actually determine how often and how many cigarettes you smoke. The kidney is the major organ which dictates the fate of nicotine and the most important factor in either nicotine elimination or reabsorption is urinary pH. When the urine is more acidic (pH of 5.5 or less) more nicotine is excreted. When the urine is more alkaline, more nicotine is reabsorbed.

Urinary pH can be controlled by, and is most sensitive to, the foods you eat. Foods which contain high levels of phosphorus, sulfur and chlorine tend to be **acid-forming foods** and will **lower urinary pH.** In general these tend to be meat, chicken, eggs, and fish, with the exception of shrimp. Cereals, grains and some nuts are also acid-forming. **Base-forming foods** create a more alkaline urine and **increase urinary PH.** These foods contain potassium, calcium, magnesium, and sodium and include most fruits, vegetables, dairy products and most nuts. Whether you prefer gradual or abrupt withdrawal, you can safely change your diet to help control nicotine elimination.

A high-alkaline diet may help you withdraw from nicotine more gradually. Nicotine will stay in the body for a longer period of time, serum levels will decrease more slowly and side effects will be minimized.

Increase these base-forming foods:

- Limit meats, chicken and fish to three to five oz. per day
- Shrimp
- Dairy products: milk, cheese, yogurt (choose low-fat)
- All fruit with exception of cranberries, plums, prunes and prune juice
- All vegetables except asparagus and corn
- All grains and legumes except lentils and rice
- Almonds, brazil nuts, chestnuts and filberts
- Water and mineral water

If you prefer to quit "cold turkey" and go through the withdrawal effects quickly, the high-acid diet which will quicken nicotine excretion.

Increase these acid-forming foods:

- Meats, chicken and fish
- Cranberries, plums, prunes and prune juice
- Asparagus and corn
- Lentils and rice
- Peanuts, pecans and walnuts

Reference

The preceding section is based upon information from:

Ogle, J. *The Stop Smoking Diet*. New York: M. Evans & Co., 1981

Stop Smoking Diets

In order to get you on your way, you will find a Seven-Day high-alkaline gradual withdrawal diet plan, starting on page 336, and a Seven-Day high-acid abrupt withdrawal diet plan, starting on page 340. All of the breakfasts, lunches and dinners can be interchanged within their own groupings and one specific meal does not need to follow another.

Each day, regardless of the meals you choose, your total consumption will add up to approximately 1300-1500 calories. This is a high-carbohydrate plan with sixty percent of the calories coming from carbohydrate, twenty percent protein and twenty percent fat. If weight loss is **not** one of your goals, choose snacks from the appropriate lists to increase calories as needed.

The meals included are quick and easy to prepare at home with minimal ingredients and most of them can be ordered in a restaurant.

High-Alkaline "Gradual Withdrawal" Breakfasts

1 cup melon
1 cup hot oat bran cereal
2 Tbsp raisins
2 Tbsp almonds
½ cup skim milk

½ grapefruit
1 whole-wheat English muffin
2 Tbsp part-skim ricotta cheese
2 Tbsp apple butter

1 small whole-grain bagel (heat bagel
   and cheese under broiler until cheese
   melts)
1 oz. part-skim mozzarella cheese
½ small melon

½ cup orange juice
2 whole-grain toaster waffles
1 Tbsp almond butter
2 Tbsp all-fruit jam

1 cup fresh berries
3 4-inch pancakes
2 Tbsp all-fruit jam
½ cup plain nonfat yogurt

1 cup cold Nutragrain cereal
1 cup skim milk
1 small banana

¼ cup low-fat cottage cheese
1 tsp vanilla
¼ cup frozen strawberries (thawed)
2 Tbsp all-fruit strawberry jam
2 crepes (Blenderize cottage cheese
   and vanilla. Add strawberries to the
   mixture. Roll strawberry mixture in
   crepes and top with jam. Warm in
   350 degree oven for 10 minutes.)

* Reminder,
   Tbsp = Tablespoon
   tsp   = Teaspoon

No Ifs, Ands, or Butts

High-Alkaline "Gradual Withdrawal" Lunches

Plain meat sandwich:
    2 slices whole-grain bread
    2 oz. turkey, ham or roast beef
    lettuce, tomatoes, sprouts and
    cucumber mustard, BBQ sauce or
    horseradish
1-2 pieces fresh fruit (avoid plums)

Green salad with no-oil dressing
2 cups minestrone soup
1 whole-grain roll or 6-8 crackers

Combine:
    2 cups sliced fruit (avoid plums)
    1 cup plain nonfat yogurt
    1 Tbsp concentrated apple juice
    1 Tbsp almonds
6-8 whole-grain crackers

1 large baked potato stuffed with:
    2 Tbsp plain nonfat yogurt
    1 Tbsp parmesan cheese
    1 Tbsp chives
1-2 pieces fresh fruit (avoid plums)

Hamburger on a bun with:
    2 oz. hamburger patty
    lettuce, tomatoes, pickle
    catsup, mustard or BBQ sauce
1 individual-portion pack of pretzels

Tossed salad with no-oil dressing
3 slices small cheese pizza with
    mushrooms, onions and peppers
4 oz. sherbet

Shrimp cocktail
2 cups vegetable soup or
    salad with no-oil dressing
1 cup fresh fruit compote (avoid plums)

Reminder,
   Tbsp = Tablespoon
   tsp   = Teaspoon

High-Alkaline "Gradual Withdrawal" Dinners

1   12-inch flour tortilla, oven crisped
    and topped with:
    ½ cup pinto beans (refried in
        minimal vegetable oil)
    1 Tbsp each green chilies, jalapeno
        peppers and salsa
    1 oz. shredded sharp cheddar cheese
    shredded lettuce and diced tomatoes
1   cup fresh fruit salad

1   cup tomato-based soup
3   oz. orange roughy steamed and
    topped with:
    1 tsp each almonds and capers
1   baked potato with plain nonfat yogurt
1   cup steamed spinach
1-2 whole-grain rolls
4   oz. fresh fruit sorbet

Green salad with no-oil dressing
2   cups linguini with ½ cup red sauce
2   Tbsp parmesan cheese
1-2 slices Italian bread
4   oz. ice milk

Tossed salad with no-oil dressing
2   cups vegetarian chili (avoid corn)
2   slices whole-grain bread
½   cup frozen yogurt

1   cup broth-based soup
3   oz. BBQ chicken thigh
1   large baked potato topped with
    low-fat cottage cheese
½ cup steamed French beans
3-4 almond cookies

Italian salad with no-oil dressing
4   cheese ravioli topped with
    ½ cup marinara sauce
2 slices Italian bread
4 oz. spumoni

Vegetable relish tray with blended
    low-fat cottage cheese and herbs
BBQ Steak kabobs:
    3 oz. flank steak, cubed
    ½ cup pineapple chunks
    6 cherry tomatoes
    sliced green pepper
    steak sauce to brush on kabobs
1   small sweet potato topped with:
    2 Tbsp pineapple juice

Reminder,
    Tbsp = Tablespoon
    tsp   = Teaspoon

Snacks For The High-Alkaline "Gradual Withdrawal" Diet

Snack	Amount	Calories
Carbohydrate Snacks		
Ak-Mak crackers	5	125
3-ring pretzels	14 small	154
RyKrisp	3	90
Bread sticks	4	164
Melba toast	8	122
Graham crackers	5	117
Animal crackers	13	153
Banana	1 large	160
Cantaloupe	½ melon	120
Oranges	1 medium	80
Pineapple	1 cup	120
Dates, pitted	4 medium	115
Apricot halves	7	106
Figs	2	108
Raisins	2 ounces	104
Carrots	1 medium	25
Celery	1 stalk	10
Radishes	10 small	15
Broccoli, cauliflower	1 cup	25
Cherry tomatoes	5	25
Protein Snacks (choose nonfat or low-fat when possible)		
cottage cheese	¼ cup	55
yogurt,plain	½ cup	40
frozen yogurt	½ cup	80-100
cheese	1 oz.	55-75
almonds, brazil nuts	¼ cup	210

High-Acid "Abrupt Withdrawal" Breakfasts

1 cup hot oat bran cereal
2 Tbsp chopped prunes
2 Tbsp chopped pecans
2 Tbsp apple butter

1 fresh apple or pear
1 poached egg on
1 whole-wheat English muffin

6 oz. cranberry juice
1 egg plus 2 egg white omelet with:
   onions, peppers, ½ oz. diced ham
¼ cup pizza sauce (optional)
2 slices whole-grain toast with
   1 tsp margarine

6 oz. cranberry juice
2 whole-grain toaster waffles
1 Tbsp peanut butter
2 Tbsp all fruit jam

6 oz. cranberry juice
1 small whole-grain bagel with:
2 Tbsp peanut butter
2 Tbsp apple butter

1 fresh apple or pear
3 4-inch pecan pancakes
¼ cup all fruit jam

½ cup mixed fruit
1 corn tortilla, oven crisped and
   topped with:
   2 egg whites scrambled with
   1 tsp each green chilies and salsa
¼ cup pinto beans
   (refried in minimal vegetable oil)

Reminder,
   Tbsp = Tablespoon
   tsp = Teaspoon

High-Acid "Abrupt Withdrawal" Lunches

Hamburger on a bun with:
   3 oz. hamburger patty
   lettuce, tomatoes, pickle
   catsup, mustard or BBQ sauce
1 individual-portion pack of pretzels

Plain meat sandwich:
   2 slices whole-grain bread
   3 oz. turkey or chicken
   2 Tbsp cranberry sauce or
      plum sauce
1 piece fresh fruit

1 cup sliced fruit topped with:
   2 Tbsp walnuts
   1 tsp sesame seeds
8-10 melba toast with
2 Tbsp peanut butter

1 cup egg drop soup
2 cups stir-fry chicken and vegetables
   with plum sauce
½ cup steamed rice
1 fortune cookie

Green salad with no-oil dressing
2 cups lentil soup
1 whole-grain roll or 6-8 crackers

1 large baked potato stuffed with:
   1 oz. flaked tuna
   ¼ cup steamed onions and
      green pepper
   1 Tbsp dijon mustard
½ cup fresh fruit compote

Tossed salad with no-oil dressing
2 cups chicken rice soup
1 whole-grain roll or 6-8 crackers

* Reminder,
  Tbsp = Tablespoon
  tsp   = Teaspoon

High-Acid "Abrupt Withdrawal" Dinners

Green salad with no-oil dressing
2   cups linguini with ½ cup red clam
       sauce
1-2 slices Italian bread
4   oz. dessert wine

Tossed salad with no-oil dressing
2   cups chili con carne
2   small pieces corn bread
4   oz. sherbet

Green salad with no-oil dressing
BBQ steak kabobs:
       4   oz. flank steak, cubed
       ½ cup apple chunks
       6   cherry tomatoes
       sliced green pepper
       steak sauce to brush on kabobs
Place on 1 cup steamed brown rice
1   small sweet potato topped with
       2   Tbsp concentrated apple juice

2 corn tortillas, oven crisped and
       each topped with:
       1   oz. cooked lean ground beef
       ½ cup pinto beans
          (refried in minimal vegetable oil)
       1 Tbsp each green chilies,
       jalapeno peppers and salsa
       shredded lettuce & diced tomatoes
½ cup Spanish rice
½ cup fresh fruit salad

1   cup sherried consume
4   oz. BBQ chicken
1   large baked potato topped with
       BBQ sauce
½ cup steamed French beans
3-4 peanut butter cookies

Italian salad with no-oil dressing
4   beef ravioli topped with:
       ½ cup marinara sauce
2   slices Italian bread
4   oz. Italian ice

1   cup tomato-based soup
4   oz. orange roughy steamed and
       topped with
       1   tsp walnuts and capers
1   baked potato stuffed with
       steamed mushrooms and asparagus
       cuts
1-2 whole-grain rolls
4   oz. fresh fruit sorbet

* Reminder,
   Tbsp = Tablespoon
   tsp   = Teaspoon

Snacks For The High-Acid "Abrupt Withdrawal" Diet

Snack	Amount	Calories
Carbohydrate Snacks		
Corn muffin	1	191
Rice cakes	4	140
3-ring pretzels	14 small	154
Rice crackers	5	100
Bread sticks	4	164
Melba toast	8	122
Popcorn, plain	2½ cups	115
Graham crackers	5	117
Animal crackers	13	153
Cracker Jacks	1 box	120
Plums	2 medium	120
Prunes	4 halves	120
Protein Snacks (choose nonfat or low-fat when possible)		
Peanuts, pecans, walnuts	¼ cup	210

About The Author

Julie Waltz Kembel is the education director of the Health & Healing Center at Canyon Ranch health and fitness resort in Tucson, Arizona. She designs programs and instructional manuals, and provides individual and small group instruction in many areas of lifestyle change. In addition, Julie is an adjunct clinical instructor in the Department of Family and Community Medicine, University of Arizona College of Medicine.

Julie holds bachelor's and master's degrees in special education from Wayne State University in Detroit, Michigan. Her professional background includes thirteen years with the Department of Psychiatry and Behavioral Sciences, University of Washington, Seattle; three years in hospital administration; and eleven years at Canyon Ranch. In addition, Julie is a consultant to business and health care organizations, provides seminars for health care professionals and corporate management and employees, and maintains a private counseling practice.

Julie is author of *Winning the Weight and Wellness Game*, available in student and instructor editions, and *ROLE Play: Personalities in Action*. She and her husband, Bob, own and operate Northwest Learning Associates, Inc., publisher of instructional books for health education and behavior change.

From The Publishers

We hope you've enjoyed *No Ifs, Ands, or Butts: A Smoker's Guide to Kicking the Habit*. But even more, we hope that you have found this book to be informative and helpful.

This book is the result of more than ten years of intensive work and development. The ideas, techniques, and tools presented have helped hundreds of former smokers become non-smokers. Each of these former smokers is a unique individual. No single tool or technique works equally well for all of them. Similarly, the tools and techniques which work for you are unique. We would like to know what worked for you and to hear about your experiences with *No Ifs, Ands, or Butts*. Your feedback will help us assist other smokers as they seek to "kick the habit."

If you would like to share your feedback, experiences, or other comments with Julie Waltz Kembel, please write to her at the following address:

Northwest Learning Associates, Inc.
Attn: Julie Waltz Kembel
3061 N. Willow Creek Drive
Tucson, AZ 85712-1381

Available From Northwest Learning Associates:

Winning the Weight and Wellness Game. The award winning book that combines Food Management, Exercise, and Relaxation into the most comprehensive weight management and wellness program we've ever offered. Twenty-five insightful chapters take you from Preparing for Change through Putting It All Together. Whether you're using this book individually or as part of a supervised program, *Winning the Weight and Wellness Game* has it all. 336 pages, paperback. Catalog number WIN-STD, $17.95 plus 3.00 shipping. Quantity discounts available for group purchases.

Winning the Weight and Wellness Game: Instructor Guide. Designed for the wellness professional, the instructor's guide gives you everything you need to prepare, plan, and implement your own Winning the Weight and Wellness Game program. The comprehensive planning worksheet helps you identify and set program goals. Sample templates provide ready-to-use programs of 6, 8, and 10 week durations. Twenty-one lesson enhancements allow you to add breadth and depth with information not contained in the basic manual. 296 pages, comb bound for ease of use. Catalog number WIN-INST, $39.95 plus $3.50 shipping.

ROLE Play: Personalities in Action. Clicks, clashes, and chemistry—that's what happens when different personalities come together. This book brings you fresh insight into the ROLE personality plays in your decisions, interactions, and relationships. Get set for some surprises—and a lot of fun, too—when you read and share this with others. This is an excellent resource for learning to understand others and respond to them in ways that promote positive outcomes. Paperback. Catalog number ROLE-STD, $14.95 plus $3.00 shipping.

No Ifs, Ands, or Butts: Instructor Guide. Provides suggested individual and group applications, a reference outline, objectives for each chapter of the book, and helpful supplementary information. Catalog number SM-INST, $39.95 plus $3.50 shipping.

Important Ordering Information:

Use the form on the next page to order any of the above items. Or, for faster service, call our 24-hour "record-a-message" number at 520-881-0877 or our FAX number at 520-881-0632 to place your order. Quantity discounts are available on all items. Please write or call for current information.

Northwest Learning Associates, Inc.
3061 N. Willow Creek Drive
Tucson, AZ 85712-1381
Phone: (520) 881-0877 FAX: (520) 881-0632

Sold To:

Name:

Firm:

Address:

City, State, Zip:

Ship To:

Name:

Firm:

Address:

City, State, Zip:

Telephone:

Date:

Purchase Order Number:

Qty	Cat. Number	Description	Amount

Subtotal	
Arizona Residents add 7% Sales Tax	
Shipping and Handling	
Total	

No Ifs, Ands, or Butts:
A Smoker's Guide To Kicking The Habit

This book provides you with a comprehensive guide to kicking the smoking habit. In it, you will find a blueprint for achieving your independence from cigarettes. This blueprint has helped many other smokers kick their habit— now it can help you.

Section I focuses on your decision to quit. It will help you examine your readiness for change and your commitment to quitting. You will learn:

✔ What you should do before you begin. How you can examine your reasons for quitting and determine your readiness to quit.

✔ How to prepare yourself for the changes associated with quitting.

✔ What happens to your body when you smoke.

✔ How you can change your mind and attitude about smoking.

Section II guides you through the process of quitting. This practical, results oriented section will teach you:

✔ Tools that will help you accomplish change.

✔ What you should expect during withdrawal and how you can prepare for it.

✔ How to manage yourself without cigarettes. And, how to maintain yourself as a nonsmoker.

✔ How to develop nonsmoking plans and strategies that fit your particular lifestyle.

Section III enables you to maintain your progress. It provides proven techniques that will show you:

✔ How you can prevent relapses. And, how you can recover should they occur.

✔ How to avoid weight problems after you quit.

✔ How exercise can help you feel healthier.

✔ What steps you can take to achieve lifelong freedom from smoking.